FOOTSTEPS
OF THE
CHEROKEES

▲▲▲▲▲▲▲▲

FOOTSTEPS OF THE CHEROKEES

▲▲▲▲▲▲▲▲

A GUIDE TO THE EASTERN

HOMELANDS OF THE

CHEROKEE NATION

Vicki Rozema

John F. Blair, Publisher
Winston-Salem, North Carolina

Third Printing, 2000

*The paper in this book meets the guidelines
for permanence and durability of the
Committee on Production Guidelines
for Book Longevity of the
Council on Library Resources.*

Front cover—

Lake Santeetlah, Snowbird Mountains, North Carolina

Library of Congress Cataloging-in-Publication Data

Rozema, Vicki, 1954—

    Footsteps of the Cherokees : a guide to the Eastern homelands of
the Cherokee Nation / Vicki Rozema.

         p.   cm.

    Includes bibliographical references (p.   ) and index.

    ISBN 0-89587-133-5 (alk. paper)

    1. Cherokee Indians—Southern States. 2. Indians of North
America—Southern States. 3. Southern States—Description and
travel. I. Title.

E99.C5R93 1995

975'.004975—dc20   95–18092

DESIGN BY DEBRA LONG HAMPTON

MAPS BY LIZA LANGRALL

PRINTED AND BOUND BY R. R. DONNELLEY & SONS

To

Chris, Laurel, and Ed
for their love and support.

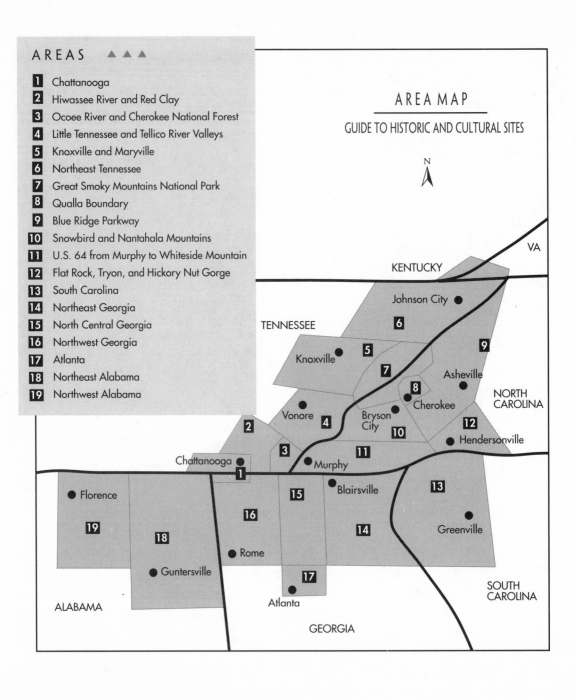

AREAS ▲ ▲ ▲

1. Chattanooga
2. Hiwassee River and Red Clay
3. Ocoee River and Cherokee National Forest
4. Little Tennessee and Tellico River Valleys
5. Knoxville and Maryville
6. Northeast Tennessee
7. Great Smoky Mountains National Park
8. Qualla Boundary
9. Blue Ridge Parkway
10. Snowbird and Nantahala Mountains
11. U.S. 64 from Murphy to Whiteside Mountain
12. Flat Rock, Tryon, and Hickory Nut Gorge
13. South Carolina
14. Northeast Georgia
15. North Central Georgia
16. Northwest Georgia
17. Atlanta
18. Northeast Alabama
19. Northwest Alabama

AREA MAP

GUIDE TO HISTORIC AND CULTURAL SITES

N

KENTUCKY
VA
TENNESSEE
NORTH CAROLINA
SOUTH CAROLINA
ALABAMA
GEORGIA

Johnson City
Knoxville
Asheville
Vonore
Bryson City
Cherokee
Hendersonville
Chattanooga
Murphy
Florence
Blairsville
Greenville
Rome
Guntersville
Atlanta

TABLE OF CONTENTS

▲ ▲ ▲

PREFACE

▲ ▲ ▲

A few years ago, on a trip to Montana, I met a young man at the Little Big Horn National Monument who was "half Cherokee and half Texan." He was a tourist like myself, but he was also on a pilgrimage to learn more about his Native American roots. The young man expressed dismay that the other visitors paid so much attention to the legend of General George Custer and the Seventh Cavalry and very little to the information on chiefs Crazy Horse and Sitting Bull and the Sioux and Cheyenne Indians who fought at the Little Big Horn.

This man, in his mid-twenties, said he'd only recently taken an interest in learning more about his Native American ancestry. His mother was a full-blooded Cherokee from Oklahoma, but he and his brothers had been raised in the panhandle of Texas. He'd never been east of the Mississippi, so I encouraged him to come visit his ancestral homelands in the southern Appalachians. I told him that my home, Chattanooga, was near the Red Clay Council Grounds and New Echota, two of the former capitals of the Cherokee Nation. And the home of John Ross, the principal chief of the Chero-

kees at the time of the their removal from the East, was just across the state line in Georgia. From Chattanooga, I advised, it was only a short drive over the mountains to the Cherokee Indian Reservation in North Carolina.

Like most people who grew up in the South, I was very aware of the Native Americans who once lived in the area. How could I not be? All over the south, place names like Chickamauga, Hiwassee, Chattahoochee, Unicoi, Tennessee, Oconee, and Tuscaloosa are constant reminders of their presence. There are names like the Sequoyah Caverns, Alabama Boulevard, Ocoee Street, Cherokee Realty, Cherokee Auto Repair, Cherokee Shopping Center, Cherokee Pharmacy, Cherokee Freight, and the Cherokee Area Council of the Boy Scouts. Everywhere one goes in the South, there are names that serve as reminders of the first Americans.

But like most Southerners, my knowledge of the Native Americans and the early history of our region was spotty. I had spent many hours hiking and driving in mountains that bear Native American names. I had visited Red Clay and New Echota and had grown up with the knowledge that my great, great-grandmother was full-blooded Cherokee. But I really knew very little about how these people, my ancestors, lived or how they were driven away.

My love of the southern Appalachians has manifested itself in my photography for many years. As most photographers know, the best images are taken by those who know their subject. Thus, my interest in Cherokee history and folklore grew out of a desire to know more about the areas I was photographing. I'm not sure when, or why, I decided to start working on a book about the Cherokee heritage in the southern Appalachians, but I know the idea grew out of a fondness for the land. It grew out of a desire to understand the people, the lore, and the history of the region where I was born and have lived all my life. It was nurtured by a wish that my children would have a better understanding of their ancestry than I did. Finally, I wanted to share the history and the beauty of my homeland with others.

This book began as a short, photographic guide to scenic drives and a few, select Cherokee historic and cultural sites. While working on the book, I kept discovering new sites and historical information (at least new to me) which were so interesting that

I had to include them in the book.

Although I have spent several hundred hours researching this book, I hope readers will recognize it as a guidebook and not an academic treatise. In my research for the book, I encountered anomalies, anachronisms, disputed sites, and even quarreling local historians. I have tried to resolve these problems by locating additional sources or checking references. In some cases, I have presented more than one viewpoint, or made a judgment as to which source seemed most reliable. Since time constraints prevented me from checking thousands of original land records and papers in state and federal archives, I may not have made the correct choice in every situation. But I hope this book will inspire some readers to learn more about the early history of their community and to do additional research.

The sites in this book were chosen using the following criteria: historical or cultural significance, accessibility, proximity to other sites, beauty, educational opportunities, time restrictions, my personal fondness for the site, and my ability to locate the site. Due to time constraints, I limited my search to an area bounded on the west by the Tennessee River and on the north by the Kentucky and Virginia state lines. However, I made a few exceptions to my self-imposed restrictions, such as Betsy Pack's property in Jasper, Tennessee, and Cumberland Gap National Historic Area in Tennessee, Kentucky, and Virginia. While I tried to include sites which were more significant in Cherokee history than in Euro-American history, this distinction was often difficult to make. The documented history of the Cherokees is inevitably linked with the history of European settlers. Most of what we know about Cherokee history has been written by Euro-Americans.

One of the problems I encountered in writing this book was the dilemma of which sites were candidates for graverobbing or vandalism. Looting of prehistoric Native American sites is a major problem in the United States, and the Southeast is particularly susceptible because of the number of Woodland and Mississippian-era sites in our region. I have tried to avoid revealing any burial, bluff shelter, or other prehistoric sites which have not already been published, or are not already well-known or protected. In a few instances, I was asked by local authorities not to reveal specific locations, and in each case, I honored that request. I would like to remind readers that all Native American burial sites are protected by state and federal laws. In fact, all private and public lands are protected by law from vandalism, trespassing, or any form of looting. So the best policy to follow when you find Native American artifacts is to report them to on-site authorities, but don't pick them up. And please remember that sites on private property should be viewed from the road to avoid trespassing.

The locations of many of the Cherokee villages are now underwater, victims of man's progress. It is ironic that so much of the archaeological research which has been done on Cherokee sites is a result of rushed efforts to study the sites before they were lost forever under the waters of recreational lakes or power and flood-control projects. Other sites have fallen victim to development or to man's ignorance of the importance of these sites. But fortunately, there are a few sites left worth preserving, and there is a growing interest in Native American culture and history which could be the salvation of many of them. I hope this book will inspire a few readers to become involved in local preservation efforts so future generations can learn more about our Native American heritage.

Footsteps of the Cherokees is organized in two main sections. The first part is a historical and cultural overview which will help place the locations described in the second part into historical perspective. The second part, a guide to scenic, cultural, and historical locations, contains maps, photographs, and detailed directions to each site. I have listed hours of operation, entrance fees, and information phone numbers for museums, parks, and other attractions. This information was current at the time we went to press, but some of this information will undoubtedly change. It is advisable to call ahead to verify hours of operation if you are planning a trip and don't want to be inconvenienced. I have also included a bibliography of references used for this book. I recommend the books and articles in this bibliography for more in-depth reading about the Cherokees and the locations described in the book.

The photographs in the book help illustrate what will be found when you reach your destination. For some of the more remote sites, they will help answer the question, "Am I in the right place?" Although I had a large collection of color slides of the region before I started this project, I found that they did not convert to black-and-white with the quality I desired, so only a few have been used in the book. Most of the photographic images used in *Footsteps of the*

Cherokees were taken within the last year, using black-and-white print film. I wanted to use more "people shots" from the Cherokee Indian Reservation in North Carolina, and from powwows around the region, to illustrate that the Cherokee culture is alive and thriving, but the need for model-releases limited the use of these images to only a few pictures. And since I was on a tight schedule, the scenic shots weren't always photographed at the best time of day or year. But I think they do justice to the beauty of the region, and I hope that a few weeks after folks have visited a site, they can turn back to the photographs in the book and be reminded of an exciting hike in the mountains or an interesting drive along a river.

I hope you receive as much pleasure from exploring the mountains and valleys of the Cherokees as I have. And I hope you enjoy learning a little more about the history and culture of some of the first Americans. I wish you good reading and happy exploring as you follow in the *Footsteps of the Cherokees*.

ACKNOWLEDGMENTS

▲ ▲ ▲

This book has benefited from the suggestions and recommendations of many people. Special thanks go to Larry Beane of Russell Cave National Monument, George Frizzell of the Hunter Library at Western Carolina University, Nicholas Honerkamp of the Jeffrey L. Brown Institute of Archaeology at the University of Tennessee at Chattanooga, and Rickey Butch Walker of the Lawrence County (Alabama) Schools Indian Education Program, for providing additional resources and time to this project. My thanks to Marc Carpenter for loaning me books and journals from his collection and for providing ideas for topics.

This book would not have been possible without the darkroom artistry of Janet Stewart Coots of Bridgeview Black and White in Chattanooga, Tennessee. Janet processed nearly all of my black-and-white film for this project and printed over 140 black-and-white images.

Special thanks must also go to the staffs of the following libraries, where I spent many interesting hours: The Chattanooga-Hamilton County Bicentennial Library, The Lupton Library at the University of Tennessee at Chattanooga, The John C. Hodges Library at the University of Tennessee at Knoxville, the James D. Hoskins Library at the University of Tennessee at Knoxville, the Atlanta History Center, and the Hunter Library at Western Carolina University. My thanks to all libraries and organizations, including the Tennessee Valley Authority, who participate in the inter-library loan system. It was a special treat to receive an original, 1849 copy of Charles Lanman's, *Letters from the Allegheny Mountains*, through inter-library loan.

My appreciation to the professionals at John F. Blair, Publisher, especially Debbie Hampton, Liza Langrall, Carolyn Sakowski, and Andrew Waters.

I would also like to thank the many individuals who reviewed parts of this book or provided information: Margie Douthit of the Cherokee Historical Association; Shirley Lawrence of the Friends of the Cherokee Memorial; Scott Alexander of Oconee Station State Park; Carol Borneman of Cumberland Gap National Historic Park; Joe Distretti and Jeff Wells of Fort Loudoun State Historic Area; the reenactors of The Independent Company of South Carolina; Dr. Jefferson Chapman of The Frank H. McClung Museum; John Wilson of *The Chattanooga Free Press*; J. C. Thacker of Sunset, South Carolina; Jack T. Wynn of the United States Forest Service in Gainesville, Georgia; Curtis Hill of the Archaeological Laboratory of Jacksonville State University; David Perry of Tallulah Gorge State Park; Mike Johnson of Sheffield Parks and Recreation Department; Emma Jordan of the Fort Payne Depot Museum; John Chambers, DeKalb County Historian; tom kunesh of Chattanooga, Tennessee; Ray Zimmerman of Chattanooga, Tennessee; Russ Whitlock of the Museum of North Carolina Minerals; Faye Harper of the Southern Highland Craft Guild; Phil Noblett and Ina Parr of the Blue Ridge Parkway; Scott Stegenga of Table Rock State Park; Mac Copeland of Keowee-Toxaway State Park; Jim Brown of The Tennessee River Gorge Trust; Stacy Tilley of Audubon Acres; Steve McAloon of Reflection Riding; the staff of New Echota State Historic Site; Libby Bell of Etowah Indian Mounds State Historic Site; Eric Williams of Ninety Six National Historic Site; Penny McLaughlin of Tipton-Haynes Historic Site; Herb Roberts of Sycamore Shoals State Historic Area; Marlene Jones of the Sam Houston Schoolhouse; Carroll Hamilton of the Sequoyah Birthplace Museum; Barbara Broach of the Florence Department of Arts and Museums; Jim Atkinson of the Natchez Trace Parkway; Linda Grant of Toccoa Falls College; Wally Woods of Fort Mountain State Park; Joy Goodwin of the Chieftain's Museum; Ken Rush of the Ducktown Basin Museum; Robert McGinnis of James White's Fort; Cherry Payne of the National Park Service, Long Distance Trails Group Office; Terry Seabolt of the Dahlonega Gold Museum State Historic Site; Jeanette Pike of Noccalula Falls and Turkeytown Association of the Cherokee; Robert Hughes of Zion Hill Baptist Church; Gail Gomez of Kituwah; Tony Tonacio of the Kingston Parks and Recreation Department; Joan Greene of the Museum of the Cherokee Indian; Mary Black of the Moccasin Bend Chapter of the Daughters of the American Revolution; Muriel Spoden of Kingsport, Tennessee; Larry Luckett of the Brasstown Ranger District; Alice White of the Cherokee County Historical Museum; Dave Redman and Debbie Mintz of Cherokee Tribal Travel and Promotion; Lois Osborne of Red Clay State Historic Park; Nancy Gray of The Great Smoky Mountains National Park; Peggy Sellers of Blowing Rock Attractions; Bob Stiles of the John Ross

House Association; Hurley Badders of the Pendleton District Commission; Karen Gibbs of Hendersonville, North Carolina; Joe Nicholson of the Wayah Ranger District; Quentin Bass of the Cherokee National Forest; Pat Lancaster of the Pisgah Ranger District; Glen McConnell of the Cheoah Ranger District; Gerald F. Schroedl of the University of Tennessee at Knoxville Department of Anthropology; and Nancy Beck of the Chattahoochee River National Recreation Area.

And finally, my heartfelt thanks to my children, Laurel and Chris, and to my parents, Mr. and Mrs. Robert T. Bell, for their patience and support. To my husband Ed, on our twentieth anniversary, thanks for many hours of childsitting and camera-equipment hauling, for your companionship on weekend excursions, and for being a wonderful sounding board.

FOOTSTEPS
OF THE
CHEROKEES

THE PRINCIPAL PEOPLE

▲ ▲ ▲

Great Smoky Mountains National Park

They called themselves the *Ani-Yun-Wiya*, The Principal People. No one knows where the Cherokees came from, or how long they have lived in the Southeast. Their language is of the Iroquois family, suggesting they may have migrated from the north. Their Muskogean neighbors called them *Tciloki*, or "people of a different speech." The Cherokees adopted this name as *Tsalagi*, which later became "Cherokee."

Cherokee legend indicates, and some historians believe, the Cherokees arrived in the southern region of the Appalachian Mountains only a few years before the Europeans arrived in the Southeast. Other historians, however, point to archaeological evidence found in pottery, tools, and customs that suggests they were in the Southeast several hundred years, perhaps over a thousand years, before the Europeans arrived.

THE PREHISTORIC INDIANS

The early history of the Native Americans of the southeastern United States is usually divided into four cultural development periods: Paleo-Indian, Archaic, Woodland, and Mississippian. These cultural periods began at different times in various regions of the Southeast and frequently overlapped with developmental phases in other parts of North America. Evidence of these prehistoric cultures is scattered across the Southeast. A brief examination of the major characteristics of these cultural periods will help place the history of the Cherokee culture into perspective.

The Paleo-Indian period began with the migration of the first band of Pleistocene hunters and gatherers into the region, ten thousand to thirty thousand years ago. These ice-age hunters used spears to kill large animals such as mammoths, mastodons, camels, and horses, all of which became extinct in North America around 8000 or 9000 B.C. As glacial ice receded, and large game disappeared due to overhunting and climate changes, North American Indians entered an economic and cultural phase known as the Archaic period.

Southeastern Indians of the Archaic period, which began around 8000 B.C. and ended around 1000 B.C., were nomadic hunters and gatherers, occasionally living in caves or taking temporary shelter beneath rocky outcrops. Evidence that Native Americans of the Southeast were living in caves as early as 7000 B.C. can be found at Russell Cave National Monument in Alabama.

During the Woodland period, which began around 1000 B.C. and lasted for about two thousand years, eastern North American Indians built a number of earthworks of varying size and function. Ancient stone fortifications, like those at Old Stone Fort State Park in south central Tennessee and Fort Mountain State Park in north Georgia, are similar to sites in Kentucky and Missouri. Several effigy mounds, mounds built in the shape of an animal or geometric design, have been identified as belonging to the Woodland period. The Rock Eagle Mound in Georgia is an effigy mound believed to have been built in the Woodland period. The purpose of these stone complexes and of the effigy mounds are not known, but many archaeologists believe their purpose may have been ceremonial. Other mounds built by Indians are clearly burial mounds.

The Mississippian period began around 700 to 900 A.D. and was at its height from 1200 to 1400 A.D. Mississippian cultures

Museum of the Cherokee Indian

declined rapidly after the arrival of De Soto in 1540 A.D. The culture of this period is believed by some archaeologists to have originated on the Mississippi River, between St. Louis, Missouri, and Vicksburg, Mississippi. It gradually spread southeastward and southwestward along the tributaries of the Mississippi. It probably reached the southern Appalachians around 1000 A.D. The Mississippian cultural period saw an increase in the populations of Native American people, as well as an increase in the number of towns. The Mississippian Indians began building flat-top earthen mounds, which served as foundations for temples, mortuaries, and houses. These mounds have been found all over the Southeast, primarily near waterways, where most of the towns were located. Significant mound sites located in the Cherokee territory include the Nikwasi and Nacoochee mounds, which were occupied by the Cherokees when the first Europeans arrived, and the now-destroyed Peachtree Mound near Murphy, North Carolina.

The relationship of the Cherokees to the southeastern Mississippian culture is not clear. Some archaeologists believe the historic Cherokee culture is part of a continuum of local culture, particularly in the Appalachian summit area of western North Carolina. Others characterize the Chero-

kees as an invading force from the north, who adopted parts of the Mississippian culture of the people they had driven off. The Cherokees were not known as mound builders, but they used mounds built by earlier cultures, some of whom may have been ancestors.

Indian Corn or Selu

CHEROKEE LIFE AND CUSTOMS

Archaeologists and historians have been able to discover a great deal about the lifestyle of the early Cherokees and their predecessors.

Food played an important role in determining the Cherokees' way of life. During the Mississippian period in the Southeast, Indians began to rely on crops and became less dependent on gathering nuts, berries, and other seasonal foods than they had

Fort Loudoun State Historic Area

been in earlier periods. Corn and beans were the most important crops that the early Indians learned to cultivate. They also learned to grow several other crops, including squash and tobacco. But corn was the staple crop of the Cherokees and played an important role in their daily lives, as well as their belief system. *Selu* was the Cherokee name for corn and the name of the first woman in the Cherokee belief system. The mythical *Selu*, it was believed, oversaw the crops. Likewise, Cherokee women had the primary responsibility for agricultural duties, from planting to harvest. When the corn was ripe, the women presented it to the village in a sacred ritual, the Green Corn Ceremony.

While Cherokee women had primary responsibility for farming, the men hunted, fished, and trapped. The weapon of choice during the Archaic period was the *atlatl*, a tool for throwing spears, which gave way to the bow and arrow during the Woodland and Mississippian periods. Early points for arrows were made by chipping flint, other stone, and occasionally bone. Cherokees also used deer antlers, turkey spurs, or pieces of metal as points. Bows were shaped of sycamore, yellow locust, or hickory, then soaked in bear oil before they were seasoned by fire. Bows and arrows were frequently used against larger game such as deer, while traps, blowguns made of hollow cane reeds, and thistle darts were often used for smaller animals like rabbits.

Black bears were common throughout the Cherokee territory and were usually hunted in the fall when they were fattest. Bear grease was highly prized and was stored in large clay pots in the floor of Cherokee houses. Cherokee hunters sometimes used scorched honey as a bait to attract bears to an area. Bears might be shot with arrow tips poisoned with mayapple roots. Occasionally they were trapped using a metal-spiked, hollow log set in a hole in the ground that had been baited.

The white-tailed deer was the most important source of meat for the Cherokees, due partly to its abundance. Hunters usually stalked deer early in the morning or late in the evening during the fall and winter. The Cherokees sometimes used a whistle, made by splitting a laurel twig and inserting a piece of rhododendron or laurel in the cleft, to attract the deer.

Fish were also an important source of food. Methods of fishing included the use of traps and nets. One ingenious method of catching fish involved building a dam across a stream and poisoning the water by dropping ground buckeyes into it. This killed the fish which were trapped there but caused no harm to humans when the fish were eaten. Smaller fish were boiled with corn meal to make a soup, while larger fish were roasted or fried. The scales of gar were sometimes used as arrow points.

Cherokee village life centered around the *anaskayi*, or council house, which was sometimes set on top of a ceremonial mound. The villagers gathered at the *anaskayi* to debate important issues. While politics was male-dominated, prominent females often spoke at council. Cherokee villages were ruled by these local councils and chose their own chiefs. The concept of a "Principal Chief," a leader of the entire Cherokee tribe, did not evolve until the eighteenth century.

Each village chose two chiefs, the "White Chief" and the "Red Chief." Village life revolved around the seasons, and the roles of the chiefs depended on what time of year it was. In winter, the "Red Chief," or war chief, often presided over meetings because winter was the time for hunting and war. The "White Chief" was more important during the summer season because he oversaw planting and other domestic affairs. Summer was the time for planting, peace, and ceremony. Six major summer festivals, including the Green Corn Ceremony, celebrated spring planting and the harvest season.

Central to the Cherokee culture was the clan system. There were seven clans: Deer, Wolf, Paint, Bird, Holly, Blind Savannah, and Long Hair. (The exact translation of the clan names is unclear. The last four clan names have also been translated as the Red Paint, Blue Paint, Wild Potato, and Twister clans.) Clan kinship was matrilineal. Children were members of their mother's clan, and after marriage, men remained in their mother's clan. Clan regulations, with rules on domestic issues such as marriage and child rearing, were developed and overseen by women. The clan regulations played an integral part in Cherokee life. When they were broken, the violators were often beaten by female members of the clan. Most villages had all seven clans represented among its people. Council houses were often built with eight sides. One side was dedicated to the entrance, and the other seven sides honored the seven clans.

Recreation was an important part of village life. Many villages had ball grounds for playing stick ball, the forerunner of lacrosse. The game was played using sticks with nets, which were used to carry a ball made from a stuffed animal skin. Apparently this was a very popular pastime for the whole village, and the ball games were taken very seriously. The games reached high levels of frenzied play, the no-holds-barred play often resulting in serious injuries and death. Other forms of sport included bow-and-arrow competition and chunkey. Chunkey was a game played by rolling a disc of stone across a level playing field and then throwing sticks at the stone to see who could get the closest to it.

Like the customs and government of village life, many of the Cherokee myths and religious practices were tied to the seasons. The new year began in the fall when the fire in the council house was extinguished and renewed. After cleaning out the old ashes from their hearths, women went to the council house to bring home some of the new fire. The ceremony was symbolic of a new year beginning free of sins or problems.

The Cherokee belief system, like all belief systems, developed an explanation for how the world was made. It described how plants, animals, and people came to play their roles in the universe. It also sought to create order in the world. The Cherokees believed that the earth was a great floating island in a sea of water, suspended at each of its four corners by a cord hanging down from a rock sky. Before the island was created, all the animals lived in *Galun lati*, the sky above the rock. Since it was very crowded there, they sent the water beetle down to explore the great sea.

9 ▲ ▲ ▲

View of Qualla Boundary, the Cherokee Indian Reservation

He dove beneath the waters and brought up mud, which formed the island earth. While the land was still soft, the great buzzard came down and flew all over the earth to see if it was ready for occupancy. When the great buzzard became tired while flying over the center of the great island, his giant wings struck the earth, making valleys. When he beat his wings upward, he pushed the earth up, creating the mountains. Thus, the Cherokees believed, the mountainous homelands of the *Ani-Yun-Wiya* were at the center of the earth.

THE ARRIVAL OF
THE WHITE MAN

▲ ▲ ▲

THE SPANISH EXPEDITIONS

The first Europeans to venture into Cherokee territory were the members of the De Soto party, who arrived in the region in 1540. Landing near Tampa Bay off the coast of Florida in May 1539, De Soto embarked on a journey across the Southeast which would take four years and end in tragedy for many Native Americans, as well as for De Soto himself. The expedition included over 600 soldiers, 100 servants, 240 horses, pigs, and an arsenal of weapons. The primary purpose for the expedition was to search for the gold and riches that the Spaniards believed were located throughout the New World. The exact route of De Soto's expedition is unclear, but it is believed· he traveled north into Georgia, then east to central South Carolina, where he encountered a female ruler at the town of Cofitachequi (near present-day Camden, South Carolina). Leaving South Carolina, his army moved northwest into North Carolina, then crossed the Blue Ridge Mountains into eastern Tennessee. Somewhere near present-day Knoxville, they turned south and crossed eastern Tennessee, making their way to the capital village of the Coosa chiefdom, near present-day Carter's Dam in North Georgia. De Soto followed the Coosa River into Alabama and fought a major battle on the Alabama River with the Alibamo chief, Tasculuza, before turning northwest into Mississippi, Arkansas, and Texas. Returning to the Mississippi River, the expedition built brigantines and sailed down the river to the Gulf of Mexico, and then on to Panuco in the territory of Mexico. The expedition ended in September 1543. There were only three hundred survivors of the expedition, not including the Indian captives the Spanish brought to Mexico. De Soto had died on the Mississippi River in May 1542.

This unsuccessful search for gold cost the lives of a countless number of Indians. Many died of smallpox and other European diseases. The Native Americans had never been exposed to these diseases, and therefore, had no immunities to them. In many areas, disease may have preceded De Soto's arrival. This probably was due to Indians who came in contact with the Europeans, or infected Indians, then traveled to other villages, transmitting disease throughout the

Nantahala Gorge - Andrews

area. De Soto often encountered villages that were hit by epidemics shortly before he got there. The diseases brought by Europeans were so deadly, that estimates by scholars suggest up to 95 percent of the Native American population of the Southeast may have been wiped out in the first two hundred years of contact with whites. Disease was not the only cause of Indian deaths. De Soto, himself, was directly responsible for killing many Indians. Some died while serving as slaves for the Spanish. Others were killed when they could not point De Soto in the direction of non-existent mines.

In 1567, another Spaniard, Juan Pardo, ventured into what is now western North Carolina, looking for gold. Pardo probably came in contact with the Cherokees during his expedition, although it is not known for certain. By the end of the sixteenth century, there had been several Spanish expeditions to establish mines in the Cherokee territory.

THE CHEROKEES
AND THEIR NEIGHBORS

In the years following the Indians' first contact with the Spanish explorers, contact with the whites increased. The sixteenth, seventeenth, and early-eighteenth centuries were years of increasing trade between the Cherokees and white explorers, as well as between the Cherokees and neighboring tribes. Due to the increase in trade, competition for farmland and hunting grounds grew. Relationships between neighboring tribes became volatile, and border disputes between the Indians often turned violent and bloody. French and British operatives often encouraged and supported the violence between the tribes to further their influence in the area.

During the first half of the seventeenth century, the Cherokee and Creek Indians were in an almost constant state of warfare. These skirmishes lasted for decades, until a decisive battle occurred at Taliwa, near present-day Ball Ground, Georgia, around the year 1755. About five hundred Cherokees defeated a force of nearly one thousand Creeks, forcing the Creeks to immediately abandon their town on Nottely Creek, near present-day Blairsville, Georgia. Soon afterwards, the Cherokees and Creeks briefly became allies in a war against the colonists, but the boundary between the two nations remained in dispute for many years. As a result of their victory at Taliwa, the Cherokees claimed land seventy miles south of Atlanta, though they

13 ▲ ▲ ▲

*Stone historical marker marks
the trail of the Indian War Path that
passed by the Long Island of the Holston River.*

never moved to the southernmost region.

The Cherokees also struggled with other neighboring tribes. They experienced years of hostilities with the Shawanos, or Shawnees. The Shawnees lived in the Ohio River Valley and the Cumberland River area in middle Tennessee and Kentucky. The Cumberland River was marked on many early maps as the "River of Shawano." The Shawnees were old allies of the Creeks, and soon came into conflict with the Cherokees. During the Shawnee wars, the Chickasaws—who lived in northern Alabama, northern Mississippi, and western Tennessee—came to the aid of the Cherokees. The Cherokee and Chickasaw warriors forced the Shawnees north to the Ohio River around the year 1710. For many years, the warring tribes continued to fight each other along the Cumberland River, until the area was virtually abandoned except for hunting parties. Later, the Shawnees allied with the Delawares, who occupied lands in present-day Pennsylvania, New York, New Jersey, and Delaware. The Delawares were embroiled in a long war with the Cherokees that lasted until 1768. The last major battle between the Cherokees and Shawnees took place in Tazewell County, Virginia, in 1786.

The near-constant state of warfare among Indians caused the boundaries of the tribes to fluctuate. By the eighteenth century, most Cherokee towns were located in three areas: the "Lower Towns," concentrated along the Savannah River in northeast Georgia and western South Carolina; the "Middle and Valley Towns" in the extreme northeast area of Georgia and southwest North Carolina along the Little Tennessee and Tuckasegee rivers; and the "Overhill Towns" in eastern Tennessee along the Hiwassee, Tennessee, and Tellico rivers.

Although the various tribes spoke different languages, the language barrier did not seem to inhibit trade among the Indians. The Cherokees traded soapstone, used to make tools, for conch shells from the coast. The shells were made into ceremonial and ornamental objects including gorgets and ear pins. Ancient trade and war paths followed the route of bison through the mountain passes and along valley floors.

THE FRENCH AND BRITISH INFLUENCE

Trade with Europeans continued to grow during the various conflicts between the tribes. European traders used the Indians' ancient paths to establish trade throughout the Cherokee territory. By the early eigh-teenth century, English traders began to build stores in Cherokee territory, where they exchanged goods brought by horse from South Carolina. French traders from the Gulf Coast also traded with the Cherokees. The fur and skin trade flourished during this period, as Cherokees developed a taste for European goods such as blankets and metal tools. By the end of the eighteenth century, thousands of deerskins and other pelts had been traded to the Europeans. By the middle of the nineteenth century, the gray wolf, eastern bison, eastern elk, and river otter had disappeared from most of the eastern landscape due to trapping and hunting by white hunters as well as Indians.

Political intrigue among the European powers increased tensions between the tribes. The French held Canada, Louisiana, and the Mississippi Valley. The Spanish were in Florida, and the British occupied most of the Atlantic seaboard. Agents of these countries sought to establish allies among the various tribes of Native Americans, and they often manipulated tribes against one another.

The slave trade between the Indians and the Europeans also increased tensions between those two groups, as well as between the various Indian tribes. Warring tribes often took prisoners in battle, then sold the captives to the Europeans as slaves. The Cherokees probably would have tortured and killed their prisoners had they not been bought by traders for the slave market. These unfortunate Indians worked alongside African slaves on coastal rice and tobacco plantations.

In 1715, the issue of slavery began a conflict between the Cherokees and the colonists of Charles Towne (now Charleston, South Carolina). In that year, the Cherokees learned the colonists had shipped Cherokee captives to the West Indies to serve as slaves. Charles Towne also wanted the Cherokees to declare peace with the Creek Indians, but the Cherokees balked at this demand. The Cherokees needed Creek slaves to trade for guns and ammunition. In the same year, Colonel George Chicken took a detachment to Tlanusi'yi on the Hiwassee River (near the present-day town of Murphy, North Carolina) to discuss peace and to resolve the slave and weapons issues. Colonel Chicken agreed to send guns and white soldiers to assist the Cherokees in their wars against tribes with whom the English were still at war. In 1721, the Cherokees made their first land cession to the British, giving up a strip of land between the Saluda, Santee, and Edisto rivers. It was a small strip that was hardly used by the Cherokees, but it was of importance to the expanding Charles Towne colony. In return the Cherokees were granted an end to the Cherokee slave problem and to unfair trade practices.

In 1730, a colorful character named Alexander Cuming, an unofficial representative of the King of England, visited the Cherokees and succeeded in gaining a pledge of loyalty to the British crown. Stopping in the Overhill Town of Tellico (present-day Tellico Plains, Tennessee), Cuming met the local chief, Moytoy, who declared his allegiance to King George II. Later, during council at Nikwasi (present-day Franklin, North Carolina), Cuming declared Moytoy "Emperor" of all Cherokees. Cuming took two chiefs and five prominent Cherokees back to England to meet the king. One of the young warriors who accompanied Cuming on this trip was Attakullakulla. Attakullakulla, also known as "Little Carpenter," would come to play an important part in the relations between his people and the white man in the following years.

The first Christian mission in Cherokee territory was established at Tellico by Christian Priber, a French Jesuit, in 1736. Priber was liked by the Cherokees and quickly gained influence. He drew up a scheme of government for the Cherokees, modeled after European governments. His plan called for a capital to be established at the Overhill Town of Great Tellico, with the principal medicine man as emperor, and Priber as the emperor's secretary. For four years, Priber drew Cherokees to the French. He was able to persuade many Cherokees that the smallpox epidemic of 1738, which killed nearly half the Cherokees, was sent by the English. Oconostota, the most powerful of the Overhill war chiefs, bore the scars of the terrible disease on his face for the rest of his life. He sided with the French, possibly due to Priber's influence. During this time, a rift developed between Oconostota and Attakullakulla, who was now a prominent leader of the Cherokees and remained loyal to the English.

The British began to grow concerned about the increasing French influence among the Cherokees. When they perceived Priber was a threat, he was intercepted by British traders on his way to Fort Toulouse (near present day Montgomery, Alabama) and taken to Fort Frederica in Georgia, where he later died.

In 1746, the English learned that two French agents were in the Overhill area trying to persuade the Cherokees to ally with the French. The French agents argued that the English intended to take the Cherokees' land. They told the Cherokees the French would give them better trade terms without threatening their hunting grounds. The British also heard reports that the French planned to build a fort in the Overhills. To solidify their relations with the Cherokees, the British proposed to build two forts in Cherokee country: Fort Prince George was to be built in northern South Carolina near Keowee, the principal town of the Lower Cherokees; and Fort Loudoun would be built on the Little Tennessee River near the principal Overhill Town of Chota. The forts were also to provide protection for the Cherokee towns while the Cherokee warriors, under Ostenaco, aided the British in fighting Shawnees, who were allied with the French.

Progress on Fort Prince George proceeded quickly, due to its closer proximity to the British colonies. However, it took several years for the money to be allocated for the building of Fort Loudoun. Finally, in 1756, the remote outpost in the heart of the Cherokee Overhill country was completed. Trade with the Indians living near Fort Loudoun began immediately. All materials and supplies for Fort Loudoun came through Fort Prince George. Obtaining supplies from Fort Prince George was difficult, with many miles of isolated mountainous terrain separating the forts. For three years the garrison at Fort Loudoun

Reenactors of the Independent Company of South Carolina - Fort Loudoun

maintained an uneasy peace with the Cherokees. French agents continued their activities in the area, and there were occasionally violent misunderstandings between the Cherokees and English.

In 1756, Cherokee warriors went to Virginia to assist the British in their war against the French. Many of the Cherokees became dissatisfied with their treatment and inadequate compensation and began to slip away. One band of Cherokees took some horses from Virginia settlers on their return home. The settlers followed the Cherokees, and a skirmish took place in which several settlers were killed. Over the next few years, several skirmishes occurred between Cherokees and whites.

In response to these skirmishes, Governor William Henry Lyttleton of the South Carolina colony (as the Charles Towne colony was now known) demanded the surrender and execution of every Indian who had killed a white man in the area. In December 1759, a delegation of prominent Cherokees came to Fort Prince George for peace talks. On Lyttleton's orders, the delegation was captured and imprisoned at the fort. Oconostota was among these prisoners. They were to be held as hostages at Fort Prince George until the murderers were apprehended.

Attakullakulla came to the fort and was able to arrange the release of several of the Cherokees, including Oconostota. On February 16, 1760, Oconostota summoned Lieutenant Richard Coytmore, commander of Fort Prince George, to meet with him outside the fort. During the meeting, the Cherokees opened fire and killed Coytmore. The English soldiers then killed the remaining Cherokee prisoners, which caused the Cherokees to begin a siege of Fort Prince George that lasted several months.

Captain Paul Demeré, commander at Fort Loudoun, realized that the siege at Fort Prince George placed his own fort in peril. First, he cut rations. Then on March 20, 1760, the Cherokees opened fire on Fort Loudoun and continued attacking for four days. The Cherokees then fell back and began a siege of the fort. On June 2, the Cherokees appeared to abandon the siege, but when two soldiers slipped out of the fort to find food, they were both killed. Meanwhile, Fort Prince George was relieved in early June by Colonel Archibald Montgomery's British troops, who were on an expedition to destroy several Lower Cherokee towns. The mountains, and concern for his wounded soldiers, prevented Montgomery from continuing to Fort Loudoun to relieve Demeré and his men.

Conditions at Fort Loudoun were miserable during the summer of 1760. On August 6, Captain Demeré and the Overhill chiefs, including Oconostota, finally reached some terms. The garrison and its weapons were to be turned over to the Cherokees in return for safe escort of all the soldiers to Fort Prince George. Two days later, the garrison marched out of the fort in the direction of Fort Prince George. That night they made camp at Cane Creek on the Tellico River. The next morning, the soldiers discovered their Indian escort had slipped away during the night. After reveille, they found themselves surrounded by Indians. Both sides opened fire. Approximately twenty men and women from the fort were killed, including Demeré. Captain John Stuart, a favorite of Attakullakulla, was the only junior officer who was spared. Stuart had accompanied

Attakullakulla on diplomatic missions to Fort Prince George and Charles Towne, and Attakullakulla trusted him. Attakullakulla may have arranged for Stuart to be spared, or the Captain may have been saved by Oconostota so he could direct the transport of Fort Loudoun's cannon over the mountains for use against Fort Prince George. Whatever the reason for Stuart's salvation, the Cherokee plan to attack Fort Prince George with the cannon never came about. Attakullakulla managed to rescue Stuart from his captors and return him safely to the British. The other survivors of Fort Loudoun were taken captive and moved to various Cherokee towns. Many were eventually killed. Some were later traded for goods or ransomed to the governments of Virginia and Carolina. Fort Loudoun was occupied briefly by Cherokee families and later burned.

The reason for the massacre has been subject for much speculation. One theory is that the Cherokees felt deceived when they discovered the garrison had buried some of its gunpowder. Another theory is that the chiefs had never been able to reach a consensus on the issue of safe escort of the garrison, and the dissenting chiefs decided to attack. A third theory is that the Cherokee justice system practiced blood revenge, or clan revenge. The number of Fort Loudoun soldiers killed equalled the number of Cherokees killed at Fort Prince George. This is the appropriate number in terms of clan revenge. Whatever the reason, in 1761, the English launched a vengeful retaliation on the Lower and Middle towns, destroying fifteen communities and hundreds of acres of corn and beans. A letter written by Lieutenant Francis Marion, who later became known as the "Swamp Fox" during the American Revolution, described the awful tasks performed by the British soldiers:

> We proceeded, by Colonel Grant's orders, to burn the Indian cabins. Some of the men seemed to enjoy this cruel work, laughing heartily at the curling flames, but to me it appeared a shocking sight. Poor creatures, thought I, we surely need not grudge you such miserable habitations. But when we came, according to orders, to cut down the fields of corn, I could scarcely refrain from tears. Who, without grief, could see the stately stalks with broad green leaves and tasseled tops, the staff of life sink under our swords with all their precious load, to wither and rot untasted in their mourning field.

In December 1761, Attakullakulla met with Governor Bull at Charles Towne and negotiated a treaty with the South Carolina colony. Two months later, the Cherokees signed another peace treaty with the Virginia colony at the British fort on the Long Island of the Holston River (present-day Kingsport, Tennessee). Attakullakulla persuaded the British to appoint John Stuart as "head white man" in the Cherokee territory. In the late 1760s, Stuart sent two competent deputy commissioners, John McDonald and Alexander Cameron, into Cherokee territory. Cameron was given land in Long Canes country (present-day Abbeville County, South Carolina) by the Cherokees, and McDonald settled near the ruins of Fort Loudoun. These sympathetic men managed to reestablish friendly relations with the Indians that lasted about thirteen years. Cameron and Stuart would go on to play important roles in influencing the Cherokees to side with the British during the American Revolution.

Cades Cove was known by the Cherokees as Tsiya'hi or "Otter Place."

CONFLICTS WITH
THE SETTLERS

▲ ▲ ▲

THE RISE OF NANCY WARD
AND DRAGGING CANOE

Tensions continued to rise between the Cherokees and the American colonists in the years after the attack on Fort Loudoun and the brutal retaliation that followed. During this period, Nancy Ward and Dragging Canoe emerged as important Cherokee leaders. Although they were cousins, they came to play very different roles in the Cherokees' relations with the whites.

Nancy Ward was a niece of Attakullakulla and first rose to prominence during the battle of Taliwa in 1755. In the battle, the Cherokees found themselves heavily outnumbered by the Creeks. Nancy Ward was then a teenage girl, known as Nanyihi. Her husband, Kingfisher, was shot and killed, and Nanyihi took up his gun and rallied the outnumbered Cherokees to victory. The warriors who returned to the village of Chota declared Nanyihi a great warrior, and the young, widowed

Nancy Ward's grave - Benton

mother of two was given the title of *Ghighau*, sometimes translated as "Beloved Woman" or "Most Honored Woman." As *Ghighau*, Nanyihi sat with the peace and war chiefs at council meetings and served as head of the Woman's Council. She was also responsible for preparing the "Black Drink," a concoction made from the winterberry shrub (*Ilex vomitoria*). The Black Drink ritual was a sacred purification rite performed by warriors before battle and during several religious ceremonies.

Some time after Kingfisher was killed, Nanyihi married an English trader named Bryant Ward. After this marriage, Nanyihi's name became Nancy Ward. Marriages between traders and Cherokee women were fairly common. These mixed marriages produced several future leaders of the Cherokee nation, including George Lowrey, John Ross, and Sequoyah. Upon marriage, which was a simple ceremony where the bride and groom exchanged gifts as a token of their promise to be good partners, the white man was accepted into the tribe.

Nancy Ward's cousin, Dragging Canoe, was the son of Attakullakulla. He was born about 1732 and was just a few years older than Nanyihi. He received his name from an incident that occurred when he was a young boy. He wanted to accompany his father on an expedition to fight the Shawnee. Attakullakulla refused to let him go, but the young warrior hid in a dugout canoe, which the war party was taking along. When his father discovered him, Dragging Canoe was told he could go with the war party if he could portage the canoe to the next river. The young boy dragged the canoe across the land, and the warriors gave him the name of Tsiyu Gansini, "Dragging Canoe." As Dragging Canoe grew older, he emerged as a bold leader of the Cherokees.

Both Nancy Ward and Dragging Canoe were raised in the capital town of Chota, but their opinion of how to deal with the settlers could not have been more different. In the years that followed, Nancy Ward continually advised the Cherokees to make peace with white settlers and to avoid violent retaliations. Dragging Canoe became a leader of a band of fierce renegades determined to hold out against the whites' encroachment on Cherokee land. Both played important roles as the tensions grew between white settlers and the Cherokees.

THE WATAUGA SETTLEMENT

In 1763, a proclamation by King George III forbid British settlement and land grants beyond the crest of the Appalachians. Europeans who had already settled in the west were to leave the region. This "proclamation line" was very unpopular with colonists, as well as with Virginia land companies like the Ohio Company and the

Loyal Land Company, whose plans for land speculation in the west were temporarily thwarted.

Despite this proclamation, settlers continued to pour into the territory on the west side of the Appalachians. The colonial government found they were unable to enforce this new law in the remote wilderness. The first permanent settlers came to the Watauga Valley, located in northeast Tennessee. Members of the William Bean family from Virginia, were the first to settle in the area in 1769. Others soon followed the Beans, and the Sycamore Shoals area (present-day Elizabethton, Tennessee) became a rendezvous point for these settlers.

This settlement probably survived because Cherokee warriors in the area were away fighting the Chickasaws. At first, the Cherokees seemed willing to work out agreements with the settlers in the Watauga Valley. A variety of treaties were signed between Cherokee chiefs and settlers. This often led to confusion, since it was seldom clear what authority the various chiefs had to represent the Cherokees in these treaties. This problem would continue to plague the Cherokees throughout their history of dealing with the whites.

In 1771, John Donelson (a Virginian who later helped found Nashville), Attakullakulla, and Indian agent Alexander Cameron, conducted a survey that determined the Wataugans were in violation of a 1770 treaty with the Cherokees. Attakullakulla took pity on the settlers and agreed the boundary line could run down the south fork of the Holston River to Long Island (at present-day Kingsport, Tennessee). This legitimized some of the settlers' claims, but not all. Cameron ordered the Wataugans who were in violation of the boundary to leave. Refusing to leave, William Bean and a settler named James Robertson traveled to Chota in an attempt to work out their own agreement. There, they learned the chiefs and British agents disagreed about the boundary. Bean and Robertson found chiefs who were willing to lease land, gave them gifts, and worked out a new agreement. They got approval for the agreement from John Stuart, still the head British agent in the territory, over the opposition of Cameron.

When Attakullakulla went to Watauga to work out details of the new lease, he wrote to Stuart:

> Father . . . I will eat and drink with my white brothers, and will expect friendship and good usage from them. It is but a little spot of ground that you ask, and I am willing that your people should live upon it. I pity the white people, but they do not pity me. . . . The Great Being

Sycamore Shoals State Park - Elizabethton

above is very good, and provides for everybody . . . he gave us this land, but the white people seem to want to drive us from it.

Attakullakulla and the Wataugans agreed to a ten-year lease of land in return for five thousand dollars in trade goods, muskets, and household items. To complicate matters further, Jacob Brown, who lived near Sycamore Shoals, met with Oconostota and other chiefs and worked out a separate lease with them.

The Wataugans met in May 1772 to draw up "Written Articles of Association," which officially established the Watauga settlement. This document was of historical significance because it is the first constitution west of the Appalachians, and the first drawn up by native-born Americans.

The years between 1772 and 1774 were peaceful years for the Wataugans and the Cherokees, as well as for the American colonists and England. By 1774, however, the Cherokees were becoming unhappy. They had made the 1771 agreement on the basis that they could continue to hunt on the lands they leased to the settlers, and that no more whites were to settle in the area. Yet settlers continued to pour over the mountains. Several of the younger Cherokees protested the agreement because it was made with only a few of the older chiefs.

The governor of North Carolina ordered the Wataugans to leave Cherokee land, but the white settlers ignored the order. Tensions grew between the Watauga settlement and the Cherokees when the cousin of Chief Ostenaco was murdered at a horse race at Sycamore Shoals in 1774. To defuse the situation, another treaty meeting was arranged for March 1775.

Daniel Boone, acting as an agent for the Transylvania Company, arranged the meeting at Sycamore Shoals. The Indians were treated to games, festivities, and food by the Wataugans and the Transylvania Company. The Transylvania Company proposed to purchase twenty million acres of land from the Cherokees in exchange for wagons and cabins full of gifts and goods. In addition, the Wataugans proposed to purchase the rights to their settlements.

Representing the Cherokees, the great chiefs Oconostota, Attakullakulla, Willanaugh, and Old Abram of Chilhowee were attired in the typical eighteenth-century clothing adopted by many Cherokees. This attire consisted of European-style match coats with ruffled shirts and leggings. On their chests they wore gorgets and British medals. The assemblage also included twelve hundred braves with colorful tattoos, as well as Cherokee women and children.

After Attakullakulla gave a speech in support of the treaty, his son, Dragging Canoe, rose and made an eloquent speech against it:

> The white man makes treaties only to break them. He is not satisfied with the land beyond the mountains, or the land beside the Watauga, or the land along the Nolichucky. Now he wants still more. And what we do not give him, he will take anyway until our whole Nation is gone from this earth. . . . Old men make paper talks; young men fight for what is theirs. I will not lose these lands without a fight.

In spite of Dragging Canoe's prophetic words, the elder chiefs signed the purchase on March 17, forfeiting the entire Cumberland River watershed, plus the southern half of the Kentucky River watershed—an area of twenty million acres. On March 19, for an additional two thousand pounds, the Wataugans bought outright the land they had been leasing.

A week before the signing, Daniel Boone left Sycamore Shoals with a party of axemen and began blazing a trail through the Cumberland Gap. Early in April, the first settlers followed and founded Boonesborough on the banks of the Kentucky River. The royal governors of Virginia and North Carolina said the purchase, the largest private or corporate land deal in United States history, was illegal, but again, the settlers ignored the commands of the colonial government.

VIOLENCE ON THE FRONTIER

In the fall of 1775, the Wataugans declared their support for the American cause against the British. The British sought the help of Dragging Canoe and the Cherokees in fighting the Americans. They tried to convince the Cherokees the land cession the Cherokees made at Sycamore Shoals had encouraged the settlers to declare independence. The Cherokees soon pledged their loyalty to John Stuart and the British.

In anticipation of trouble with the Cherokees and the British, the Wataugans built Fort Caswell, also known as Fort Watauga, at Sycamore Shoals. They also began construction on Fort Lee on Limestone Creek, near the Nolichucky River.

In May 1776, a fourteen-man delegation of Shawnee, Ottawa, Mohawk, Delaware, and Mingo warriors arrived in the Overhill area to seek an alliance with the Cherokees to fight the white man's encroachment on Indian lands. The young Cherokees accepted the northern Indians' war belts,

Monument marking original site of Fort Watauga - Elizabethton

Long Island on the Holston River, and Carter's Valley (west of present-day Kingsport, Tennessee).

Nancy Ward, who was no doubt present during many of the councils, warned the Wataugans of the impending attack. The motives for Nancy Ward's warning are subject for speculation, but some historians feel that she may have remembered the results of the Fort Loudoun and Fort Prince George attacks, which resulted in the burning of many Cherokee villages. Ward may have been trying to prevent another war with the whites, which her people could not win, or she may have taken pity on the settlers. In later years, one of her favorite sayings was, "The white men are our brothers. The same house shelters us, and the same sky covers us all."

The settlers had been expecting renewed trouble for some time. When Nancy Ward's messengers arrived with confirmation of the attack, Lieutenant John Sevier, leader of the Watauga militia, abandoned the incomplete Fort Lee, and the settlers moved to the safety of Fort Watauga.

The Cherokee war party first arrived at the deserted Fort Lee. After burning it, they split forces. The Raven of Chota headed toward Carter's Valley with his forces, Dragging Canoe moved toward Long Island, and Old Abram of Chilhowee ad-

while the elder Cherokees looked on in disappointment. Soon after this meeting, the older chiefs received an ultimatum from Colonel William Russell of Virginia to control Dragging Canoe and oust the British advisors, or face an invasion of Cherokee country. In response, seven hundred warriors headed north in mid-July to attack the Watauga and Nolichucky settlements, vanced toward Sycamore Shoals, which was under the command of Colonel John Carter, Captain James Robertson and John Sevier. The Raven's party moved into the largely abandoned Carter's Valley, burning cabins and destroying crops. Dragging Canoe was wounded in the thigh and defeated at Long Island by a combined force of Virginia and local militia.

On July 21, 1776, at daybreak, the Cherokees under Old Abram alarmed several women who were milking cows outside Fort Watauga. All the women near the fort escaped to the safety of the fort before the gates were closed except a tall woman named Catherine Sherrill. When she reached the wall of the fort, Catherine was pulled to safety by John Sevier. Sevier would marry her four years later.

Abram's assault with three hundred warriors lasted three hours and was driven back with some loss to the Indians. Soon after the first attack, the Indians learned of Dragging Canoe's defeat, withdrew from gun range, and set up siege positions. They harassed the settlers for two to three weeks. Inside the fort there was suffering and sickness. Most of the losses to the settlers were due to carelessness. In one incident, James Cooper and a youngster named Tom Moore were sent out to collect boards to repair a roof. Cooper was shot and scalped trying to swim across a stream, while Moore was captured and taken to the village Tuskegee, where he was burned at the stake. By the time Colonel Evan Shelby arrived to relieve Fort Watauga, Old Abram and his warriors had left the scene.

Although most of the settlers were able to reach Fort Watauga, Mrs. William Bean was not so lucky. Before the attack, Mrs. Bean had been captured and taken to Old Abram's camp. She was tied to a stake to be burned but was freed by Nancy Ward. The *Ghighau* told the Indians she could use Mrs. Bean's instructions in the making of butter and cheese.

In late July, Georgia, Virginia, and Carolina militias marched into Cherokee country and attacked the Lower, Middle, and Valley towns. In October, over twenty-one hundred militia, under the command of Colonel William Christian, left Fort Patrick Henry on Long Island for the Overhill Towns, where they met with no opposition. The Virginians burned Tuskegee, where young Moore had been burned alive a few weeks before. They then sacked three towns loyal to Dragging Canoe before returning home.

The elder Cherokee chiefs met with North Carolina and Virginia commissioners at Long Island and agreed to remain neutral. They could not speak for Dragging

Canoe, who continued to be hostile. A treaty talk was also held at De Witt's Corner in South Carolina, where all but a small western strip of land in South Carolina was ceded to the whites. The Overhill Cherokees made the cessions because their people were desperate. Their towns were crowded with refugees from the burned-out Middle Towns.

While the settlers continued to build new forts and stockades on the frontier, the disgruntled Dragging Canoe and some loyal followers moved to Chickamauga Creek, just east of Lookout Mountain in southeast Tennessee. Cherokee rebels were joined by refugees from the Lower Towns, which had just been ceded to South Carolina, as well as dissidents from other tribes. This band, known as the Chickamaugans, soon included a thousand warriors. In 1777, Five Killer, the son of Nancy Ward and Kingfisher, joined the Chickamaugans.

Chickamauga Creek at Audubon Acres - Chattanooga

Alexander Cameron also went to live with the Chickamaugans. Cameron and John Stuart, staunch Tories, still working as British agents, offered the Chickamaugans supplies to fight the American rebels.

Governor Patrick Henry of Virginia sent Colonel Evan Shelby and six hundred North Carolina and Virginia volunteers to raid the Chickamaugan towns in April 1779. Eleven towns were destroyed, and stores of British ammunition were confiscated. Undaunted, Dragging Canoe moved his Chickamaugan villages southwest to the foot of Lookout Mountain, an area which would be easier to defend. These new villages, called the "Five Lower Towns," were Lookout Town, on the east side of Lookout Creek near present-day Tiftonia, Tennessee; Crow Town, near present-day Stevenson, Alabama; Long Island, at present-day Bridgeport, Alabama; Runningwater, near present-day Haletown, Tennessee; and Nickajack, near present-day Shellmound, Tennessee. From these new locations, Dragging Canoe continued to stage raids on settlers who moved further and further west, blatantly encroaching on Indian land.

In October 1780, while the Wataugans were away fighting the British at the Battle of Kings Mountain in South Carolina, the Chickamaugans saw a chance to attack the settlements along the Nolichucky and Watauga rivers and rid themselves of the fierce Watauga militia. The Cherokees made plans for war, and British agents brought supplies to aid their efforts. Again, Nancy Ward, whose daughter was now married to Joseph Martin, a Virginia agent to the Cherokees, warned the settlers. She sent word of the impending attack on the Watauga settlements to John Sevier, who had just returned from Kings Mountain. In December 1780, Sevier and three hundred Overmountain Men, as the Wataugan fighting force had come to be called, engaged the Indians at Boyd's Creek. Two weeks later, Sevier's forces proceeded to the Cherokee capital town of Chota and burned it. The Wataugans then destroyed the other principal towns in the Overhill territory: Tellico, Citico, Chilhowee, Hiwassee, Chistowee, Toqua, and many more. Nancy Ward and her family were taken prisoner and placed under the protection of Joseph Martin who was living at Long Island on the Holston River.

Attakullakulla was now dead, and Oconostota was very old. Old Tassel, who would become principal chief in 1782 after Oconostota's death, was official spokesman for the Cherokees at a treaty meeting held in July 1781, at Long Island. Tassel blamed the recent troubles on Dragging Canoe and

British agent Alexander Cameron. Nancy Ward also spoke on behalf of her people:

"I know that white people think that a woman is nothing, but we are your mothers. . . . Our cry is for peace. This peace must last forever. Let your women's sons be ours and let our sons be yours. Let your women hear our cry."

Colonel Christian, who had spared Chota during the Virginia militia raid on the Overhill Towns in 1776, possibly as a favor to Nancy Ward, replied:

> Mother, we have listened to your talk. It is humane. No man could hear it without being moved by it. Such words and thoughts show that the human nature is the same everywhere. Our women shall hear your words, and we know they will feel and think of them. We will not quarrel with you, because you are our mothers. We will not meddle with your people if they will be still and quiet at home and let us live in peace.

The Long Island treaty was one of the few treaties in which whites did not ask for a cession of land.

As soon as the treaty meeting was over, Nancy, her son Five Killer, and his wife Catherine, returned to Chota where they adopted orphans left from the town's destruction months earlier. The Overhill Cherokees were forced to endure hunger and desperation for the next two years. Food was extremely scarce, and as whites continued to encroach on their land, game became scarce.

In 1781, the American Revolution ended with the surrender of Cornwallis at Yorktown. After a long and bitter war with England, Congress wanted peaceful and fair terms with the Cherokees. However, both the federal and state governments found it difficult to control the actions of the settlers on the frontier. In 1784, North Carolina, unable to control John Sevier or the western settlers, ceded the lands of the Wataugan and Nolichucky settlements to Congress. In protest, the Wataugans established a self-proclaimed State of Franklin. In November 1785, Congress called for a new treaty meeting at Hopewell, South Carolina, which returned land in the southern part of Franklin, including the capital town of Greeneville, to the Cherokees. The last clause of the treaty also gave the Cherokees license to harass any settlers who remained in their territory six months after the treaty was signed. Unfortunately, affairs between the Cherokees and whites worsened, and Congress was not prepared to deal with them properly. In trying to enforce the Treaty of Hopewell, the Cherokees killed several settlers in the northern area of their nation. Dragging Canoe also

Kuwa'hi, the "Mulberry Place." According to Cherokee legend, the bears have townhouses under Clingmans Dome and three other peaks.

raided an illegal settlement at Muscle Shoals, Alabama, killing John Donelson, one of the founders of Nashborough (Nashville, Tennessee). As punishment for the raids on white settlers, the Cherokees were forced into the Treaty of Coyatee in which they surrendered all of their land north of the Little Tennessee River.

In 1787, the *Kentucke Gazette* reported that the general assembly of the State of Franklin was concerned about frequent attacks by Chickamaugans and Creeks on travelers in Kentucky and Cumberland. A Kentucky militia of about seventy-five men under the command of Colonel John Logan, went to the Chickamaugan settlements where they killed seven Cherokees who were friendly to the whites. One of those killed was a chief of the village of Chota. Joseph Martin, agent to the Cherokees, rushed to Chota to prevent reprisals. Tensions between the Cherokees and the Frankliners continued to escalate, and after a few isolated instances of settlers being killed, many of the inhabitants of the settlements below the French Broad River began to move into small forts. Joseph Martin believed the Chickamaugans, not the local Cherokees, were responsible for the recent murders, and with this argument,

he managed to postpone some reprisals from the settlers. However in May 1788, eleven members of the John Kirk family, who lived twelve miles south of present-day Knoxville, were killed. Colonel John Sevier led a reprisal raid against the Overhill Towns and burned Hiwassee. John Kirk, Jr., the son of the murdered family, vowed revenge and joined a group of militia commanded by Major James Hubbard, one of Sevier's men. The militia, acting without the knowledge of Sevier, went to Chilhowee where Colonel Hubbard invited Old Abram, chief of Chilhowee, Old Tassel, chief of Chota and principal chief of the Overhills, and Old Abram's son to a meeting across the river from the village. Old Abram and Old Tassel were known to be friendly toward the whites, and both sides displayed white flags. However, Hubbard ushered the Cherokees into a building, then allowed young John Kirk, Jr., to attack the unsuspecting Indians with a tomahawk. Five or six Indians were killed, including the two chiefs and Abram's son. After the death of their principal chief, Old Tassel, the Cherokees moved their capital from Chota to Ustanali (near present-day Calhoun, Georgia).

View of Parksville Lake and Sugarloaf Mountain from Chilhowee Mountain

FEDERALIZATION AND CHRISTIANIZATION OF THE CHEROKEES

▲ ▲ ▲

THE CHEROKEES REBUILD

The end of the American Revolution found most Cherokees suffering from great hardships. Few towns remained, and the once-bountiful fields were destroyed. President Washington and the federal govern- ment decided that the Cherokees must become "civilized." To most whites, this meant the Cherokees had to evolve from a hunting society to an agrarian one. They also had to learn to read, write, speak English, and become Christians. While Washington seemed sincere in his desire to help the Cherokees survive, many supporters of the "civilization" effort had an ulterior motive—to obtain more of the Cherokee land for white settlement.

In 1791, at White's Fort on the Holston River (present-day Knoxville, Tennessee), the United States and the Cherokees negotiated another treaty, the Treaty of Holston. This treaty was significant in several respects: it clearly defined boundaries between the Cherokee lands and the United States, gave Cherokees the right to punish transgressions against them under their own laws, and provided resources for the "civilization" program.

Many Cherokees welcomed the program because they realized how vulnerable their villages were to further destruction. Others, like Chief Bloody Fellow, sought to stave off starvation. Of the treaty, he wrote, "The treaty mentions ploughs, hoes, cattle, and other things for a farm; this is what we want. Game is going fast away among us. We must plant corn and raise cattle, and we desire you to assist us."

It was several years before the program to federalize the Cherokees began in earnest. Hostilities between the Chickamaugans and the settlers continued. Dragging Canoe died in 1792, but his mixed-blood successor, Chief John Watts, continued raids against whites for two more years.

In 1784, North Carolina, in an effort to distance themselves from the volatile Watauga settlers, ceded all of its lands west of the Alleghenies to Congress. William Blount was appointed governor of the region which was known as "The Territory South of the Ohio River." Later it would become Tennessee. The independent State of Franklin eventually dissolved.

In 1793, a meeting occurred between some representatives of Governor Blount and Chief Hanging Maw. During the meeting, local militia acting on their own initiative, attacked the Cherokee delegation. The militia killed several Cherokee headmen and burned Hanging Maw's home. The representatives of Governor Blount narrowly escaped with their lives but were able to stop the militia from killing the rest of Hanging Maw's people.

This attack convinced Chief Hanging Maw he needed protection from violent settlers. In 1794, Chief Hanging Maw persuaded Governor Blount to build a blockhouse on Cherokee land. Hanging Maw believed this blockhouse would protect his friendly people from further raids. Blount believed the Tellico Blockhouse would also serve to keep the Indians under control. In 1795, Congress passed the "Factory Act," which provided for the "establishment of trading houses within the Indian tribes." Under this act, the Tellico Blockhouse was enlarged to house both a military garrison and a trading post.

Agents from Washington were sent to teach the Cherokees farming techniques, such as plowing and fence-building. The government also established gristmills and employed blacksmiths. Women, who were eager to learn to spin and weave, were provided with cotton seed, looms, and spinning wheels. Soon, the Cherokees were producing more fabric than they could use and were selling raw cotton and cloth to the federal agents.

Ironically, the Chickamaugans, who had fought so long and hard against the encroachments of the whites, were some of the most successful in embracing the new lifestyle and economy brought by the federalization program. The southern chiefs Will, Doublehead, and John Watts had more success in obtaining goods for their people than the mountain Cherokees. Newly established Cherokee farms in the south produced thriving corn, cotton, and bean crops.

One of the first to take the advice of the Indian agents in the federalization program was The Ridge. The Ridge was born around 1770 or 1771, at Hiwassee, now in Polk County, Tennessee. His mother was half Deer Clan, half Scottish. His father was full-blooded Cherokee. When the Hiwassee towns were burned, The Ridge's father put his family in canoes and left the area. They floated down the Hiwassee River to the Tennessee River, past the site of present-day Chattanooga. They settled on Sequatchie Mountain, "the place of the grinning possum," which is now known as Walden's Ridge, Tennessee. Here the family was safe from the problems in the Overhill and Middle towns.

As a young boy, The Ridge was called Nung-noh-hut-tar-hee, or "The Pathkiller." As a young man, he obtained the name Kah-nung-da-cla-geh, "the man who walks on the mountaintops," because when he was asked how he reached camp, he would reply, "I came along the top of the mountain." Later in his life, white men shortened this to The Ridge out of respect because it implied "one who could see far."

In 1788, The Ridge's father moved his family back to the Hiwassee River. They settled in Chestowee, "the rabbit place." While they were living there, a new war broke out between settlers and Cherokees in 1788. At the age of seventeen, The Ridge took his first scalp in a raid on soldiers who were resting in an orchard near Citico, on the Little Tennessee River.

The Ridge later moved to Pine Log (in present-day Bartow County, Georgia) where he was chosen to serve at the regional

Cherokee council held at Oostanaula (near present-day Rome, Georgia). The Ridge wanted to establish a farm to support his family. On the advice of Moravian missionaries and government agents, he left Pine Log and moved to Oothcaloga Creek (near present-day Calhoun, Georgia). The Ridge, like other Cherokees who moved to the area, cleared land for corn and cotton, built a log house, and planted apple and peach orchards. The Ridge also established a store, operated a ferryboat, and purchased slaves to run his growing plantation. The rich Oothcaloga lands soon became known as the garden spot of the Cherokee country.

The Ridge's success as a farmer and businessman was repeated by other Cherokees. James Vann, half Scot and half Cherokee, also became a wealthy planter. In 1804, he built a large brick mansion at Spring Place, Georgia. Vann, who had three wives and five children, was known to be a drinker and a bit of a scoundrel. He killed his brother-in-law, John Falling, in a duel. In 1809, Vann was killed by one of Falling's relatives. Vann's house and part of his land was inherited by his son Joseph, who was an even shrewder businessman than his father. When Joseph was forced off his land in 1835 by the state of Georgia, "Rich Joe Vann's" holdings included 800 acres of cultivated land, 42 cabins, 6 barns, 5 smokehouses, a grist mill, a sawmill, a blacksmith shop, and a trading post. Joseph Vann also held as many as 110 Negro slaves.

By the early 1800s, many southern Cherokees had undergone a significant transformation in their traditional lifestyle and culture. Many abandoned their towns and were living as nuclear families in log cabins. They tended small farms, even though these were still usually owned by the tribe, and became as proficient in agriculture as their white neighbors. Women were no longer primarily responsible for planting the crops. Still others developed entrepreneurial skills and purchased mills, stores, and ferries.

There were factions of traditionalists who clung to old Cherokee values and customs, but the majority of Cherokees changed. Although the white men thought of this "civilizing" trend as an abandonment of traditional values, several scholars now conclude that the "progressive" Cherokees were merely acquiring skills to survive economically and politically—not abandoning their culture.

In 1801, the Moravians, whose mission headquarters was in Salem, North Carolina, asked James Vann for land to establish a mission. Vann consented, and the school at Spring Place opened in March 1802.

Missions representing various religious groups were later established all over the Cherokee territory. Other mission sites included Brainerd, established in 1817 on Chickamauga Creek in Chattanooga, Tennessee; Carmel, established in 1819 on the old Federal Road east of Oothcaloga; and Creek Path, established in 1820 near Guntersville, Alabama. Progressive Cherokees like James Vann and The Ridge supported the missions because they believed their people must be able to read and write the white man's language to survive in the changing world. The missions established boarding schools so the young Cherokees would not be under the influence of their "savage" parents. Away from their families, young Cherokees could be taught the white man's ways and religion. The missions and mission schools later played an influential role in trying to protect the rights of the Cherokees from greedy Georgians and the federal government.

THE CREEK WAR AND THE EMERGENCE OF ANDREW JACKSON

In 1813, the frontier was shocked by the news of a great massacre at Fort Mims in the Mississippi Terrritory (now Alabama).

At this battle, 250 white men, women, and children were butchered by a faction of the Creek Confederacy known as the "Red Sticks."

There were several factors which led to this confrontation between the white settlers and the Creek Confederacy. For several years the great Shawnee war chief, Tecumseh, had tried to unite the northern and southern Indians into a confederation aimed at stopping the spread of white settlement. Tecumseh's efforts took the form of a religious movement, and this movement gained many supporters among the Indians. British agents in Canada encouraged Tecumseh and supplied his followers with goods and ammunition for an uprising against the Americans. Members of the Upper Creeks, a faction of the Creek tribe centered on the Tallapoosa River, enthusiastically embraced Tecumseh's message. An Upper Creek called Red Eagle joined Tecumseh's confederacy and led the group known as the "Red Sticks." Although some Cherokees were in favor of joining Tecumseh and the Creeks, The Ridge and other prominent chiefs convinced the Cherokees to side with the Americans.

After the attack on Fort Mims, Governor Blount of Tennessee immediately ordered Andrew Jackson, of Nashville, and Major General John Cocke, of eastern

Tennessee, to raise large militias to fight the Red Sticks. Colonel Return J. Meigs, an agent to the Cherokees serving at the Hiwassee Garrison, was ordered by the secretary of war and the governors of Tennessee and Georgia to enlist the Cherokees in the struggle against the Creeks. Meigs was able to persuade The Ridge and other sympathetic Cherokees to join Jackson and Cocke's forces in fighting the Creeks. Members of the Lower Creeks, another faction of the Creek tribe, centered on the Chattahoochee River, also joined the struggle against their fellow tribe members.

The Ridge and his recruits met General James White at the Hiwassee Garrison. While White's forces were on their way to join Jackson, they received word that the Cherokee village of Turkeytown (present-day Gadsden, Alabama), was in danger of attack by the Red Sticks. White led his detachment to Turkeytown and successfully relieved the town from the Creek threat. In their first battles with the Creeks, The Ridge and the Cherokees took several Creek prisoners, who were brought back to the Hiwassee Garrison and then dispersed throughout the Cherokee Nation.

During the war against the Red Sticks, The Ridge was promoted to the rank of Major and earned the distinction of being one of only six Cherokees who were commissioned as officers in the United States Army during the conflict.

The Tennesseans, eager to gain revenge for the massacre at Fort Mims, fought zealously against the Creeks. Of the battle of Tallushatchee, young David Crockett wrote, "We shot them like dogs." The decisive victory came in March 1814, at the Battle of Horseshoe Bend on the Tallapoosa River. Under cover of darkness, the Cherokees swam the river and stole the Creek canoes before the battle. They then joined Jackson's forces in a fierce struggle that left nearly seven hundred Creek warriors dead.

In 1815, The Ridge and several other chiefs were granted an audience with President Madison in Washington. The purpose of this visit was to settle the Cherokee-Creek boundary dispute and to seek compensation for damages received during the Creek War. In a treaty signed in March 1816, four million acres of land were returned to the Cherokees, and $25,600 in damages were awarded. As a condition of the treaty, the Cherokees granted the United States the right to build roads in the Cherokee territory. This last clause also permitted the Cherokees to establish taverns along the roads. A second treaty on the same date ceded the last of the Cherokee lands in South Carolina to the United States for $5,000.

The Little Snowbird Creek, Snowbird Mountains

Andrew Jackson, who ignored the courageous support the Cherokees had given him at the Battle of Horseshoe Bend, was enraged by the March treaty and set about to undo it. On September 14, 1816, he succeeded in obtaining a new treaty with a faction of the Cherokees. He was able to do this largely through the use of bribes to eight Cherokee chiefs. In this treaty, the Cherokees ceded 1.3 million acres for $5,000, plus a large annuity. This settlement was boycotted by many leading Cherokees on the grounds that it was made with a small clique representing only a minor faction of the tribe.

In May 1817, the Cherokee Council of Chiefs met to discuss the latest land cessions, and the increased pressure on the tribe to move west. Nancy Ward, now old and unable to attend, sent her son Five Killer to read a message from his mother to the sixty-seven chiefs at the Amovey Council:

> Our beloved children and the head men of the Cherokee Nation, we address you warriors in council. We have raised all of you on the land which we now have, which God gave us to inhabit and raise provisions. We know that our country has once been extensive, but by repeated sales has become circumscribed to a small tract, and never have thought it our duty to interfere in the disposition of it till now. If a father or mother was to sell all their lands which they had to depend on, which their children had to raise their living on, that would be indeed bad. We do not wish to go to an unknown country. We have understood some of our children wish to go over the Mississippi, but this act of our children would be like destroying your mothers. Your mothers, your sisters, ask and beg of you not to part with any more of our lands. We say ours. You are descendants and take pity on our request, but keep it for our growing children for it was the good will of our creator to place us here, and you know our father, the great president, will not allow his white children to take our country away. Only keep your hands off of paper talks, for it is our own country. If it was not, they would not ask you to put your hands to paper. For it would be impossible to remove us all, for as soon as one child is raised, we have others in our arms, for such is our situation and will consider our circumstance.
>
> Therefore, children, don't part with any more of our lands but continue on it and enlarge your farms and cultivate and raise corn and cotton. And we, your mothers and sisters, will make clothing for you, which our father, the president, has recommended to us all. We don't charge anybody for selling any lands, but we have heard such intentions of our children. But your talks become true at last, and it was our desire to forewarn you all not to part with our lands.
>
> Nancy Ward, to her children Warriors, to take pity and listen to the talks of your sisters, although I am very old,

yet cannot but pity the situation in which you will hear of their minds, I have great many grandchildren which I wish them to do well on our land.

Five Killer read the names of the twelve other women who signed the petition and delivered Nancy Ward's walking cane, which represented her official vote. This was Nancy Ward's last act as *Ghighau*. In 1822, she died at her home at Womankiller Ford on the Ocoee River (near Benton, Tennessee).

On June 20, 1817, a new commission, consisting of Andrew Jackson, General David Meriweather of Georgia, and Governor Joseph McMinn of Tennessee, gathered at the United States Agency to the Cherokees at Calhoun, Tennessee, on the Hiwassee River. Again, Jackson negotiated with a small group of chiefs and used well-placed bribes to secure a treaty. The treaty was signed by several chiefs who had already moved west. Only a few eastern chiefs signed the treaty. In the treaty, the United States agreed to supervise the removal to Arkansas of all Cherokees who wished to go west.

Among the signers of the treaty was Chief John Jolly. Jolly lived on Hiwassee Island for many years until he was persuaded by his adopted son, Sam Houston, that the Cherokees' best chance to preserve their way of life was to move west. In 1809, Jolly's older brother, Tahlonteeskee, had been forced to move west with 1,130 fellow Chickamaugans when he was threatened with assassination by the Jefferson administration. Tahlonteeskee became the first principal chief of the Western Cherokees. When he died in 1820, his brother, Jolly, succeeded him as principal chief of the Western Cherokees.

As a result of the 1817 treaty, Governor McMinn succeeded in persuading between 3,500 and 5,000 Cherokees to move west. In 1818, Chief John Jolly led a flotilla of 331 Cherokees to Arkansas. This group included a half-blood named Sik-wa-yi.

Sik-wa-yi, or Sequoyah, was born about 1760 in the village of Tuskegee, five miles from the Cherokee capital of Chota. His English name was George Gist. His father may have been George Washington's friend, Nathaniel Gist, who spent many years among the Cherokees as a hunter and soldier.

Sequoyah was a silver craftsman by trade. As a young man he moved from the Overhill area to Wills Town (present-day Fort Payne, Alabama). He served as a private in the Creek War and fought at the Battle of Horseshoe Bend.

Although Sequoyah could not read or write, he began working on a Cherokee

Brasstown Bald - Blairsville

syllabary around 1809. After moving to Arkansas, he continued his work. While he was developing the syllabary, he faced much ridicule by his fellow Cherokees. After twelve years of work, his young daughter became the first Cherokee to learn the syllabary because she was the only one in his family who believed in what he was attempting.

In 1821 Sequoyah brought messages written in his partially completed syllabary from Cherokees in the West to their friends and relatives in the East. In 1822, after refining his syllabary, he returned to Arkansas carrying letters with him. Correspondence between east and west grew. Within a year, thousands of Cherokees had learned to read and write using the new syllabary.

In 1825, David Brown, a Cherokee, began translation of the New Testament into Sequoyah's syllabary. By September, four gospels had been translated. The American Board of Missions commissioned and paid for a printing press. It was shipped from Boston and arrived in New Echota in January 1828. Elias Boudinot, a Cherokee school teacher and The Ridge's nephew, was commissioned to serve as editor-in-chief of the new newspaper, the *Cherokee Phoenix*. The weekly paper, printed in both Sequoyah's syllabary and in English, was distributed throughout the Cherokee Nation, as well as in parts of the United States and Europe.

Bluff of the A'tla'nuwa - Chattanooga

JOHN ROSS AND THE CHEROKEE NATION

▲ ▲ ▲

THE CHEROKEE GOVERNMENT FORMALIZES

The 1820s were remarkable years for the Cherokees. They experienced a rapid increase in literacy due to Sequoyah's easy-to-learn syllabary. They also completed a successful transformation to a commercial agrarian economy. Perhaps most importantly, the decade saw a trend toward centralization and formalization of the Cherokee government, a movement that resulted in the Cherokee Constitution. As the Cherokee government became more sophisticated, the federal government in Washington was confronted with a new group of powerful Cherokee leaders who were politically savvy.

In May 1817, the Cherokees created a National Committee in an effort to prevent questionable treaties, such as the 1816 treaty in which 1.3 million acres of land were ceded in return for bribes. The National Committee consisted of thirteen respected leaders including The Ridge and Charles Hicks, who was Principal Chief Pathkiller's friend and advisor. This move established a bicameral legislature, the existing National Council coordinating with the new National Committee. However, the infant Cherokee government was unable to stop Andrew Jackson's treaty of July 1817, which arranged for the voluntary removal of Cherokees to the West. One of the first tasks of the new National Committee was to attempt to sort out this ambiguous treaty. This effort resulted in a new treaty which

was signed in 1819. This new treaty included provisions for Cherokees to receive 640-acre lots "for life," provided they became United States citizens. Most Cherokees rejected the offer, refusing to become citizens of the nation that persecuted them. However, many Cherokees accepted the offer, including Nancy Ward and Yonaguska, leader of the Oconaluftee Cherokees in North Carolina.

THE RISE OF JOHN ROSS

In November 1818, a young mixed-blood Cherokee named John Ross accepted the position of president of the National Committee. As a member of the influential McDonald family, John Ross had a privileged upbringing which uniquely qualified him for leadership in the Cherokee Nation. His grandfather, a Scot named John McDonald, had a trading post at Fort Loudoun in the mid-1700s. There, McDonald met and married Anne Shorey, daughter of another Scot, William Shorey, and a full-blood Cherokee named Ghigooie. McDonald and Anne moved to the Chickamaugan settlements, where McDonald was appointed British agent to the Lower Cherokees. Along with John

Stuart and Alexander Cameron, McDonald encouraged the Chickamaugans to side with the British during the Revolution. McDonald, who carried on extensive trade throughout the Spanish territories, became a Spanish agent to the Cherokees in 1792. McDonald was skilled at playing the American, British, and Spanish governments against each other. His influence with the Cherokees was so strong that all three governments sought his assistance. Governor William Blount of the Tennessee territory, unaware of McDonald's $500 annual pension from the Spanish, enthusiastically recommended McDonald to the secretary of war because of his influence with the Cherokees. He was appointed a United States agent to the Cherokees in May 1793.

In 1785, McDonald rescued a young Scottish trader from the hands of the Chickamaugans at Lookout Mountain. The man, Daniel Ross, had come to trade with the Chickasaws, but McDonald persuaded Ross to begin trading with the Cherokees. Within a year, Daniel Ross had married McDonald's daughter, Mollie. In 1788, the Ross and McDonald families moved to Turkeytown, where Daniel and Mollie's third child, John, was born on October 3, 1790. The families moved several more times before settling at the foot of Lookout Mountain.

Although John Ross was only one-eighth Cherokee, he was still racially categorized as an Indian. He was raised among the Cherokees and participated in the Green Corn Ceremony and other traditional ceremonies. Although he was not fluent in Cherokee, and never learned the alphabet invented by Sequoyah, he was fully accepted by the Cherokees. They affectionately called him Tsan Usdi, or Little John. He later gained the name of a mythical bird: *Cooweeskoowee.*

For their early education, John, his brothers, and his sisters had a tutor. John and his brother, Lewis, later became students at the mission of Reverend Gideon Blackburn in Chickamauga. Later they attended an academy at Southwest Point, now Kingston, Tennessee.

Ross entered military service in October 1813, as a second lieutenant in a company of mounted Cherokees under the command of Colonel Gideon Morgan, Jr. Although Ross fought at Horseshoe Bend with Jackson's forces in March 1814, his military career was not particularly noteworthy. Ross left military service only two weeks after Horseshoe Bend, and during much of his service, he was on leave with his family. Later in life, he rarely spoke of his personal experiences in the Creek War.

In 1813, Ross married Elizabeth Henley

Brown—who was usually known by her Cherokee name, Quatie. She may have been full-blooded Cherokee, but more likely her father was a Scottish trader, and her mother was probably the sister of the Cherokee judge, James Brown. Quatie and John had six children, five of whom lived to adulthood. Ross's four sons served in the Union army during the Civil War. His oldest son James was killed during the war.

Also in 1813, John Ross became a partner with Timothy Meigs, son of the United States agent to the Cherokees, Return J. Meigs. Ross and Timothy Meigs ran a supply business that thrived on government contracts. After Timothy died in 1815, Lewis Ross became John's new partner. John Ross was still active in his own business interests when he assumed the leadership of the National Committee in 1818.

Although he had been raised by the Cherokees and had married a Cherokee woman, Ross had a white man's educational, social, and economic advantages. Exactly why he chose to dedicate his life to the Cherokees is unclear. He may have been propelled into Cherokee politics because of the Cherokees' need for leaders who could speak English fluently and who could understand the white man's treaty-making policies. The times demanded an educated man who understood Cherokee ways, who was dedicated to the cause of protecting their land, and who could deal with the federal and state governments on their own terms.

In the mid-1820s, John Ross moved to the head of the Coosa River, now Rome, Georgia, where he could pursue his activities in Cherokee politics more easily. His home was only thirty miles from New Echota, and three miles from The Ridge's home and business. His new farm at Coosa thrived, as had his other business ventures. By the mid-1830s, Ross's orchards consisted of 170 peach, 34 apple, 9 pear, 5 quince, and 5 plum trees. The Coosa plantation also boasted a blacksmith shop, smokehouses, stables, and quarters for 19 slaves.

In January 1827, old Pathkiller died. Two weeks later, Charles Hicks, the second chief of the Cherokees, also died. John Ross, as president of the National Committee, and The Ridge, as speaker of the National Council, served as temporary leaders of the Cherokees until the National Council convened in October. They chose Elijah Hicks, brother of Charles Hicks, to fill out Pathkiller's term as principal chief. That same year, under the leadership of Ross and The Ridge, the Cherokees wrote a constitution that formally declared their intention to remain in their homeland and to govern themselves.

The constitution was modeled after the United States Constitution but differed in several respects. It declared the boundaries of the Cherokee nation and stated that the land belonged to the nation as a whole. No individual could sell his land and use the earnings to move west. The constitution also called for the election of a principal chief once every four years. In the fall of 1828, under the terms of the new constitution, Ross was elected principal chief of the Cherokees, a title he would hold until his death in 1867.

THE MOUNTING PRESSURE TO MOVE WEST

The Cherokees' efforts to formalize their government did not go unnoticed by the state and federal governments. A number of states, particularly Georgia, felt threatened by the new Cherokee Constitution. In 1802, Georgia made a compact with Congress that ceded much of the Cherokee land in Georgia to the federal government. In return, Congress agreed it would eventually eliminate Cherokee claims to Georgia land. In response to the Cherokee Constitution, Georgia tried to pressure Congress to honor the 1802 agreement. One reason the Cherokee territories were coveted by the expansionist state governments was that many areas were rich in ore. Other Cherokee territories were prime cotton-growing land. In July 1829, gold was discovered in a section of the Cherokee Nation in the North Georgia mountains. The discovery attracted a stampede of prospectors.

Georgia accused the Cherokees of violating the principal of state sovereignty and called for the abolishment of the Cherokee Constitution. They forbid the National Council from meeting within the Georgia boundaries. They also passed a series of discriminatory acts designed to isolate the Cherokees, thus encouraging them to move west. Provisions of the acts included prohibiting the Cherokees from mining their own gold or testifying against whites in Georgia courts. Another provision abolished the Cherokee court system.

In 1831, Georgia declared that Cherokee land was to be surveyed and divided into tracts. This move was preparation for transferring the land to white settlers. In 1833, Georgia held a lottery that awarded the

Guide at Oconaluftee Indian Village
Courtesy of Cherokee Historical Association

land of Ross, The Ridge, Vann, and all other Cherokees to lucky Georgians.

Appeals to President Jackson to consider the plight of his former allies were fruitless. In 1830, Congress passed a removal bill sponsored by Jackson. The bill stated that the Cherokees could move to the West on a voluntary basis. However, it provided no protection for the Cherokees from pressure by states that encouraged the removal.

The Cherokees' efforts to keep their land had many supporters among the missionaries to the Cherokee Nation. To deal with the dissident missionaries, the Georgia legislature ordered that all whites living on Indian lands had to be licensed by the state. Whites living in Cherokee territory also had to swear allegiance to the Georgia legislature. The state legislature created the Georgia Guard to enforce the new laws. In September 1831, eleven missionaries were captured by the Georgia Guard and convicted of violating the new Indian laws. Nine of the missionaries accepted pardons and quickly took assignments in the Cherokee West, while Samuel A. Worcester and Elizur Butler remained in captivity.

Encouraged by a number of leading legal minds and influential friends, such as Senator Daniel Webster, the Cherokees turned to the United States Supreme Court for help. In 1830, former attorney general, William Wirt, prepared to challenge Georgia's authority in a case that sought to overturn the murder conviction and hanging sentence of a Cherokee named George Tassel. Georgia ignored the summons and expedited Tassel's execution.

In a second suit, brought in 1831, Wirt requested an injunction against Georgia for its many violations against Cherokee sovereignty. In this case, the United States

Supreme Court determined that the Cherokee nation was a "domestic dependent nation." As such, it had no standing before the court. In 1832, in *Worcester v. Georgia*, the Supreme Court ruled that Georgia had no legal power over the Cherokees and ordered the state to release Worcester and Butler. However, Georgia ignored the decision and kept the missionaries in jail.

In 1832, Cherokee council meetings were moved across the Georgia line to Red Clay, Tennessee, because of Georgia laws prohibiting Cherokees from meeting, except to cede lands. To the dismay of many Tennesseans, Cherokee refugees from Georgia moved their homes to Tennessee. Ross moved his home to Red Hill, Tennessee, and was a frequent houseguest at the home of his brother, Lewis, who lived nearby on the Hiwassee River. After his release from jail in 1835, Dr. Elizur Butler, the physician and missionary who had been imprisoned in Georgia, established a home near Red Clay.

THE TREATY OF NEW ECHOTA AND THE TRAIL OF TEARS

It is not clear at what point The Ridge began to have misgivings about the wisdom of fighting to maintain the Cherokee Nation in the East. The Ridge's change of heart may have been influenced by a discouraging visit to Washington, or by his nephew and *Phoenix* editor, Elias Boudinot. In August 1832, Boudinot resigned as editor of the *Phoenix* because of differences of opinion with Ross over editorials on the removal issue. In October, The Ridge introduced a resolution to the National Council to begin negotiations on a removal treaty.

Ross worked diligently over the next several years to unite the nation and give it hope that their eastern homeland would survive. He went among the people, encouraging them to plant their crops and continue life normally. The pro-removal forces, which included Ross's brother, Andrew, argued that the Cherokees should negotiate a favorable removal treaty while they could. They claimed that John Ross was being naively optimistic in his belief that support from the courts would prevail over a powerful president and states that seemed determined to push them out.

In 1835, one hundred pro-removal Cherokees met in New Echota to negotiate a new treaty. The treaty party consisted of several prominent Cherokees including The Ridge, Elias Boudinot, and Andrew Ross. The infamous Treaty of New Echota, signed December 29, 1835, relinquished all lands in the East in exchange for land in the West and five million dollars. Fifteen thousand Cherokees signed a petition to protest the treaty, but the United States Senate ratified the treaty by a majority of only one vote. The deadline for final removal was set for May 23, 1838.

While John Ross's faction lobbied in Washington to stop the treaty, the pro-removal group prepared to move west. In early January 1837, the first party to emigrate under the New Echota Treaty departed. This party of six hundred aristocratic Cherokees traveled with Negro slaves and droves of oxen overland through Kentucky, Illinois, Missouri, and Arkansas, reaching their new homelands in time to put in spring crops.

In the East, federal troops and local volunteers were busy constructing stockades in preparation for the forced removal of the remaining fifteen thousand Cherokees who were under the leadership of John Ross. The work was distasteful to many of the white soldiers, including their leaders who were sympathetic to the Cherokees' situation. General John Ellis Wool, commander of the federal troops, asked to be relieved from the unpleasant task, while Brigadier General R. G. Dunlap, commander of the Tennessee volunteers, threatened to resign his commission. Eventually General

Winfield Scott was put in command of seven thousand federal troops charged with rounding up the Cherokees.

As the May 28 deadline approached, it became obvious that the Cherokees were not preparing for removal. Scott issued a proclamation encouraging the Cherokees to move on their own accord to waiting areas at Gunter's Landing (Guntersville, Alabama), Ross's Landing (Chattanooga, Tennessee), or the Hiwassee Agency (near Charleston, Tennessee), where they would receive food, clothing, and shelter until water transportation heading west could be arranged.

Scott attempted to make the removal as humane as possible. On May 17, Scott ordered his troops to show "every possible kindness" to the Cherokees and to arrest any soldier who inflicted "a wanton injury or insult on any Cherokee man, woman, or child." Although Cherokee men were to be disarmed when captured, Scott ordered that they be assured their arms would be returned when they reached their new lands in the West.

General Scott ordered the roundup to begin on May 26, 1838, in Georgia and be continued ten days later in Tennessee, Alabama, and North Carolina. In spite of Scott's wishes to treat the Cherokees in a Christian manner, many hardships were

Red Clay State Park - Cleveland

inflicted on them. Families were given only an hour to pack belongings when the troops descended on their homes. Parents and children were separated, some never to be reunited, when troops visited a cabin while a husband or son was away.

The first Cherokee group to be forcibly emigrated numbered about eight hundred and left Ross's Landing on June 6, 1838. They followed a route down the Tennessee River to the Ohio, Mississippi, and Arkansas rivers. About mid-June, two more groups followed from Ross's Landing. George Lowrey, second principal chief under John Ross, and a group of Cherokee leaders including Lewis Ross, complained about the treatment of the June deportees. They persuaded Scott to delay further emigration until fall, when the season most likely to produce disease was over. John Ross was in Washington at the time the request was made. Although the leaders were acting without authority from Ross, Scott granted the request.

Nearly thirteen thousand Cherokees spent the summer in miserable conditions in overcrowded camps that were ripe with disease. Whiskey was smuggled into the camps by white peddlers, and many Cherokees sought relief from the oppressive conditions by drinking themselves into oblivion. Hundreds died that summer.

Some historians believe more Cherokees died in the camps than on the trail west.

When Ross returned from Washington, he persuaded Scott to allow the Cherokees to supervise their own removal in the fall. He also negotiated funds to buy supplies and transportation for his people. Ross's plan was to form thirteen groups of about one thousand people and begin departure in September. Due to the extended drought, departure was delayed until October 1. In a final council held at Rattlesnake Springs (near present-day Charleston, Tennessee), the Eastern Cherokees voted unanimously to continue their old constitution and laws upon arrival in the West.

The thirteen parties that left their homelands in the fall of 1838 did not fare well. Although Cherokee scribes tried to record deaths, no one is certain how many Cherokees died on the journey. Ross later stated that 424 emigrants died on the trail, but the number was probably much larger. Historians estimate between four and six thousand Cherokees died during the removal of 1838-39.

John G. Burnett, a United States Army private who participated in the removal, later wrote:

> [I] witnessed the execution of the most brutal order in the history of American

warfare. I saw the helpless Cherokees arrested and dragged from their homes, and driven at the bayonet point into the stockades. And in the chill of a drizzling rain on an October morning, I saw them loaded like cattle or sheep into 645 wagons and headed toward the West. . . .

The trail of the exiles was a trail of death. They had to sleep in the wagons and on the ground without fire. And I have known as many as twenty-two of them to die in one night of pneumonia, due to ill treatment, cold and exposure. Among this number was the beautiful Christian wife of Chief John Ross. This noble-hearted woman died a martyr to childhood, giving her only blanket for the protection of a sick child. She rode, thinly clad, through a blinding sleet and snow storm, developed pneumonia and died in the still hours of a bleak winter night.

The long painful journey to the West ended March 26th, 1839, with four thousand of silent graves reaching from the foothills of the Smoky Mountains to what is known as Indian territory in the West. And covetousness on the part of the white race was the cause of all that the Cherokees had to suffer.

The Cherokee Removal of 1838-39 became known as "The Trail Where They Cried" and later as "The Trail of Tears." Chief Junaluska, who fought alongside Andrew Jackson in the Creek War, later said: "If I had known that Andrew Jackson would later drive us from our home I would have killed him that day at Horseshoe Bend."

In the spring of 1839, the Trail of Tears survivors joined other Cherokees in northeast Oklahoma. The new emigrants, Ross's followers, far outnumbered the Old Settlers and the Treaty Party Cherokees who were already living in the West. The Old Settlers were the Cherokees who had moved west before the Treaty of New Echota and included the followers of Tahlonteeskee and John Jolley, who were now dead. The Old Settlers, or Western Cherokees, now had three chiefs, John Brown, John Looney, and John Rogers. Sequoyah was also considered one of the Old Settlers. The Treaty Party Cherokees included The Ridge, his son John Ridge, and Elias Boudinot. They were the Cherokees who emigrated voluntarily after the Treaty of New Echota. The three factions clashed over many issues. Ross's followers, the National Party, wanted to revise the government of the Western Cherokees, and the Old Settlers wanted the new emigrants to live under the existing government. Sequoyah and Reverend Jesse Bushyhead assisted in mediation between the two groups. Meanwhile, the Treaty Party was trying to undermine the power and influence of Ross by spreading lies about the new arrivals. In one case, they reported to military personnel and William

Bald River Falls, Cherokee National Forest near Tellico Plains

Armstrong, superintendent of Western Indians, that some of the new emigrants near Camp Illinois were planning to attack the camp. The rumor proved false, but this, and other rumors, damaged Ross's reputation with the local military authorities.

On June 22, 1839, mounting tensions between the factions culminated with the murders of The Ridge, his son John, and Ridge's nephew, Elias Boudinot. The Ridge was ambushed and shot from his horse that morning on the Arkansas Road. His son, John, was dragged from his bed at daybreak and stabbed twenty-seven times in front of his wife and children. Elias Boudinot was stabbed in the back and hacked with a tomahawk by men who had

asked him to fetch medicine for sick members of their family. Boudinot's brother, Stand Watie, escaped with his life only because a Choctaw was sent to warn him about the murders of the others. Stand Watie immediately blamed Ross for the murders, though Ross denied any involvement. The murders were reminiscent of those of Cherokee Chief Doublehead and Creek Chief William McIntosh, who had participated in land cessions without the consent of their respective tribal governments and were then brutally killed. To this day, many believe the Ridges and Boudinot were killed for their role in the Treaty of New Echota.

Oconaluftee River

THE EASTERN CHEROKEES REBUILD

▲ ▲ ▲

THE CHEROKEES WHO REMAINED BEHIND

While the bulk of the Cherokee Nation struggled to settle their differences and begin to rebuild their lives in the West, a small band of Cherokees, who had managed to avoid removal, began their own struggle to hold onto lands in North Carolina. Many Cherokees managed to escape removal by claiming to be "Black Dutch," or something other than Cherokee. Some hid deep in the forested mountains and managed to avoid the troops. Other Cherokees were allowed to stay because they had become United States citizens under the provisions of the 1819 agreement with the federal government.

Under the Treaty of 1819, in which Cherokee lands in North Carolina were ceded to the federal government, forty-nine families in North Carolina chose to accept 640-acre reservations and become citizens of the United States. These Cherokees were traditionalists, who had no problems severing their ties with the progressive government of the Cherokee Nation. Unfortunately, these Cherokees had to deal with many of the same problems as the Cherokees who lived in the heart of the Cherokee Nation. Shortly after the 1819 agreement, the state of North Carolina sold their reservations, then admitting its mistake, paid the Cherokees for the land they had lost.

A few Cherokees, like the influential Euchella, moved across the Little Tennessee River into Cherokee lands after receiving his money. Others, like Euchella's father-in-law, Yonaguska, chose not to rejoin the Cherokee Nation. Yonaguska and other Cherokees settled along the Oconaluftee River.

Yonaguska adopted a white boy named William Holland Thomas who grew up to become a trader. He also became a spokesman for the Oconaluftee Cherokees and helped purchase tracts of land as they became available. The largest of these tracts, known as the Qualla Boundary, was acquired piecemeal. This is the area where the present-day town of Cherokee, North Carolina, is located. When the New Echota Treaty was signed, Thomas went to Washington to argue that the treaty did not apply to the Oconaluftee Cherokees because they were North Carolina citizens, not members of the Cherokee Nation.

The Oconaluftee Cherokees found themselves in a precarious position while Thomas was in Washington attempting to convince the government that they should be allowed to stay. The Oconaluftee Cherokees had sympathy for the plight of the other Cherokees during the roundup, but they did not wish to jeopardize their own situation by aiding the refugees. One of the refugee groups, a man named Tsali and his family, killed two soldiers during the roundup and escaped into the mountains. Pressure was placed on the Oconaluftee Cherokees to aid in the arrest of the Tsali band.

Thomas enlisted the aid of Euchella, who was subject to the removal because he lived inside the Cherokee Nation boundary. Euchella and his men captured Tsali's men and executed them, thereby securing permission for Euchella and the Oconaluftee Cherokees to remain in their eastern homelands.

WILLIAM THOMAS AND THE CHEROKEES IN THE CIVIL WAR

Once the Eastern Cherokees were granted permission to stay in North Carolina, they enjoyed a brief period of peace before the Civil War began. During the conflict, Thomas organized a legion of Cherokees to fight for the Confederacy by defending the mountain passes. They were stationed at Strawberry Plains, near Knoxville, when they weren't engaged in bushwhacking Union soldiers or guarding Alum Cave in the Smoky Mountains. In June 1862, they were sent to Chattanooga for a brief period to participate in the fighting there. While in Chattanooga, Thomas captured an errant Union soldier. At that point, each of his men vowed to take a Union prisoner before the war was over.

In September 1862, the Confederates learned that Union forces were planning to move from southwest Virginia into eastern Tennessee by way of the gaps south of the Cumberland Mountains. Thomas's two Cherokee companies were ordered to the region to protect the gaps. On September 13, First Lieutenant William S. Terrell led the Indians into Baptist Gap, ten miles north of Rogersville, Tennessee, near the Virginia state line, where they were ambushed. Fighting continued until September 15, when Terrell ordered Second Lieutenant Astoogatogeh, grandson of Chief Junaluska, to charge the Yankees. In the attack, Astoogatogeh was killed, and the enraged Cherokees fought with renewed strength, driving the Yankees from the gap. Angry at the loss of their popular leader, the Indians took scalps from the dead Union soldiers. The event made the newspapers, and many people, especially Union supporters, were outraged by the scalping. While their reputation as fierce Confederate warriors was enhanced, causing many of the Union forces to fear the Cherokee soldiers, Thomas was upset. He was concerned how the image of "the savage Indian" would harm their chances of earning equal rights and citizenship. It was later reported that the scalps were returned to be buried with the Union soldiers.

In February 1864, about three hundred of Thomas's men were camped at the mouth of Deep Creek on the Tuckasegee River (present-day Bryson City, North Carolina) when they were surprised by federal soldiers under the command of Major Francis M.

Davidson. The Cherokees scrambled to a cliff and fought a close, fierce battle. According to Davidson, two hundred Cherokees were killed in this battle. Thomas, on the other hand, insisted only two or three of his men were killed. Twenty or thirty Cherokees were captured and taken to Knoxville, Tennessee.

While in prison, some of the men learned for the first time that they were fighting for slavery and converted to the Union cause. Others pretended to pledge their loyalty to the Union. After release, they returned to Thomas and informed him the federal government had offered five thousand dollars for his scalp.

During the final year of the Civil War, most of Thomas's troops were sent to Virginia, where many died in battle. In the fall of 1864, most of the survivors rejoined Thomas in North Carolina, but some of the others were present at the final siege and surrender of Richmond.

THE CHEROKEE RESERVATION

Hard times fell on the Oconaluftee Cherokees after the Civil War. Immediately following the war, the Cherokees were ravaged by a smallpox epidemic that took many lives. To make matters worse, Thomas and the Oconaluftee Cherokees were in great debt, and the Cherokee lands were threatened by creditors. However, in 1868, the Eastern Band drew up a constitution, and the federal government officially recognized them as an Indian tribe separate from the Western Band. The United States also brought a lawsuit on behalf of the Cherokees that salvaged the Cherokee lands from creditors but placed the land in trust with the federal government.

In the 1880s, the legal status of the Eastern Band of Cherokees was again brought into question. Nimrod Jarrett Smith, who was now chief of the Eastern Band, applied for and received a corporate charter from the state of North Carolina in 1889. This ingenious move gave the Eastern Band of the Cherokee Indians the right to own property, enter into contracts, and bring suits to court. But the federal government continued to treat the Cherokees as wards of the government.

At the turn of the century, the main source of income for many Eastern Cherokees was timber. Although most of the good timber had been sold by 1900, the sale of pulpwood and tanbark continued into the

The Eternal Flame at Red Clay State Park

1920s. "White Cherokees," people who managed to claim Cherokee ancestry either legitimately or non-legitimately, owned much of the Cherokee lands.

By the depression, the Eastern Cherokees were in much need of Roosevelt's New Deal, which brought help through work-relief programs. The federal government hoped to turn the Qualla Boundary, as the Eastern Cherokee reservation was called, into a tourist attraction and incorporate it into the Great Smoky Mountains National Park when it opened in 1934. However, the Cherokees resisted the plan. Instead, the Qualla Boundary remained largely outside the park boundaries, and the Cherokees formed cooperatives to market their baskets and other crafts. The tourist industry is still the most important source of income in the Qualla Boundary, although the Eastern Cherokees have invested in other businesses such as a mirror manufacturing company, trout farms, and high-stakes bingo.

Today, the Qualla Boundary consists of about fifty-six thousand acres held in federal trust for the Cherokees. The largest tract of land is the area where the town of Cherokee is located. This, plus the Snowbird tracts, the Tomotla, and the Thomas tract, all located in southwest North Carolina, comprise the Eastern Cherokee Res-

ervation. Approximately seven thousand Cherokees live on or near the reservation, which is divided into six voting precincts: Yellowhill, Birdtown, Big Cove, Painttown, Wolftown, and Cheroah. Each precinct elects two representatives to the tribal council every two years and participates in the election of the principal and vice chiefs every four years. Tribal council meetings are open to the public and have been compared to New England town meetings.

The Eastern and Western Cherokees, though separated by many miles, have maintained friendships and family ties. In April 1984, a historic joint-council met at Red Clay to reaffirm the bonds of their common heritage. Both groups have overcome enormous obstacles to maintain their Cherokee identity and generate a renewed interest in their culture.

The words of William Ross, spoken at the funeral of his uncle John Ross in May 1867, at Park Hill, Oklahoma, impart the spirit and tenacity of the Cherokee people. They pay tribute not only to Ross, but to all of the *Ani-Yun-Wiya*, The Principal People—survivors against all odds:

> It is proper, that here, should his dust mingle with kindred dust, and that a suitable memorial should arise, to mark the spot where repose the bones of our great-

est chieftain. It will keep alive within our bosoms a spirit of patriotism. It will impart strength and hope in the hour of adversity. It will teach us to beware of domestic strife and division. It will serve to unite us more closely in peace, in concord, and in devotion to the common welfare. It will soften our asperities and excite the thoughtful youth of our land to patience, to perseverance, to success and to renown.

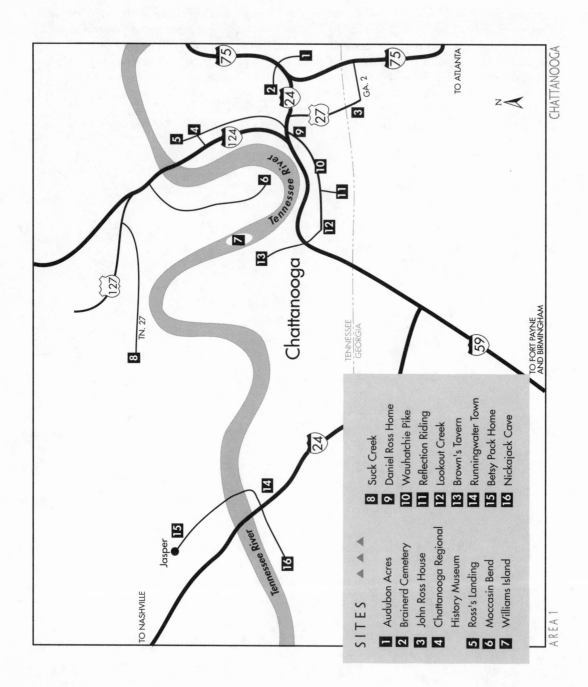

SITES ▲ ▲ ▲

1 Audubon Acres   8 Suck Creek
2 Brainerd Cemetery   9 Daniel Ross Home
3 John Ross House   10 Wauhatchie Pike
4 Chattanooga Regional   11 Reflection Riding
   History Museum   12 Lookout Creek
5 Ross's Landing   13 Brown's Tavern
6 Moccasin Bend   14 Runningwater Town
7 Williams Island   15 Betsy Pack Home
                   16 Nickajack Cave

Chattanooga

Tennessee River

TENNESSEE
GEORGIA

GA. 2

TO ATLANTA

TO FORT PAYNE
AND BIRMINGHAM

TO NASHVILLE

Jasper

TN. 27

N

CHATTANOOGA

AREA 1

Chattanooga Nature Center at Reflection Riding

CHATTANOOGA

▲ ▲ ▲

The city of Chattanooga lies east of the Grand Canyon of the Tennessee, a deeply-incised canyon formed by the Tennessee River as it cuts its way through Walden's Ridge on the Cumberland Plateau. The canyon, which separates Signal Mountain on the northern side from Raccoon and Lookout mountains to the south, forms a natural gap in the mountains. A number of Indian trade paths were established through this gap.

One of the most-traveled of these paths was the Great Indian War Trail, also known as the Great Indian Warpath. The trail ran from Virginia and east Tennessee, through the canyon, to Alabama. The Chickamauga Path was a path that entered the area from north Georgia and led to Kentucky. The Cisca and Saint Augustine Trail, which connected middle Tennessee with Florida, also passed through the area.

Many different groups of Native Americans established villages along the banks of the Tennessee River near the junction of these major trade routes. Recent excavations of Moccasin Bend and Williams Island on the Tennessee River show that Native Americans lived in the Chattanooga area for approximately fourteen thousand years. Villages and burial mounds built during the Woodland and Mississippian periods were established on both banks of the Tennessee River. When the Chickamaugans moved into the area in the late 1700s, the mountains and the turbulent waters of the Tennessee River Gorge provided natural protection for their lower towns and enabled them to control westward traffic through the area. In the early 1800s, several Cherokees established farms and industries along the river's fertile banks.

Chattanooga was once called A'tla'nuwa, or "Hawk's Hole," by Native Americans, for a bluff on the south side of the river that was the legendary nesting site of a mythical hawk named *Tlanuwa*. After the Cherokees moved into the area, the settlement was called Ross's Landing because John Ross established a warehouse and boat landing on the great bend in the Tennessee River. After the Cherokee removal in 1838, the town took its name from nearby Chatanuga Mountain, now called Lookout Mountain. There have been several attempts to translate the name Chatanuga. One theory, offered by Hamilton County historian James W. Livingood, is that it means both "rock that comes to a point" in the Creek language, and "mountains looking at each other" in Cherokee. It's fitting that the city retains a name that reflects both its distinctive geography and its rich Native American heritage.

SPRING FROG CABIN AT AUDUBON ACRES

Chattanooga

A two-story log cabin named in honor of Tooan Tuh, also known as Dustu' or Spring Frog, is located in the Elise Chapin

Spring Frog Cabin at Audubon Acres

Wildlife Sanctuary at Audubon Acres. Spring Frog was a Cherokee chief who lived in the Chattanooga area prior to the Cherokee removal in 1838. He was an avid hunter, fisherman, farmer, and stick ball player. He was also a brave warrior who fought at Horseshoe Bend and Emuckfaw with Andrew Jackson during the Creek War. Thomas L. McKenney, who served many years in the Bureau of Indian Affairs in Washington, wrote the following about his friend Tooan Tuh:

"He watched the seasons, noted the changes of the weather, marked the hues of the water, and the appearances of the vegetation. . . . His friends were always welcome to this cheerful fireside, and the stranger, to use the figure of one of the noblest spirits or our land, 'never found the string of his latch drawn in.' "

Federal census records of 1835 indicate that four farmsteads were located on South Chickamauga Creek and that a Cherokee named Drowning Bear may have been the real owner of the Spring Frog Cabin. In 1842, Drowning Bear filed a claim for the loss of two houses, each ten by twelve feet, and other improvements he made on his property on Chickamauga Creek that he left behind during the removal. Today, the cabin named for Spring Frog still beckons visitors to come sit by the fireplace, or on the large front porch, and remember a time when Cherokee families lived peacefully in the area.

Visitors to Audubon Acres may cross Chickamauga Creek on a swinging bridge and follow a nature trail to an area known as Little Owl's Village. Robert Sparks Walker, a popular writer who founded Audubon Acres, suggested that the village of Little Owl, brother of Dragging Canoe, was located at the Audubon Acres Site. The village was actually located further southeast, in Georgia. The area Sparks called Little Owl's Village was actually a prehistoric Indian town, occupied from about 1500 to 1600 A.D. The site has not been extensively researched, but archaeological studies suggest that the three-and-a-half-acre area was highly congested, with thirty to forty houses and a minimum population of three hundred people. Ancient Indian trails passed through the area, and the site is believed to have been a peripheral town of the large Coosa chiefdom centered in north Georgia on the Coosawattee River. In studying the Spanish expedition of Tristan de Luna in 1559 to 1561, historian Charles Hudson places the Napochie village that was raided by the Coosas and Spaniards at the Audubon Acres site. (See Coosawattee Old Town in Area 16 for more information on the Coosas and Napochies.)

Audubon Acres offers many special events each year, including Indian Summer Days which is held each fall and features Native American and pioneer crafts. Hours at Audubon Acres are Monday through Saturday from 9 A.M. to 5 P.M., and Sunday from 1 P.M. to 5 P.M. Admission is three dollars. Information on special events at Audubon Acres may be obtained by calling 615-892-1499.

From Interstate 75 in Chattanooga, take the East Brainerd Road East exit. Follow East Brainerd Road East to the intersection with Gunbarrel Road. Turn right on Gunbarrel Road and follow the signs to Audubon Acres on North Sanctuary Road.

The well at Spring Frog Cabin

BRAINERD CEMETERY

Chattanooga

The Brainerd Mission was founded in 1817 by the American Board of Foreign Missions. Colonel Return J. Meigs, the United States agent to the Cherokees, purchased the land for the mission from John McDonald for five hundred dollars. Located on the banks of the Chickamauga River, the Christian mission was the site of the first agricultural school in the United States. Opened as part of the effort to assimilate the Cherokees into white culture, the school taught Cherokee girls how to spin and weave, and Cherokee boys were taught farming and carpentry. The Brainerd mission established ten satellite stations in the area and influenced missions established by other denominations and organizations. The success of the Brainerd program brought important visitors to the mission, including presidents James Monroe and James Madison. By 1822, there were between thirty and forty buildings on the property, which was valued at $17,390. The Brainerd Mission was closed on August 19, 1838, as a result of the Cherokee removal. Today, all that remains of the thriving mission is a peaceful cemetery, which is maintained as a garden and his-

Brainerd Cemetery

torical site by the Daughters of the American Revolution and the Sons of the American Revolution.

The cemetery is open Monday through Friday from 8 A.M. to 4 P.M. Admission is free.

To reach the cemetery from Interstate 75, take the Lee Highway West exit north of downtown Chattanooga. The cemetery is located off Lee Highway, between Eastgate Mall and the Brainerd Village Shopping Center. Access is from the eastern end of the Eastgate Mall parking lot.

JOHN ROSS HOUSE

Rossville, Georgia

The two-story log house in Rossville, Georgia, known as the John Ross House, was built by Ross's grandfather, John McDonald, in 1797. John Ross's family lived only a few miles away from this house, in a cabin built by his father Daniel Ross. Around 1808, John moved to the McDonald house, and he lived there off and on during the next twenty years. In 1827, after the death of his grandfather, John Ross again returned to the house, this time for an extended period, and made several improvements.

The house is maintained by the John Ross House Association. From June 1 through Labor Day, it is open from 1 P.M. to 5 P.M. daily, except Wednesdays. The grounds are open year-round. Admission is free. For information, call 706-866-9750.

From Interstate 24 in Chattanooga, take the Rossville Boulevard exit and drive south on Rossville Boulevard (U.S. 27). When Rossville Boulevard intersects with McFarland Avenue, continue left on Rossville Boulevard and watch for a historical marker for the Ross House on the right. Turn right at the marker. The Ross House is located in a small park, one block from Rossville Boulevard. It was moved to this location several years ago from its original location nearby.

John Ross House

Chattanooga Regional History Museum

CHATTANOOGA REGIONAL HISTORY MUSEUM

Chattanooga

The Chattanooga Regional History Museum tells the story of Chattanooga and the surrounding area, starting with its geologic history and the history of the Native Americans who have lived here for fourteen thousand years. The permanent exhibit includes Native American artifacts from the Woodland and Mississippian periods, such as stone gorgets, axes, knife blades, and drills, as well as effigy pieces and incised pottery pieces. There are exhibits on the Citico mound, Sequoyah, Brainerd Mission, the Chickamaugans, and the Trail of Tears. In addition to the permanent exhibits on the development of Chattanooga, the museum hosts rotating exhibits and special programs. It also has a discovery room, a model train room, and a gift shop.

The Chattanooga Regional History Museum is open Monday through Friday from 10 A.M. to 4:30 P.M. On Saturday and Sunday the museum is open from 11 A.M. to 4:30 P.M. The museum is closed Thanksgiving and Christmas. For information, call 615-265-3247. There is a small admission charge.

To reach the museum from Interstate 24, take U.S. 27 north to downtown Chattanooga. From U.S. 27, take Exit 1C for Fourth Street. The museum is in an old brick building on the corner of Fourth and Chestnut streets, just two blocks from Ross's Landing and the Tennessee Aquarium.

ROSS'S LANDING

Chattanooga

In 1815, John Ross asked his brother, Lewis Ross, to join him in his trading firm after the death of his original business partner, Timothy Meigs. Lewis Ross managed operations at the firm's office at the Hiwassee Garrison, while John Ross

Ross's Landing

moved back to his childhood home in Chattanooga.

John Ross constructed a ferry and warehouse on the south bank of the Tennessee River near the "Hawk's Hole," the bluff that was the nesting site of a legendary hawk named *Tlanuwa*. Ross probably chose the site because the high bluff was not subject to flooding, and because the water at the foot of the bluff was deep up to the shoreline.

In 1837, George Featherstonhaugh, a visitor in the area, described his arrival at Ross's Landing in a journal:

> After some time, they ran the canoe ashore at a beach where there was no appearance of a settlement, and told me that it was Ross' Landing. I was somewhat dismayed at first at the prospect of being abandoned on a lone beach, since these men having fulfilled their agreement had a right to be paid immediately, and time was important to them to get back that night. Upon parleying with them, however, I learnt that there was a small settlement not far from us, and that they would carry my luggage there for a reasonable gratification. Upon which I sent them immediately on, and taking a last look at the river followed the road they took. At length I came to a small village hastily built, without regard to order or streets, every one selecting his own site, and relying on the legislature of Tennessee to pass a law for the permanent arrangement of their occupations.

At the time of Featherstonhaugh's visit, the Cherokee Nation was holding its last council session at Red Clay, Tennessee, to discuss what could be done to prevent the impending removal. When the removal became inevitable, an internment camp named Camp Cherokee was built two miles east of Ross's Landing on Citico Creek. Today, Manker Patten Tennis Courts and Scrappy Moore Field are located at the site of Camp Cherokee. Another camp was built at Indian Springs, near the foot of Missionary Ridge on land now occupied by Parkwood Nursing Home and the Glenwood Subdivision.

Ross's Landing served as an important embarkation point for Cherokees headed to the West. On March 3, 1837, eleven flatboats of Cherokees departed Ross's Landing. This group of 466 Cherokees, led by The Ridge, left voluntarily. The first group of Cherokees to be forcibly moved to the West left Ross's Landing on June 6, 1838. This group of approximately 800 Cherokees was forcibly crowded onto a steamer and six flat boats for the journey west. A week later, another 875 Cherokees were shipped from Ross's Landing on six more flatboats.

In the middle of June, the final contingent of 1,070 Cherokees to depart from Ross's Landing left on foot due to a shortage of flatboats. They planned to rendezvous with flatboats downstream at Waterloo, Alabama.

Today, the visitor to Ross's Landing can only imagine what it may have looked like in the early 1800s. The level of the Tennessee River is much higher now, due to Nickajack Dam. And the waterfront has been reconfigured by the construction of a marina and the Riverfront Parkway. A large area along the riverfront is now called Ross's Landing, but it is believed Ross's original ferry may have been located on the east end of the present-day landing near the Market and Walnut Street bridges.

A visit to Ross's Landing should begin at the plaza around the Tennessee Aquarium, where the story of Chattanooga is told in artistic designs set in the pavement. Across the Riverfront Parkway and near the water is a bronze sculpture paying tribute to the Cherokees. Walkways leading east from Ross's Landing take the visitor under the Market Street Bridge to the approximate site of John Ross's original ferry. A few paces further, a staircase leads up to the Walnut Street pedestrian bridge. From the bridge there is an excellent view of the white bluffs of Hawk's Hole and of Maclellan Island, which was inhabited by early Native Americans.

To reach Ross's Landing from the Chattanooga Regional History Museum, drive or walk north on Chestnut Street 2 blocks to the Tennessee Aquarium. From Interstate 24, take U.S. 27 north to downtown Chattanooga and take Exit 1C for Fourth Street. Turn left at the first corner onto Chestnut Street and park near the Tennessee Aquarium.

MOCCASIN BEND

Chattanooga

Designated as both a National Historic Landmark and a National Register of Historic Places District, Moccasin Bend is considered by many to be the most important archaeological complex located inside a United States city. The thousand-acre strip of land is a peninsula formed by a great bend in the Tennessee River at Chattanooga, just before the point where the river cuts through the mountains to the west. It takes its name from its shape, which is reminiscent of a moccasin. Seven burial mounds, built between 200 and 1000 A.D.,

Moccasin Bend

are located on the toe of the bend. Several other important archaeological sites are on Moccasin Bend. On the western shore lie the sites of Mallard's Dozen, a Native American village dated about 400 B.C.; Vulcan, dated to 1335 B.C.; and Hampton Place, an Indian village from the 1500s that had extensive contact with Spanish traders. Due to a significant number of Spanish artifacts found at Hampton Place, some archaeologists believe De Soto or Juan Pardo visited here, and that it might have been the center of the province of Chiaha or of Coste-Tali, both of which were chronicled by the De Soto expedition.

Moccasin Bend was in the heart of Chickamaugan territory and provided an excellent vantage point from which to attack intruders. In the early 1800s, Moccasin Bend was the eastern terminus of Brown's Ferry. John Brown lived and farmed on Moccasin Bend and operated a tavern across the river. (See the Brown's Tavern section later in this chapter.)

Moccasin Bend and Brown's Ferry played a significant role during the battle for Chattanooga in the Civil War. In August 1863, Union artillery units were placed along Stringer's Ridge on the eastern shore of the bend. The Union artillery shelled Chattanooga from this strategic position for several weeks, probing Confederate positions in preparation for an attack on the city. On September 9, Union forces entered and occupied Chattanooga under protection of artillery fire from Moccasin Bend. Later that month, after a rout by the Confederates at the Battle of Chickamauga, Union troops retreated to Chattanooga and were surrounded on the east, west, and south sides by Confederate forces. Union forces held Chattanooga and Moccasin Bend, but their supply lines were cut by the Confederate forces, and the besieged city faced starvation. On October 27, Union troops assaulted Confederate troops at Brown's Ferry, and on October 29, Union forces drove the Confederates out of the western part of Lookout Valley in the Battle of Wauhatchie. These two victories opened Union supply lines from Bridgeport, Alabama, to Chattanooga. Later, Chattanooga was turned into a staging area for Union forces to begin their long march to Atlanta. The remains of Civil War wagon roads, cannon emplacements, bivouacs, and camps can still be seen at Stringer's Ridge on Moccasin Bend.

The future of Moccasin Bend is the subject of much controversy. Over the last fifty years, there have been many proposals to both protect and develop Moccasin Bend.

A proposal to build an amphitheater on Stringer's Ridge was recently defeated by local preservationists including archaeological, Civil War, Native American, and wilderness groups who oppose any new major construction on Moccasin Bend. These groups support establishment of a greenway or park on Moccasin Bend, which will utilize existing structures and promote the history of the bend while protecting the environment.

Meanwhile, looters have disturbed over one thousand Native American burial sites on Moccasin Bend. These acts of vandalism have prompted the establishment of the Native American Reserve Force (NARF). Working under the auspices of the Hamilton County sheriff's department, the armed NARF volunteers from the Chattanooga InterTribal Association patrol Moccasin Bend to prevent looting and poaching. The restricted burial sites are clearly posted, so visitors to the bend should not worry about accidentally wandering into prohibited areas.

Beautiful views of Lookout Mountain and the Tennessee River await the visitor at Moccasin Bend. The Blue Blazes Historic Loop Trail is a nature walk with several signs explaining Civil War and Native American sites.

From Interstate 24 in downtown Chatta-nooga, take U.S. 127 North. After crossing the Tennessee River, take the Manufacturer's Road exit and turn right (west). Drive approximately 0.5 mile on Manufacturer's Road and take a left turn onto Hamm Road. Hamm Road meets Moccasin Bend Road in 0.7 mile. Take a left turn on Moccasin Bend Road, which will lead you toward Moccasin Bend Hospital. The hospital campus is closed to non-business traffic from 6 P.M. to 6 A.M. During the day, when the hospital area is open, you can park in the visitor's parking lot and walk to a view of the Tennessee River. The Blue Blazes Historic Loop Trail is located halfway between the hospital and Hamm Road, on Moccasin Bend Road. You can park at the Blue Blazes Trail when the hospital area is closed.

WILLIAMS ISLAND

Chattanooga

Williams Island is a 450-acre island in the Tennessee River, on the west side of Chattanooga. It is listed on the National Register of Historic Places. Many important archaeological sites on the island provide evidence of man's fourteen-thousand-year history in the Chattanooga area. Native

American sites dating from 12,000 B.C. to the 1800s have been identified on the island. One of the most significant finds on Williams Island was the 4-acre village of Talimico, occupied from approximately 900 A.D. to 1650 A.D. The palisaded village contained a temple and burial mounds, a central plaza, and hundreds of wooden houses. Talimico, and nearby Hampton Place, had extensive contact with early Spanish explorers and may have been a stop on De Soto's 1540 expedition.

In 1776, Bloody Fellow founded a large village which spread from Brown's Valley to Williams Island. The village, Tuskegee Town, was destroyed in 1779 by Colonel Evan Shelby but was soon reoccupied by followers of Cutteotoy (also Cotetoy). After raids by John Sevier in 1782, most of the Chickamaugans moved further south to the five Lower Towns.

Around the year 1800, John Brown, a mixed-blood Cherokee who became prominent in the area, ran a ferry across the Tennessee River at Williams Island. He was also known as the best guide for navigating the treacherous waters at the Narrows and the Suck along the Tennessee River.

In 1986, Williams Island was purchased by the state of Tennessee with assistance from the Tennessee River Gorge Trust.

Officially named Williams Island State Archaeological Park, the island is managed by the trust which offers ongoing environmental tours and educational excavations. The island is reached by a ferry from the north bank of the Tennessee, but access is restricted to those with permission. The Tennessee River Gorge Trust has recently given the Chattanooga InterTribal Association's Native American Reserve Force permission to patrol the island to prevent grave looting. For information, contact the Tennessee River Gorge Trust at 615-266-0314.

The best place to view Williams Island is from Signal Point on Walden's Ridge. Signal Point also offers a view of the Tennessee River Gorge.

To reach Signal Point from downtown Chattanooga, take Interstate 24 to U.S. 27 North. Cross the Tennessee River on U.S. 27 North and take the Signal Mountain exit to U.S. 127, also known as Signal Mountain Boulevard. Signal Mountain Boulevard turns into Taft Highway, which you follow up the mountain. When you reach the top, turn onto Signal Mountain Boulevard, and then turn left again onto Mississippi Avenue. Mississippi Avenue becomes James Boulevard. In about 1 mile, turn left onto Signal Point Road and drive 0.3 mile to the parking area for Signal Point.

Near the mouth of Suck Creek

THE SUCK ON THE
TENNESSEE RIVER

Chattanooga

Many early pioneers traveled west on the Tennessee River, but the strange geography of the river prevented it from becoming the great highway that other rivers, such as the Ohio River, had become. The obstacles that lay along the river were legendary. Thomas Jefferson wrote about one of the river hazards, the Suck, in his *Notes on Virginia*: "Above the Chickamogga towns is a whirl-pool called the Sucking pot, which takes in trunks of trees or boats, and throws them out again half a mile below."

The Indians called the treacherous spot Untiguhi, for "pot in the water." The Cherokees believed the Suck was a haunted whirlpool, where a house full of people lived on the bottom of the river. The inhabitants reached through the beams of their house to pull travelers into the depths.

In later years, obstacles like the Suck made it impossible for steamboat captains to traverse the entire length of the river. Instead, steamboat lines operated on sections of the river between these obstacles, such as the sections from Knoxville to Chattanooga and from Chattanooga to Decatur. In some cases, railroad lines were built to transport passengers around the treacherous sections.

One of the early emigrant parties to encounter the Suck was the Donelson party. In December 1779, John Donelson packed up his and several other families and set out from Fort Patrick Henry (at present-day Kingsport) for the Big Salt Lick (present-day Nashville). After a delay of about two months, the flotilla of thirty flatboats and canoes resumed their journey, reaching the Chickamaugan settlements in early March. One night, they stopped at a deserted Cherokee town at the mouth of Chickamauga Creek, which had been burned the year before by Colonel Evan Shelby, and then continued down the river. They soon came into sight of the Chickamaugan village of Settico, now called Citico, and noticed canoes of painted warriors following them. The Donelson boats approached another town on the southern bank of the river near an island in the river. The Indians in this village tried to convince the party to use the channel around the island closest to the town. Instead, Donelson chose the channel on the northern side of the island, placing the party close to Moccasin Bend. On Moccasin Bend, Indians were lying in ambush in the canes along the river. The Indians fired on the party and killed a young man named Payne.

The rear boat was occupied by twenty-eight family members and friends of Thomas Stuart. The Stuarts had agreed to stay in the rear because the occupants of the boat were carrying smallpox. The Chickamaugans decided to concentrate their attack on the Stuart boat and captured it. All of the people on the boat were killed, except for the six-year-old son of John Stuart who was spared and later ransomed. Ironically, many of the Chickamaugans died from smallpox contracted from the Stuart party.

The rest of the Donelson party, including Rachel Donelson, the future wife of Andrew Jackson, continued toward the treacherous river gorge. In an excerpt from Samuel Cole Williams' *Early Travels in Tennessee Country*, Donelson described what happened next:

> We are now arrived at the place called Whirl, or Suck, where the river compressed within less than half its common width above, by the Cumberland Mountains, which juts in on both sides. In passing through the upper part of these narrows, at a place described by Coody, which he termed the 'boiling pot,' a trivial accident had nearly ruined the

expedition. One of the company, John Cotton, who was moving down in a large canoe, had attached it to Robert Cartwright's boat, into which he and his family had gone for safety. The canoe was here overturned, and the little cargo lost. The company, pitying his distress, concluded to halt and assist him in recovering his property. They had landed on the northern shore, at a level spot, and were going up the place, when the Indians, to our astonishment, appeared immediately over us on the opposite cliffs, and commenced firing down upon us, which occasioned a precipitate retreat to the boats. We immediately moved off. The Indians, lining the bluffs along, continued their fire from the heights on our boats, below, without doing any other injury than wounding four slightly. Jennings' boat is missing.

Johnathan Jennings' boat had run into a large rock jutting out from the northern shore at the Suck. Mrs. Jennings heroically rescued the boat, which had become partly immersed, while miraculously dodging bullets. Donelson wrote, "Their clothes are very much cut with bullets, especially Mrs. Jennings." The Donelson party eventually made it to Big Salt Lick but only after additional hostile encounters with Indians.

In 1913, Hales Bar Dam was completed and the treacherous Suck—along with the Pan, the Skillet, and other dangerous points along the Tennessee River—was tamed.

While the Suck has disappeared, there is still a scenic drive along the north shore of the Tennessee River that passes by the former location of this legendary obstacle. Suck Creek Road, once called the Cherokee Trail and thought by at least one local historian to have been used by a group of Cherokees leaving Ross's Landing on the Trail of Tears, passes by the former location of the tumbling shoals. The road turns north at the mouth of Suck Creek, where the Suck was located, and follows the picturesque creek up the mountain. At Suck Creek, the scenic drive along the river may be continued by using Kelley's Ferry Road, also known as Mullens Cove Road. Kelley's Ferry Road leads past the former locations of other famous obstacles along the Tennessee River, including Deadman Eddy, the Pot, the Skillet, and the Pan.

From Interstate 24 in downtown Chattanooga, take U.S. 27 North across the river to the Signal Mountain exit. Turn right (west) onto Signal Mountain Boulevard which is U.S. 127. At the base of Signal Mountain, turn left onto Tn. 27 West and follow the road along the Tennessee River for 4.1 miles. This is Suck Creek Road. At the point where the road begins to turn away from the river, it crosses a point near the mouth of Suck Creek which is the former site of the Suck.

DANIEL ROSS HOME AND CHATTANOOGA CREEK

Chattanooga

Chatanuga Town, located on Chattanooga Creek where it empties into the Tennessee River, was established during the winter of 1776-77 by followers of Dragging Canoe. Because of its geographical layout, Dragging Canoe chose this location for his village. There was a small island in the Tennessee River between Chatanuga Town and Moccasin Bend. The island made it easy to cross the river from the bend to the town during seasons when the water was low. In later years, the island became known as Ross's Tow or the Tow Head.

In September 1788, General Joseph Martin, on his expedition to destroy the Chickamaugans, led a group of 450 East Tennessee militiamen into Chatanuga Town. He hoped to surprise the inhabitants, but he found the town deserted. One of Martin's men, George Christian, described the town as having "a good many houses built quite scattering with a large Council House in near the center." After entering Chatanuga Town, a portion of the expedition attempted to cross Lookout Mountain. The expedition was met by a Chickamaugan war party and, after a fierce battle, forced to turn back. Martin buried his dead in the floor of one of the houses in Chatanuga Town before burning the town. The town was reinhabited by Chickamaugans after Martin and his men left. (See the next section, Wauhatchie Pike Greenway, for more on the 1788 Martin expedition.)

Around the year 1800, Daniel Ross built a log house at Chatanuga Town where he planted orchards and built a mill, stables, and slave quarters. He established a tannery for deerskins and maintained a stand on the Federal Road. John Ross was not born in this house, but he lived here several years before he turned eighteen. (See The John Ross House section in this chapter.)

John Ross's older sister, Jane, married Joseph Coody, who established a farm and a mission school on Chattanooga Creek near the Daniel Ross house. Coody also built a stand on the Federal Road, between Nickajack and Spring Place. Jane and Joseph moved west in 1834, where the Coody family was active in Cherokee affairs.

During the Creek War, the Cherokees allied themselves with the Americans and a supply base was built near Daniel Ross's house. The supply base was known as Camp Ross.

Today, the area around Chattanooga Creek doesn't look like it did when the small village of Chatanuga Town was located here. The Tennessee River is deeper, and the island called Ross's Tow is underwater. The meandering route of Chattanooga Creek has been tamed by channels and commercial development, and its marshlands have disappeared.

From Ross's Landing or downtown Chattanooga, take Broad Street south toward Lookout Mountain. From Interstate 24, or U.S. 27, take the Lookout Mountain U.S. 11/U.S. 64 exit. Turn right onto Twenty-fifth Street and go 2 blocks to Broad Street and begin following the signs for Lookout Mountain. Broad Street crosses Chattanooga Creek at Twenty-eighth Street, near the site of Chatanuga Town and Camp Ross. Continue down Broad Street another 0.5 mile to a historical marker for Daniel Ross's house, which is located on the left side of Broad Street in front of the Double Cola building.

WAUHATCHIE PIKE GREENWAY

Chattanooga

When Joseph Martin and his men arrived in Chatanuga Town during their 1788 expedition, they found an abandoned village. While most of his soldiers waited in the town, a group of one hundred volunteers ascended Lookout Mountain to look for the Chickamaugan forces. When Martin's army met a force of Chickamaugans led by Dragging Canoe, they fought on a boulder-strewn bench of the mountain. The battle was an Indian victory. Three of Martin's men were killed in the battle and five were wounded. The Chickamaugans lost one Shawnee and one Negro warrior.

One of the men killed in the battle, a Captain Bullard, resembled John Sevier. The Chickamaugans misidentified his body and assumed they had killed their most-hated enemy. A lengthy celebration occurred, only to be followed later by disappointment when they learned Sevier was still alive.

Today the battle is commemorated by a historical marker at the Wauhatchie Pike Greenway. Wauhatchie Pike was a road built around 1845 as part of the Kelly Pike, which ran from Jasper in Marion County to Dallas in Hamilton County. For many years, the Kelly Pike served as the main road from Chattanooga to Nashville and Birmingham. A 0.7-mile section of the Wauhatchie Pike has now been closed and turned into a greenway. Wauhatchie Pike was named for Chief Wauhatchie who lived in a nearby valley. Wauhatchie was severely wounded while he served in Colonel Gideon Morgan's Cherokee regiment during the Creek War.

Wauhatchie Pike is several hundred feet below the Federal Road which followed Jackson's Trace around the end of Lookout Mountain somewhere near Ruby Falls. Jackson's Trace, or Road, was originally an old Indian trail and was the primary route from east to west during the Chickamauga era. Jackson's Trace is probably the actual sight of the 1788 skirmish between Martin and the Chickamaugans.

Today, the Wauhatchie Pike Greenway provides scenic views of Moccasin Bend. To reach Wauhatchie Pike Greenway, take Broad Street from downtown Chattanooga to the foot of Lookout Mountain. Proceed up Cummings Highway, following the signs for Ruby Falls. Turn left onto Scenic Highway which crosses the Old Wauhatchie Pike just before reaching Ruby Falls. Turn left and the parking lot for the greenway will be just a short distance down the Old Wauhatchie Pike by the Sky Harbor Bavarian Inn. The greenway can also be reached easily from Reflection Riding. When leaving Reflection Riding, turn right from Garden Road onto Old Wauhatchie Pike, just before the intersec-

tion with Cummings Highway (U.S. 41 and U.S. 64.) Follow Old Wauhatchie Pike up the mountain for 1.1 miles and cross Scenic Highway to the parking lot on the other side.

CHATTANOOGA NATURE CENTER AND REFLECTION RIDING

Chattanooga

The Chattanooga Nature Center and Reflection Riding are located between Lookout Creek and the western base of Lookout Mountain. Reflection Riding refers to a 3-mile motor-trail loop that travels through the three-hundred-acre botanical garden. The garden boasts a wide variety of native wildflowers and trees that provide a continuous show of color throughout the year. The Chattanooga Nature Center is located on the grounds.

An Indian cabin, originally from North Carolina, is located on the grounds. Also located on the grounds are millstones believed to be from a mill built on Lookout Creek in 1803. Built as part of the effort to federalize the Cherokees, the mill was located near the spot where the Great Indian

War Trail and the Federal Road crossed Lookout Creek. It was operated by Dick Justice and The Glass, both Cherokees. Justice also operated a nearby ferry, located where Lookout Creek empties into the Tennessee.

A section of the Federal Road is still preserved in Reflection Riding. There are several hiking trails that begin on the grounds, including one to nearby Skyuka Springs. Skyuka Springs is named for Wyuka, a chief of Lookout Mountain Town during the Chickamaugan era. Wyuka signed the Treaty of Hopewell in 1785.

In February 1994, a new loop trail, named the Indian Profile Trail, was opened in Reflection Riding. The 2.5-mile trail received its name because it provides a view of Sunset Rock, which resembles the profile of an Indian. Local legend says that the Cherokees called the rock Do da nun-yu, meaning "Father Rock."

In addition to the historic landmarks and scenic beauty of Reflection Riding, the Chattanooga Nature Center offers a wildlife rehabilitation lab, a wetland boardwalk, wildlife exhibits, and a gift shop. The Chattanooga Nature Center and Reflection

Chattanooga Nature Center

Riding are open Monday through Saturday from 9 A.M. to 5 P.M., and Sunday from 1 P.M. to 5 P.M. For information, call 615-821-1160. There is a small admission charge.

To reach Reflection Riding from Chattanooga, take Interstate 24 west to Exit 175, the Brown's Ferry Road and Lookout Mountain exit. Turn left under the interstate and follow the signs for Lookout Mountain. Then turn left onto Cummings Highway (U.S. 41) and drive 0.7 mile. Turn right onto Garden Road at the sign for Reflection Riding. Garden Road can also be reached from downtown Chattanooga by taking Broad Street south to Cummings Highway. Take Cummings to Garden Road and turn left. Drive 1 mile to the end of Garden Road and the entrance for the botanical gardens and nature center.

LOOKOUT CREEK AND JUSTICE'S FERRY

Chattanooga

In 1779, Colonel Evan Shelby and his forces raided eleven Chickamaugan villages. After these raids, Dragging Canoe moved his operations further west to five "Lower" Towns. Lookout Mountain Town, also known as Stecoe, was one of the Lower Towns. It was located on Lookout Creek, thirteen miles upstream from the Tennessee River.

One of Lookout Mountain Town's shamans and a powerful chief was a man named Dick Justice. In 1788, he fought with Dragging Canoe against the forces of General Joseph Martin in the battle on Lookout Mountain. Justice, like many of the Chickamaugan leaders, made peace with the settlers after Dragging Canoe's death in 1792 and became a respected businessman. By 1802, he operated a ferry near the mouth of Lookout Creek, which he sold in 1818 in order to voluntarily relocate to Arkansas. The new owner of the ferry was Thomas Fox Baldridge, also a Cherokee, who operated the ferry until 1838 when he was forced to leave the area.

Cummings Highway (U.S. 41) crosses Lookout Creek near the point where Justice's Ferry was located. It is only a few miles downstream from the site of Lookout Mountain Town. From Interstate 24 or U.S. 127, take the Lookout Mountain Exit to Broad Street. Follow the Lookout Mountain signs west. At the foot of the mountain,

Broad Street turns into Cummings Highway. Follow Cummings Highway as it parallels the interstate. Cummings Highway crosses Lookout Creek 0.25 mile past the sign for Reflection Riding. This is near the point where Justice's Ferry was located.

BROWN'S TAVERN

Tiftonia

During the 1800s, several enterprising Indians built ferries and taverns along the trade paths which crossed through Cherokee territory. In 1803, a mixed-blood Cherokee named John Brown established Brown's Tavern near the ferry mentioned in the Williams Island section of this chapter. His tavern became a popular rest stop after a wagon road, connecting Fort Nashborough and Spring Place, Georgia, was completed in 1807.

The tavern is now a private residence and is not open to the public, but it may be viewed from the road. To reach the tavern from Chattanooga, travel west on Interstate 24 and take Exit 175 for Brown's Ferry Road. Turn right onto Brown's Ferry Road. The tavern is 1.1 miles on the left, near the Lookout Valley Elementary School.

Brown's Tavern

Runningwater Creek

RUNNINGWATER TOWN

Haletown

Runningwater Town was the headquarters of the legendary Chickamaugan war chief Dragging Canoe. Because this village was protected by steep banks on either side of the river, Dragging Canoe and his successor, Chief John Watts, were able to use this location as a base for their forays against white settlers. Dragging Canoe died at Runningwater Town in 1792. Ironically, he died the morning after an eagle tail dance was held in his honor to celebrate one of his victories over the white soldiers.

During the summer of 1793, a mixed-blood Cherokee trader from Chota named John Boggs visited the area and met the daughter of Chief Turtle-at-Home. Boggs married the daughter, whose name was Tsi-yah-neh-naw, and settled in Runningwater Town. He quickly established a ferry at the mouth of Runningwater Creek, where the Great Indian War Trail passed through the area. In 1794, Boggs assisted Major James Ore when Ore came to Runningwater Town in search of a Creek who had killed a white man near Knoxville. Despite Boggs's cooperation in tracking down the murderer, Ore and his troops did not spare Runningwater Town or the nearby village of Nickajack when they attacked the Chickamaugans in September of that year.

In the 1790s, the Tennessee River was only 270 yards wide at the mouth of Runningwater Creek. Today, it is 3 miles wide due to the construction of Nickajack Dam in 1967. Runningwater Town, Dragging Canoe's grave, and the site of Boggs's ferry now lie under the waters of Nickajack Lake.

Traveling west from Chattanooga on Interstate 24, take Exit 161 and turn right on Tn. 156. This section of Tn. 156 has several views of Nickajack Lake which covers the area where the former mouth of Runningwater Creek and the site of Runningwater Town were located. By turning right on Tn. 134, you can drive past the new mouth of Runningwater Creek 0.75 mile from the interstate exit ramp and take a scenic drive along the creek through the narrow gorge. If you continue on Tn. 156, it is only a short distance to the junction with U.S. 41 and U.S. 64. Turn left (west) on U.S. 41 and U.S. 64 and cross the bridge over the Tennessee River. On the other side of the bridge, on the right, is a historical marker noting the 1794 attack on Runningwater Town. From here, you may want to continue on U.S. 41/64 another 6 miles to Betsy Pack's former home in Jasper.

BETSY PACK'S FORMER HOME

Jasper

Sometime before the American Revolution, a Cherokee woman named Nannie married a Scot trader named John Lowrey.

The Lowreys and their seven children lived in the vicinity of Battle Creek near Jasper, Tennessee. The Lowrey family was closely connected with the Cherokees of this area. The oldest son John, Jr., born about 1768, married Elizabeth Shorey, the sister of John McDonald's wife, Anna. They had one daughter named Betsy. John Lowrey, Jr., lived near the mouth of Battle Creek, near present-day South Pittsburgh, where he operated a ferry and conducted a stock and cattle business. John, Jr., served as an assistant to Colonel Return Meigs and was appointed lieutenant-colonel during the Creek War. His brother, George Lowrey, married Lucy Benge, who may have been Sequoyah's half sister. George served as a major under Jackson in the Creek War and was assistant principal chief of the Cherokee Nation for thirty years.

Until the Calhoun Treaty of 1819, the Lowrey clan owned much of the land in the Battle Creek Valley. This treaty opened the area in the Sequatchie Valley below the Tennessee River to white settlement, and the territory was soon incorporated into Marion County. Due to the intolerance of white settlers, Major George Lowrey sold his holdings and most of the family moved to the Wills Valley area in Alabama.

Betsy Lowrey Pack established a ferry on

the Tennessee River. It is believed to have been located four or five miles west of Boggs's Ferry at Runningwater Town and approximately seven miles east of her father's ferry at Battle Creek. In 1815, she and her mother ran a public house on Battle Creek called Lowrey's Place. In 1822, while making plans to relocate, Betsy Pack deeded forty acres of her land for the price of one dollar to Marion County to establish a new county seat. Betsy hoped to make the county seat permanent by stipulating that if the courthouse was ever moved, the land would revert to her heirs. The commissioners accepted the land and laid out the new town of Jasper. Later, the commissioners sold some of the land donated by Betsy Pack to raise funds for the building of the Sam Houston Academy, Jasper's first public school.

From Interstate 24 west of Chattanooga, take Exit 161 and turn right on Tn. 156. From Interstate 24, the site of Runningwater Town is 0.8 mile down Tn. 156. Continue on Tn. 156 to the junction with U.S. 41/64. At U.S. 41/64 turn left (west) and cross the bridge over the Tennessee River. It is another 6 miles to the courthouse square in Jasper and the historical marker for Betsy Pack's home.

Nickajack Cave

NICKAJACK AND NICKAJACK CAVE

Ladds

Local historians have puzzled for many years over the origin of the name Nickajack. It was first used as the name of an important Chickamaugan settlement on the Tennessee River. Later it was the name for a large cave, a dam, and the lake formed by the dam, all located on the Tennessee River near the old Cherokee town. Historian Penelope J. Allen credited the name Nickajack to Jack Civil, a blacksmith and escaped slave who lived in the area for many years. Allen suggested Nickajack was a corruption of "Nigger Jack." Former Hamilton County historian Zella Armstrong wrote that Nickajack was of Cherokee origin. She suggested that the white settlers had trouble with the guttural pronunciation of the Cherokee name Ani-kusati-yi, which meant "Creek People Place."

In 1788, an incident took place that would later bring the downfall of the Chickamaugan settlements of Nickajack and nearby Runningwater Town. A boat carrying Colonel James Brown and his family left the Holston River area for Nashville. Five days into the trip, they landed at Tuskegee Island Town (on Williams Island in present-day Chattanooga) where Cutteotoy, the chief of the town, boarded the boat. Cutteotoy and two warriors acted friendly with the party, then sent runners to Runningwater Town and Nickajack. This led to an ambush of the white settlers later in their journey.

In Nickajack, John Vann, who was half-Cherokee, met the Brown party and boarded Brown's boat under a flag of truce. Vann and his forty men then killed Colonel Brown and seven of the younger men in the party. Mrs. Brown, the youngest boys, and the girls were taken captive. One of Colonel Brown's sons, Joseph, was taken

to Nickajack as the property of a young chief named Kiachatalee. Joseph remained at Nickajack nearly a year before he and two of his sisters were released in a prisoner exchange. He was soon reunited with his mother and other sister Elizabeth in North Carolina. His brother, George, was not released for several years.

In 1794, Joseph Brown was hired by General James Robertson of the Mero District militia to map a route to the Lower Towns for the purpose of an invasion. (The Mero District of central Tennessee was established in 1788 by the general assembly of the Territory of Tennessee. It included Nashville and settlements in the Cumberland region. The district was named in honor of Don Estephan Mero, a colonel in the service of Spain and, later, a governor of New Orleans.) During his captivity, Brown had noticed the various routes used by the Chickamaugans. Until Brown showed the white forces the Indian trail over the Cumberland Mountains that led down Battle Creek, the militia had not known how to penetrate the defenses of the Lower Towns. In September, Major James Ore led an expedition over Brown's route to the mouth of the Sequatchie River (near present-day South Pittsburgh). They crossed the river during the night and attacked Nickajack the next day. About seventy Cherokees were killed at Nickajack, and several more were taken prisoner. Some of the captives recognized Joseph Brown from his captivity five years earlier. Major Ore then proceeded toward Runningwater Town but met some of that town's warriors along the way. After this skirmish, Ore continued to Runningwater Town which he found deserted. Before leaving the area, Ore burned the village.

Around the year 1800, Major Ore suffered financial setbacks at his home in Grainger County and returned to Nickajack. He established a grist mill, tavern, and place to make powder at Nickajack Cave. The cave at Nickajack later became an important source of saltpeter for the Confederates, as well as a tourist attraction.

Since the building of Nickajack Dam, the cave has been flooded and closed to the public. Some random explorations by amateur archaeologists and speleologists before the flooding found evidence that suggests Native Americans used the cave for thousands of years before the Cherokees established the village of Nickajack a half mile away.

Every night at dusk, several thousand, endangered gray bats emerge from the mouth of the large cave. Each bat consumes nearly three thousand insects during its nocturnal flight. Access to a platform which gives a view of the cave is open only from April 1 to October 15. For information contact the Tennessee Valley Authority (TVA) Land Management Division at 1-800-TVA-LAND, or the Tennessee Wildlife Resources Agency at 1-800-262-6704.

Nickajack Cave is across the river from Shellmound Recreation Area, which is noted for its Indian shell middens. To reach Nickajack Cave from Chattanooga, take Interstate 24 west toward Nashville. Take Exit 161, and turn left onto Tn. 156 West. Go 5.1 miles to the TVA Maple View Public Use Area on the left. From South Pittsburgh, take Tn. 156 across the bridge at the north end of town and drive 5.3 miles to the Maple View Public Use Area. Park at the end of the parking lot and take the short path to the viewing platform near the cave.

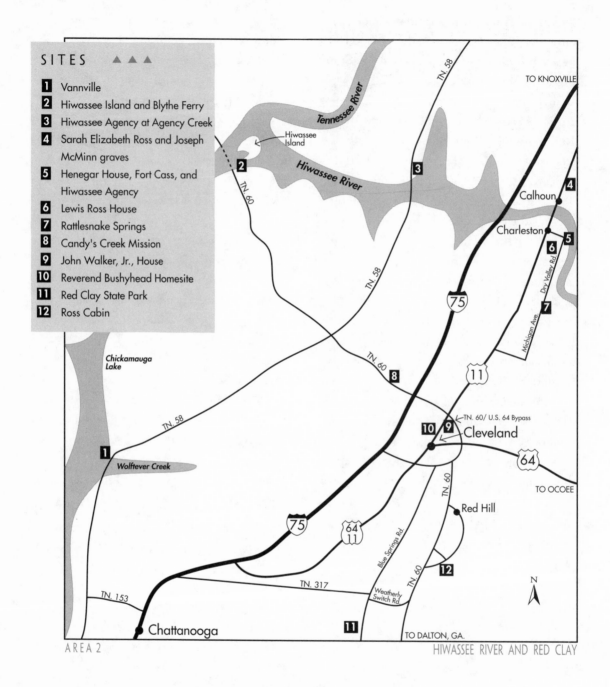

SITES ▲ ▲ ▲

1 Vannville
2 Hiwassee Island and Blythe Ferry
3 Hiwassee Agency at Agency Creek
4 Sarah Elizabeth Ross and Joseph
   McMinn graves
5 Henegar House, Fort Cass, and
   Hiwassee Agency
6 Lewis Ross House
7 Rattlesnake Springs
8 Candy's Creek Mission
9 John Walker, Jr., House
10 Reverend Bushyhead Homesite
11 Red Clay State Park
12 Ross Cabin

Tennessee River

Hiwassee Island

Hiwassee River

TO KNOXVILLE

TN. 58

Calhoun

Charleston

Dry Valley Rd.

Michigan Ave.

TN. 60

TN. 58

75

11

TN. 60

Chickamauga Lake

TN. 58

TN. 60/ U.S. 64 Bypass

Cleveland

64

TO OCOEE

Vannville

Wolftever Creek

Red Hill

64
11

TN. 60

Blue Springs Rd.

75

TN. 153

TN. 317

Weatherly Switch Rd.

N

Chattanooga

TO DALTON, GA.

AREA 2

HIWASSEE RIVER AND RED CLAY

Red Clay State Park

HIWASSEE RIVER AND RED CLAY

▲ ▲ ▲

After the Treaty of New Echota was signed in 1835, white settlers began pouring into the Cherokee Nation. Although they were in defiance of Tennessee law, the settlers wanted an early jump on the land that would be available once the Cherokees were removed. One of the first white settlers to cross the Hiwassee River into the Cherokee Nation during this land rush was Dr. P. J. R. Edwards, who was accompanied by his eleven-year-old nephew. Years later the nephew, Colonel R. M. Edwards, an attorney and historian, recalled the beauty of the last remnant of the old Cherokee Nation. He described the area where the Red Clay Council Grounds, Cherokee

Agency, and Candy's Creek Mission were located:

> When the white folks came to the county in 1835-1836, the virgin forest was almost unbroken, save a few small patches the Indians had cleared in the richest spots. The custom of the Indians was to annually burn the leaves, which kept down the young growth, the bushes being kept down, grass grew luxuriantly, and the entire country had more the appearance of a well-kept park than a forest. Along its beautiful valleys a deer might have been seen a mile or more distant, and a person could ride or drive in all directions. No wonder the Indians objected to the treaty which gave all those beautiful lands to the white race, and compelled them to seek a new home in the far-off West.

VANNVILLE

Harrison

When Dragging Canoe left the Overhill area and established the Chickamaugan towns in 1776, Ostenaco was one of the chiefs who followed him south. Ostenaco, also called Judd's Friend, and his followers settled on Ooltewah Creek, which was also known as Judd's Creek. In 1779, Colonel Evan Shelby burned Ostenaco's village.

Today, Ooltewah Creek is known as Wolftever Creek.

After Joseph Vann, a Cherokee, was expelled from his home in Georgia in 1834, he moved to a spot on the Tennessee River at the mouth of Wolftever Creek, near the former site of Ostenaco's village. He left behind a rich plantation and a stately brick mansion in Georgia, but he had already established a second plantation at Wolftever Creek. By the 1835 census, his holdings there included a mill, a ferry boat, and thirty-five houses. In 1836, he moved again to a spot on the Arkansas River where he established a steamboat line. In 1844, he was accidentally killed in an explosion aboard one of his steamboats, the *Lucy Walker*.

In 1822, the seat of Hamilton County was established on a site across the Tennessee River from the future site of Vann's plantation. Shortly thereafter, the courthouse was built on land owned by Richard Taylor and his brother, Fox Taylor, descendants of Nancy Ward. In an 1840 referendum, voters decided to move the courthouse "to the south side of Tennessee, at or within one mile of the framed house lately occupied by Joseph Vann, a Cherokee Indian, in said county." In anticipation of the vote, a land company had developed Vann's plantation and established the settlement of Vannville.

However, a town named Harrison was built next to Vanville, and the new brick courthouse was built there.

Vanville, and the original site of Harrison, are now under Chickamauga Lake. A historical marker for Vann's Town, which Vannville is often called, is located on Tn. 58, at the new mouth of Wolftever Creek.

From Interstate 75, take the Ooltewah exit and turn west on Lee Highway. After 0.1 miles turn left onto Hunter Road. Take Hunter Road to Tn. 58 (known locally as Highway 58) and turn north (right). Drive 0.6 mile on Tn. 58. The historical marker for Vann's Town will be on the left. It is located across from Wolftever Road and a subdivision.

HIWASSEE ISLAND AND BLYTHE FERRY

Birchwood

The name Hiwassee comes from *ayuhwa'si*, which is Cherokee for "savanna." Even today, the word is descriptive of the lands along the banks of the Hiwassee River, particularly the area where the Hiwassee empties into the Tennessee River. Hiwassee Island, now mostly under the waters of Chickamauga Lake, is located near the mouth of the Hiwassee River. It served as the home for many different groups of Native Americans, including Indians from the Woodland period. Later, Yuchi and Creek tribes had villages on the island. The Yuchis lived along the Hiwassee River until 1714, when the Cherokees destroyed the Yuchi town of Chestowa located there.

The Cherokees probably didn't settle on Hiwassee Island until sometime in the mid-1700s. They established a town called Cayoca (also spelled Coyocua) in the immediate vicinity of the island. Chief Oolooteeskee, also known as John Jolly, was believed to have been born at Cayoca in 1770. The island later became known as Jolly's Island. In 1809, Sam Houston came to Jolly's Island and was adopted by John Jolly and the Cherokees who lived there.

In the early 1800s, at least two ferries were located near the confluence of the Hiwassee and Tennessee rivers. Lewis Ross, brother of John Ross, operated a ferry near the western end of the Hiwassee until he moved to Charleston, Tennessee, where he established another ferry. William Blythe, Sr., who was married to the daughter of the Cherokee, Richard Fields, also established a ferry nearby. It was established sometime between 1806 and 1809 and crossed the Tennessee River at the mouth of the Hiwassee, below Hiwassee Island. Blythe Ferry, still in operation, was used by thousands of Cherokees as they traveled from Tennessee to Arkansas on the Trail of Tears.

Most of Hiwassee Island is now under the waters of Chickamauga Lake. At the time of this writing, a bridge is being built across the Tennessee River, about two miles south of Blythe Ferry. When the bridge is completed, Blythe Ferry will close after over 180 years of operation.

From Interstate 75 in Cleveland, take the Cleveland State Community College Exit and follow Tn. 60 west to the Tennessee River. Hiwassee Island is not open to the public but the remaining portion may be viewed when crossing the river on the ferry. After the ferry is closed, the best viewing point will probably be from the west bank of the Tennessee River at the former ferry landing, or from the Hiwassee Wildlife Refuge.

HIWASSEE AGENCY

Birchwood

From 1816 to 1821, an office of the

Cherokee Agency was located at the mouth of a small creek that emptied into the Hiwassee River. Eventually, the creek became known as Agency Creek. This outpost was the second of three Cherokee Agency locations on the Hiwassee River. Although there were other United States agents to the Cherokees operating throughout the Cherokee territory, the offices on the Hiwassee River became the primary location for the agency. The Cherokee Agency was moved to its first location at the mouth of the Hiwassee River in 1807, when similar operations at Fort Southwest Point (present-day Kingston, Tennessee) and the Tellico Blockhouse (present-day Vonore, Tennessee) were closed. Because the Cherokee Agency had three offices on the Hiwassee River, it was often referred to as the Hiwassee Agency. In 1816, the Cherokee Agency was moved to its second location on the Hiwassee River at Agency Creek. In 1821, the Cherokee Agency was moved to its third and final location on the Hiwassee River at Charleston, Tennessee.

In July 1817, a treaty that called for a major cession of Cherokee land and the voluntary removal of Cherokees to the West was signed at the second location. The treaty was engineered by Andrew Jackson and Joseph McMinn, the governor of Tennessee at the time.

A federally-funded study has been completed to determine the feasibility of building a Trail of Tears' interpretive park and genealogical center at the site of the old Cherokee Agency at Agency Creek. The proposed site will be one of several historic sites developed along the Trail of Tears National Historic Trail. In 1987, Congress designated that the Trail of Tears be included as part of the National Trails System. As a part of this system, road markers, provided by the National Park Service, will be erected along the land route of the Trail of Tears. These road markers were originally scheduled to be erected in 1994, but a shortage of funds has caused a delay in this project—and several of the projects associated with the Trail of Tears National Historic Trail. Local and state groups, like the Trail of Tears Association, are currently working with the National Park Service to protect important sites along the Trail of Tears. There are also plans to develop interpretive programs in locations along the trail.

For information on the Trail of Tears National Historic Trail, contact the National Park Service Long Distance Trails Group Office in Santa Fe, New Mexico, at 505-988-6888. For information on the proposed interpretive and genealogical center to be located on the Hiwassee River,

contact Friends of the Cherokee Memorial at 615-334-3923.

From Interstate 75, take the Cleveland State Community College exit and follow Tn. 60 west. This road goes past Candy's Creek, the site of a mission school for the Cherokees established in the early 1820s which will be discussed later. At the intersection of Tn 60. and Tn. 58, turn north onto Tn. 58 and cross the Hiwassee River. The site of the Hiwassee Agency office, and the proposed Trail of Tears interpretive and genealogical center, will be on the northeast shore of the Hiwassee River as you cross the bridge.

SARAH ELIZABETH ROSS AND JOSEPH MCMINN GRAVES

Calhoun

Beginning in 1815, Joseph McMinn served as governor of Tennessee for three successive, two-year terms. In January 1823, McMinn was appointed agent to the Cherokees. He served in that capacity at the Cherokee Agency office in Charleston, Tennessee, on the southern bank of the Hiwassee River, across from Calhoun. McMinn was a favorite of Andrew Jackson

Joseph McMinn's grave

Sarah Elizabeth Ross's grave

and a proponent of Cherokee removal. He reportedly used devious tactics to encourage the Cherokees' removal. To build support for the removal, he claimed that Cherokee leaders made threats on his life, and he asked the secretary of war to send troops to protect him. In another incident, he tried to convince the federal government that every white settler in Tennessee feared a Cherokee uprising. McMinn also used strong-arm tactics to intimidate his critics. He threatened to sell the Brainerd Mission in order to silence the troublesome missionaries there.

Secretary of War John C. Calhoun did not like McMinn. The Cherokee Agency had been appropriated eighty thousand dollars to aid Cherokees who wished to move west. Calhoun felt McMinn squandered the money on himself and his cronies. In 1824, McMinn died at the Cherokee Agency in Charleston and was buried in the town of Calhoun, at the Calhoun Presbyterian Church.

Two-year-old Sarah Elizabeth Ross also died in 1824. She was the daughter of Lewis and Frances Holt Ross, and the niece of John Ross. Sarah's grave is located in the Calhoun First Baptist Church cemetery.

To reach the town of Calhoun from Interstate 75, take the Calhoun exit and drive east on Tn. 163. Continue on Tn. 163 past the intersection with U.S. 11 for 0.2 mile, to a sign which reads Hiwassee Meadowland Park. Turn left and drive a short distance up the hill to a cemetery. A large granite shaft in the cemetery marks McMinn's grave. Sarah Ross's grave is directly across Tn. 163 from the Hiwassee Meadowland Park. From Tn. 163, turn right at the Calhoun First Baptist Church and drive 0.1 mile to the church cemetery.

HENEGAR HOUSE AND FORT CASS

Charleston

Around 1820, the Cherokee Agency office at Agency Creek in Meigs County was moved to Charleston in Bradley County. United States agents who served at the Charleston office at various times included Colonel Return J. Meigs, former governor Joseph McMinn, and Colonel Hugh Montgomery. Charleston was known as a gateway into Cherokee country. The area attracted many businessmen, including Lewis Ross, brother of John Ross, who established a store and ferry there.

Fort Cass was built just a little west of the Cherokee Agency office. This fort

Henegar House

became one of the headquarters of General Winfield Scott during the 1838 removal. Several thousand Cherokees were held in nearby stockades, and Charleston became the main embarkation point for the removal.

Charleston also was the home of Captain H. B. Henegar. At the age of twenty-four, Henegar, who worked for John Ross, accompanied the Cherokees west on the Trail of Tears. Soon after, Henegar returned to Charleston from Park Hill, Oklahoma, where John Ross had settled. He built a brick house with attractive gardens on the former site of Fort Cass. After his return, he wrote an account of his experiences on the Trail of Tears, which included a description of the activities in Charleston and Fort Cass:

> Charleston, Bradley County, Tennessee, on the Hiwassee River, was the starting-point and the place where the Ross party was collected. General Scott was stationed here with the United States Troops. The spot where my residence now stands was the barracks. The regular soldiers were assisted by several companies of militia; but not much difficulty was encountered in collecting the Indians, as John Ross's influence was so great that they came in at his request, he having effected a liberal compromise with the Government, the Indians being well paid for all they possessed. John

Ross took the contract for their removal, which he afterward let to Lewis Ross, who was a better businessman.

To reach the site of Fort Cass and the Henegar house from Interstate 75, take the Calhoun exit and drive east on Tn. 163. In Calhoun, take U.S. 11 south across the Hiwassee River to Charleston. From U.S. 11, turn east onto Water Street, the first road south of the Hiwassee River. Take the second right off of Water Street onto Market Street, a quiet residential street. The Henegar house, which is privately owned, is 0.1 mile down Market Street on the left. The unoccupied house can be identified by its red-brick construction and large, shady grounds. The former home of Lewis Ross is another 0.1 mile down Market Street on the right (See the Lewis Ross House, discussed in the next section.)

LEWIS ROSS HOUSE

Charleston

Lewis Ross, brother and business partner of John Ross, built his home in Charleston near the Hiwassee River when the Cherokee Agency relocated there from

Agency Creek. Lewis was a savvy business-man and established a successful trading post and ferry in Charleston. In the fall of 1838, he was entrusted by his brother with arrangements for the Cherokees' self-supervised removal. While the bulk of the Cherokee Nation traveled overland on foot and by wagon, the wealthy Lewis Ross took his family west via steamboat. In the West, Lewis Ross's business interests continued to thrive. His fortune at the beginning of the Civil War was estimated at one million dollars.

Lewis Ross's house in Charleston has been renovated several times since Ross lived there. It is privately owned and not open to the public, but it is easily seen from the street. The Henegar house, mentioned earlier, is located on the same road.

To reach the Lewis Ross house from Interstate 75, take the Calhoun exit and drive east on Tn. 163. In Calhoun, take U.S. 11 south across the Hiwassee River to Charleston. From U.S. 11, turn east onto Water Street, the first road south of the Hiwassee River. Take the second right off of Water Street onto Market Street, a quiet residential road. (These are the same directions as to the Henegar house.) The stately Victorian-style clapboard house of Lewis Ross is 0.2 mile down Market Street on the right.

Lewis Ross House

RATTLESNAKE SPRINGS

Charleston

During the long summer of 1838, between eight and thirteen thousand Cherokees were camped near the Cherokee Agency in Charleston, Tennessee. They were waiting for the weather to cool and the drought to end so they could begin their long journey west. The Cherokees lived in camps scattered throughout an area approximately twelve miles long by four miles wide. This area was located south of Charleston and also included several small forts and camps for the soldiers who were supervising the removal in case there was trouble. However, the Cherokee camps were reported to be quiet that summer and many of the troops were sent home.

An 1838 map of the area from Fort Cass on the Hiwassee River to Rattlesnake Springs, located about 3.5 miles south of the river, shows a camp for United States troops named Camp Worth located at Rattlesnake Springs. The map also shows several Cherokee camps located a short distance east of the springs on Rattlesnake Branch. Camps were also located at several points on the Hiwassee River east of Charleston, on a branch of Mouse Creek, near Chateetee Creek (now called Chatata

Creek), and at several other places between Mouse and Chatata creeks.

While John Ross made futile efforts to stop the removal during the long summer of 1838, many Cherokees died in camps. When the removal became inevitable, Cherokees assembled at Rattlesnake Springs. A council was held there, and representatives of the Cherokee Nation resolved that they would preserve their constitution in their new home in the West. The decision was made that the next detachment of Cherokee emigrants must be under way by September 1. The council also decided that thirteen detachments—of one thousand people each—would travel overland instead of by water, as originally planned. The last detachment, led by John Drew, left the Cherokee Agency on December 5, 1838. It arrived in the western territory on March 18, 1839.

In a letter, William Shorey Coodey, a nephew of John Ross, described the scene when the first detachment left in late August:

> At noon all was in readiness for moving; the teams were stretched out in a line along the road through a heavy forest, groups of persons formed about each wagon, others shaking the hand of some sick friend or relative who would be left behind. The temporary camp covered

Rattlesnake Springs

with boards and some of bark that for three summer months had been their only shelter and home, were crackling and falling under a blazing flame; the day was bright and beautiful, but a gloomy thoughtfulness was depicted in the lineaments of every face. In all the bustle of preparation there was a silence and stillness of the voice that betrayed the sadness of the heart.

Today, Rattlesnake Springs is privately-owned farmland. The area lies 3 miles southwest of Charleston and 5 miles northwest of Cleveland. The city of Cleveland is considering the area near Rattlesnake Springs for the site of a new airport. The Department of the Interior and several Native American groups have expressed concern that construction of an airport near Rattlesnake Springs might disturb the resting places of several hundred Cherokees who died there while they waited to move west. No archaeological studies have been done to determine the location of the graves.

While the future of Rattlesnake Springs and the beautiful farm land surrounding it is being considered, visitors may view the Rattlesnake Springs area. From Cleveland, take U.S. 11 north. On U.S. 11, drive 1.5 miles past the Paul Huff Parkway intersection to Tasso Road. There is no sign marking Tasso Road. The intersection of U.S.

11 and Tasso Road is marked by a muffler shop on one corner and a market with Exxon gas pumps on another corner. Turn right onto Tasso Road and drive 2 miles to Michigan Avenue. Turn left onto Michigan Avenue and watch for the Moore Farm after 2.5 miles. The springs are located at the bottom of a hill, a little north of the Moore residence. The springs and the surrounding fields where the camps were located are on private property, but they are easily viewed from the road.

CANDY'S CREEK MISSION

Cleveland

The Candy's Creek Mission school was opened February 2, 1825, by William Holland, a young man from Massachusetts, and his wife Electra Hopkins. They began their missionary work at the Brainerd Mission, which was discussed earlier, in September 1823. They were then assigned mission duties near Calhoun, Tennessee, before they were sent to Candy's Creek.

When the school at Candy's Creek first opened, it had only five or six students. The children attended classes at Holland's home. A schoolhouse, post office, church, and

Site of Candy's Creek Mission

boarding school were later established at the site. In an 1832 report to the secretary of war, Holland estimated the value of the property as somewhere between $1,500 and $1,800. This sum did not include the value of the land, which included twenty-five acres. By the time Holland closed the school in the summer of 1837, he and his wife had taught reading, writing, geography, arithmetic, and composition to over eighty-four students. One of the students, Susan Bushyhead, even taught a course in the Cherokee language to other students. Two of the students, Jesse Bushyhead and Stephen Foreman, later became prominent ministers and leaders of the Cherokees.

A historical marker for Candy's Creek Mission is located on Tn. 60 in Cleveland. The marker indicates the mission was located 0.4 mile to the east. Since Tn. 60 has very narrow shoulders, and there is not a safe place to stop near the marker, an alternative route to Candy's Creek is described here.

From Interstate 75 in Cleveland, take Exit 25. Take Tn. 60 west 1.7 miles and turn right onto Paul Huff Parkway. Then take an immediate left onto Candy's Creek Ridge Road and drive 0.6 mile to the first paved road on the left. Turn left onto this unmarked road and go 0.2 mile to where it crosses Candy's Creek.

JOHN WALKER, JR., HOUSE

Cleveland

John Walker, Jr., was the son of Major John Walker, an officer of the Cherokee force at Horseshoe Bend during the Creek War. John Walker, Jr., was also the great-grandson of Nancy Ward. Walker had two wives, which was legal and customary in the Cherokee Nation. His Cherokee wife was Nancy, who lived with her brother, Reverend Jesse Bushyhead. His second wife was Emily, a granddaughter of the Indian agent Return J. Meigs. Emily and John made their home in a two-story log house at the present site of Northside Presbyterian Church in Cleveland.

Walker was very active in Cherokee affairs, particularly in the debate about the removal process. While returning home from a council at Red Clay, Tennessee, in August 1834, he was shot, supposedly because of his support for removal. Walker is buried in Cleveland at the site of his home. A Cherokee named James Foreman was put on trial for the murder, but he escaped immediate punishment and made his way to Oklahoma. Foreman was eventually killed by Stand Watie, in an apparent act of revenge for the assassination of Walker.

A historical marker showing the site where John Walker's house once stood is located in Cleveland beside the Northside Presbyterian Church. The church is at the intersection of U.S. 11 and Paul Huff Parkway. From Interstate 75, take Exit 27 and follow the Paul Huff Parkway east into Cleveland to the intersection of U.S. 11.

REVEREND JESSE BUSHYHEAD HOMESITE

Cleveland

Jesse Bushyhead was born in 1804 near Cleveland, Tennessee. He and several brothers and sisters attended the Candy's Creek mission and school, where Bushyhead was inspired to become a minister. During the last Red Clay councils in 1837, he translated the English worship services into the Cherokee language. He also conducted services in the removal camps during the summer of 1838. George Featherstonhaugh, a British traveler who visited the Red Clay Councils, described one of the services:

> The voices of the Cherokees already at morning worship awoke me at the dawn of day, and dressing myself hastily, I went to the Council-house. Great numbers of them were assembled, and Mr. Jones, the Missionary, read out verses in the English language from the New Testament, which Bushy-head, with a singularly stentorial voice and sonorous accent, immediately rendered to the people in the Cherokee tongue, emitting a deep grunting sound at the end of every verse resembling the hard breathing of a man chopping trees down, the meaning of which I was given to understand was to call their attention to the proposition conveyed by the passage. This I was told is an universal practice also in Cherokee oratory. When they sang, a line or two of a hymn printed in the Cherokee language was given out, each one having a hymn book in his hand, and I certainly never saw any congregation engaged more apparently in sincere devotion.

Jesse Bushyhead and the elderly Chief Whitepath led a removal group from Rattlesnake Springs in 1838. At Hopkinsville, Kentucky, Whitepath died and was buried with Fly Smith, a former member of the National Council. Bushyhead and Reverend Stephen Foreman, who later became a judge of the Cherokee Supreme Court, gave the funeral addresses. In his new home in the West, Bushyhead was appointed chief justice of the Cherokee Nation. He served in that capacity until his death in 1844. His son, Dennis Wolfe Bushyhead, served as the principal chief of the Cherokee Nation from 1879 to 1891.

The site of Bushyhead's home in Cleveland, Tennessee, is now occupied by the Cleveland High and Middle School complex. From Interstate 75 in Cleveland, take Exit 27 and follow the Paul Huff Parkway east to U.S. 11. (This is the intersection where the John Walker house was located.) Turn south (right) on U.S. 11 and drive 1.25 miles to Raider Drive. Turn right at the traffic light onto Raider Drive. The schools will be on the right in 0.2 mile.

RED CLAY STATE PARK

Cleveland

In 1832, Georgia laws were put in effect that made it illegal for the Cherokees to continue to hold council meetings at New Echota. The council meetings were moved across the Georgia line to Red Clay, Tennessee. Red Clay became the seat of Cherokee government until the removal in 1838. It was at Red Clay that the Cherokee people were told their efforts to hold onto their land had failed, and that they would be forced to move to Oklahoma.

Today, the area where the Red Clay meetings took place is a state park. A replica of a Cherokee farmstead and council house at Red Clay State Park demonstrates how the Cherokees lived in the 1830s. The cool, blue spring, which provided water during council meetings, still flows there. An interpretive center houses a theater, exhibit room, and reading room. There are also several miles of hiking trails, an amphitheater, and picnic facilities. Annual events at the park include the Return of the Eternal Flame Celebration, held on the first Saturday in April, and the Cherokee Days of Recognition, held the first weekend in August.

The park is open 8 A.M. until sunset, March through November, and from 8 A.M. until 4:30 P.M., December through February. The museum hours are 8 A.M. until 4:30 P.M., March through November. December through February, museum hours

Reconstructed Council House, Red Clay State Park

are Monday through Friday from 8 A.M. until 4:15 P.M., and Saturday and Sunday from 1 P.M. until 4:15 P.M. Admission is free. For information, call 615-478-0339.

From Interstate 75, take Exit 7A near Chattanooga. Follow the signs on Tn. 317 to Red Clay State Park.

ROSS CABIN

Flint Springs

When the Cherokees established new council grounds at Red Clay in 1832, John Ross established a residence nearby. Many Cherokees stopped at his home en route to the council meetings at Red Clay. Ross also received other visitors there. In 1835, Ross persuaded John Howard Payne, author of the song "Home Sweet Home," to stay in his home when Payne arrived for the October council meeting.

The same year, government forces assembled a group of pro-removal Cherokees at New Echota to sign a removal treaty. Ross decided to travel to Washington to negotiate a separate treaty which would al-

low the Cherokees to stay in the East. On December 5, 1835, Ross was arrested at his home in Flint Springs by the Georgia Guard in order to prevent his departure to Washington. His guest, John Howard Payne, was also arrested. They were taken to Spring Place, Georgia, and held for twelve days without charges. When he was released, Ross headed to Washington. The fateful New Echota Treaty was signed in his absence.

Flint Springs has been identified by some as the location of the home Ross built. Others believe that Ross lived in a large house located in the present-day community of Red Hill, about three miles north of Flint Springs. To reach the cabin in Flint Springs from Red Clay State Park, take Red Clay Road north to Old Weatherly Switch. Turn right and go 0.45 mile to Weatherly Road, which is also Tn. 317. Drive east on Weatherly Road for 0.7 mile to Tn. 60. Turn left on Tn. 60 and drive north 1 mile to Red Hill Valley Road. Turn right on to Red Hill Valley Road and go 0.3 mile and turn right again, crossing a small creek. The replica of the Ross cabin will be on the left in 0.2 mile, next to Flint Springs.

Ross Cabin at Flint Springs

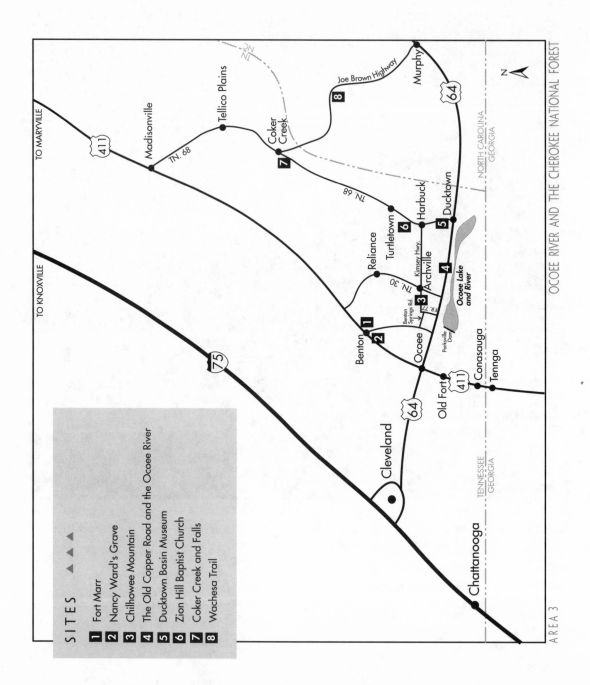

SITES ▲ ▲ ▲

1 Fort Marr
2 Nancy Ward's Grave
3 Chilhowee Mountain
4 The Old Copper Road and the Ocoee River
5 Ducktown Basin Museum
6 Zion Hill Baptist Church
7 Coker Creek and Falls
8 Wachesa Trail

TO MARYVILLE

TO KNOXVILLE

Madisonville

Tellico Plains

411

TN. 68

Coker Creek

7

Joe Brown Highway

8

Murphy

64

NORTH CAROLINA
GEORGIA

TN. 68

Harbuck

Ducktown

5

6

Turtletown

Reliance

Kimsey Hwy.

TN. 30

Archville

4

3

Benton Springs Rd.

Ocoee Lake and River

Parksville Dam

Benton

1

2

Ocoee

75

64

Old Fort

411

Conasauga

Tennga

Cleveland

TENNESSEE
GEORGIA

Chattanooga

N

OCOEE RIVER AND THE CHEROKEE NATIONAL FOREST

AREA 3

Coker Creek Falls

AREA 3

OCOEE RIVER AND CHEROKEE NATIONAL FOREST

▲ ▲ ▲

In the heart of the Cherokee National Forest is a seven stairstep waterfall known as Coker Creek Falls. Legend has it that, if you listen carefully, you can hear a Cherokee warrior and his princess wishing for a long life together. The story goes that the warrior, Coqua, would go to the spot and make a wish, shouting it into the falls. Whatever he asked for would be returned by his echo. On one occasion, he and his young maiden came to ask for a happy marriage, but they were swept over the falls to their deaths by rain-swollen waters. Legend says their ghosts still linger at the falls.

The southern Appalachians are rich in beautiful legends about tragic Indian lovers. Nacoochee Mound in Georgia, Lover's Leap at Hot Springs, North Carolina, and Noccalula Falls in Gadsden, Alabama, are just a few of the places with their own versions of this plaintive tale. The factual accuracy and original sources of these stories are probably not important. They are a colorful part of the heritage of our mountains and valleys. They reflect an interest in keeping alive the memory of the Indians who lived here. But the real beauty of our heritage is found in learning about the real people who once lived throughout the Cherokee territory.

OLD FORT MARR

Benton

Fort Marr was built in 1814 on an old military road near the town of Old Fort, Tennessee, on the Conasauga River. The blockhouse was later moved to its present location in Benton, where it is preserved in a small park.

In 1814, a military road was constructed to supply Andrew Jackson's forces during the Creek War. This road came to be known as the Federal Road. The road was built to the Conasauga River, but construction stopped temporarily due to heavy rains. The soldiers, waiting for the waters to recede, constructed a blockhouse to store supplies and to protect themselves from Indian attack.

The blockhouse, used as a supply depot throughout the Creek War, was abandoned by the military afterward. It then served as a shelter for travelers on the Federal Road. At the time of the Cherokee removal in 1838, whites feared an Indian uprising and added three more blockhouses and stockade walls at the site. The anticipated war did not happen. Instead, the Cherokees were imprisoned in the stockade during the deadly summer of 1838. The conditions inside the stockade were horrible. The area was an enclosure of only two hundred by five hundred feet, with no shelter and no provisions for sanitation. Many Cherokee families at the fort witnessed the deaths of loved ones as they waited for their turn to depart for the West.

From Interstate 75, take the U.S. 64 Bypass east around Cleveland. Continue east on U.S. 64, then take U.S. 411 north to Benton. The blockhouse is on the right side of the road, 1.1 miles north of Nancy Ward's Grave which is discussed next. The inside of the small blockhouse is not open to the public but the structure is easily viewed from the outside. Parking is permitted behind the blockhouse on the police services property.

NANCY WARD'S GRAVE

Benton

Nancy Ward, *Ghighau* of the Cherokees and friend of the white settlers, is buried on a hillside overlooking the scenic farmlands of Polk County, Tennessee. Her son, Five Killer, and brother, Long Fellow, rest

Old Fort Marr

Nancy Ward's grave

alongside her in a modest but peaceful set-ting.

It is not clear when Nancy Ward moved to Womankiller Ford on the Ocoee River. At some point in her later years, she opened an inn on the Federal Road that passed through here. Nancy's brother, Long Fellow, was a longtime resident of the area, as was her son, Five Killer. Several grandchildren and great-grandchildren were also in the area, so it was logical that she should move here in her later years.

One of Nancy Ward's great-grandchildren, Jack Hildebrand, was four when he attended his grandmother's funeral. In his book, *Recollections*, originally published in 1908, he states that Nancy Ward died in 1822—rather than in 1824 as some historians have stated. In his book, Hildebrand told of being in the room when his grandmother died. He wrote that "a light rose from her body, fluttered around the room like a bird, left through an open door, and disappeared toward Chota." It was Hildebrand who later located the site of the grave.

In the fall of 1923, approximately one hundred years after her death, the Nancy

Ward Chapter of the Daughters of the American Revolution placed a stone pyramid with a bronze tablet on the previously unmarked grave.

From Interstate 75, take U.S. 64 Bypass east around Cleveland and continue east on U.S. 64. Then turn north on U.S. 411 and watch for the roadside marker on the right, just a short distance from the intersection with U.S. 64.

Benton Springs Gazebo on Chilhowee Mountain

CHILHOWEE MOUNTAIN

Parksville

The Cherokees who lived in the Ocoee area established a network of trails that connected their villages in the Ducktown area with the Hiwassee villages. Because the walls of the Ocoee Gorge were so steep, they rarely traveled beside the Ocoee River to get from one side of the mountains to the other. Instead, they established a trail which started at the Cherokee Warpath

119 ▲ ▲ ▲

near Benton and went to the top of Bean Mountain, now called Chilhowee Mountain, following approximately the same route as present-day Benton Springs Road. The trail then dropped down to the Greasy Creek area near Archville, and climbed back up Little Frog Mountain. On the east side of Little Frog Mountain, the trail descended again to settlements in the Ducktown and Turtletown areas.

From the mid-1840s to about 1854, the Indian path over Little Frog Mountain was used to carry mail from the settlement of Archville to Ducktown. In 1853, the Copper Road was built to carry copper from the mines in Ducktown through the Ocoee Gorge. Soon after the Copper Road was built, mail carriers no longer used the Indian trail. The construction of Parksville Dam in 1912 covered much of the Copper Road with water. A new route was opened in 1920 when the Kimsey Highway was completed. This new highway generally followed the old Indian trail across Little Frog Mountain. Because of the new highway, Little Frog Mountain became known as Kimsey Mountain, but the name Little Frog Mountain still remains on most maps.

The easiest way to reach the Indian path over Chilhowee Mountain is to take U.S. 64 east from Cleveland. From U.S. 64, take F.R. 77 which leads up Chilhowee Moun-

tain. It is located next to the Ocoee Ranger office. The 6.6-mile drive up F.R. 77 to the Benton Springs gazebo provides several views of Parksville Lake and Sugarloaf Mountain. Stop at the gazebo, which will be on the left, to view the beautiful valley around Benton. Then continue on F.R. 77 several miles to Tn. 30. Drive south on Tn. 30 a short distance to Archville, and take the Kimsey Highway (F.R. 68) across Little Frog Mountain to Tn. 68. Much of this drive retraces the old Indian path, but it is very long and travels primarily over dirt roads. A shorter excursion from the Benton Springs gazebo would be to drive 0.35 mile back down F.R. 77 to Benton Springs Road and follow Benton Springs Road down the west side of the mountain. This drive is a little less than 3 miles, but the road is full of potholes and requires very slow navigation. At the bottom of the mountain, turn left on Tn. 314 to return to U.S. 64.

THE OLD COPPER ROAD AND OCOEE RIVER

Parksville

The Cherokees lived on the Ocoee River long before the first white settlers entered the area. They established several villages on the river, including one at Ducktown and one near the mouth of the Ocoee where it empties into the Hiwassee River. Ethnologist James Mooney says the name of the latter village was Ocoee or Uwaga' hi, meaning "apricot or maypop place." Another interpretation of the name Ocoee is that it comes from Ta-qwa-hi, "place of the Catawbas," referring to the fact the Catawbas once lived on the headwaters of the Ocoee. Although excavations were done at the site of Uwaga' hi many years ago, not much is known about the history of the village. The Ocoee River is better known as the home of Nancy Ward and her brother Long Fellow, who lived there during their later years. They operated an inn on the Federal Road near the western end of the Ocoee River. (See the Nancy Ward's Grave section earlier in this chapter.)

During the 1838 removal, some Cherokees hid in the mountains on either side of the Ocoee Gorge and managed to escape the United States troops. A small group of these Indians hid in the Indian Creek and Tumbling Creek areas. These creeks empty into the Ocoee River upstream (southeast) of Ocoee Dam #3, opposite Little Frog Mountain. Many of the Cherokees who

The Old Copper Road and the Ocoee River, site of the 1996 Olympic Whitewater Events

The Old Copper Road

escaped the removal from this area eventually moved to the Qualla Boundary. One Cherokee named Walkingstick did remain in the area with his wife Nancy. Eventually, he received a land grant of 160 acres at the confluence of Indian and Tumbling creeks. This area is near the present-day Tumbling Creek Campground which is located on F.R. 221.

In 1849, long after most of the Cherokees were forced to move west, a road was built to facilitate the six- and eight-mule teams that hauled copper ore through the mountains from mines near Ducktown to Cleveland, Tennessee. The "Old Copper Road," built by Cherokee labor, stretched thirty-three miles along the scenic Ocoee River. Most of this road was destroyed when U.S. 64 was built and Parksville Lake was created, but three miles of the original road remains intact.

The Ocoee River, one of the most beautiful whitewater rivers in the East, is a popular spot for rafting and kayaking. It has been chosen as the site for the 1996 Olympic whitewater events. The area is managed by the U.S. Forest Service, TVA, and the state of Tennessee, and there are camping, picnicking, and swimming facilities in the area. For more information on the Ocoee National Wildlife Management Area and the Cherokee National Forest, contact the U.S. Forest Service at 615-476-9700.

To reach the remaining portion of the Old Copper Road, take U.S. 64 Bypass east around Cleveland from Interstate 75. On the east side of Cleveland, continue on U.S. 64 East to the Ocoee Gorge. Ocoee Dam #1 and Parksville Lake are 12 miles from the junction of U.S. 64 and the U.S. 64 Bypass. Beginning at Ocoee Dam #1, U.S. 64 follows the northern edge of Parksville Lake and begins to wind through the narrow Ocoee Gorge. After U.S. 64 exits the gorge near Ocoee Powerhouse #3, it widens to four lanes where construction is being done for the 1996 Olympics. Just past the construction area, and before the road starts its steep ascent up Boyd's Gap, watch for a pull-off on the right. At the pull-off there is a dirt road and a gate. On summer weekends, there will probably be several cars parked here for swimming. Walk down the dirt road to the remnants of the original Old Copper Road.

DUCKTOWN BASIN MUSEUM

Ducktown

The area around the towns of Copperhill and Ducktown in Tennessee is frequently called either the Copper Basin or Ducktown Basin. The former name refers to the copper which was mined in the area for many years and transported over the Old Copper Road to Cleveland. Ducktown was a Cherokee village originally called

Collapsed mine shaft, Ducktown Basin Museum

Kawa'na, which is Cherokee for duck. A 1799 report of the Bureau of American Ethnology lists Ducktown as one of fifty-one Cherokee villages in existence for that year. A Cherokee named Wakoi Duck is listed on an 1807 census of Cherokees who lived in the area, but there is no evidence to support the old legend that Ducktown was named for a Chief Duck.

The Ducktown Basin Museum is dedicated to the history of this area. It is located at the site of the former Burra Burra Mine, which was one of the main mines in the basin and is now listed on the National Register of Historic Places. The museum has a film and exhibits about the history of mining in the area. It also has several exhibits describing the history of the local Cherokees, including information about the families who managed to remain after the removal. The museum is open Monday through Saturday, from 10 A.M. to 4:30 P.M. There is an admission charge. For information, call 615-496-5778.

From U.S. 64, take Tn. 68 north at Ducktown. In one quarter mile, turn right onto Burra Burra Street. The museum is located at the top of the hill.

ZION HILL BAPTIST CHURCH

Turtletown

The 1835 census recorded forty-eight Cherokee families living in the Turtletown, Ducktown, and Fightingtown areas. Most of these families were forced west in the removal. However, a few were able to escape the deportation, probably by hiding out in the mountains around the Ocoee Gorge. As time passed, the pressure to move west eased and many Cherokees who stayed in the area became active in the Turtletown community. The United Church of Christ at Zion Hill, organized in 1845, had several Cherokee members.

One of the Cherokee families that attended the church in the 1850s was the Catt family. From 1838 to the 1880s, the Catts lived in the Cold Springs Gap area of Little Frog Mountain. Sometime around 1885, some white men tried to rob the Catts, and one of the white men was killed by Johnson Catt. Fearing retaliation, the Catts fled to North Carolina but returned to Little Frog Mountain around the turn of the century.

The United Church of Christ at Zion Hill is now called Zion Hill Baptist Church. The red brick building with stained glass win-

Zion Hill Baptist Church

dows that houses the current congregation was built in 1945.

To reach the Turtletown community and the church, take Tn. 68 north from U.S. 64 at Ducktown. On the way to Turtletown you will drive along the east side of Little Frog Mountain, the home of the Catt family. Zion Hill Baptist Church is on a hill on the left side of Tn. 68, 4.85 miles from the intersection with U.S. 64. The heart of the Turtletown community is a little further north on Tn. 68.

COKER CREEK AND FALLS

Coker Creek

North Georgia is usually credited with having the first gold rush in the United States in 1828. But a small-scale gold rush had already taken place in the Coker Creek area of Monroe County, Tennessee. According to legend, whites learned of the gold in Coker Creek when a soldier noticed a gold nugget around the neck of an Indian woman. Word spread quickly, and by 1826, the Cherokees were complaining to authorities about white settlers stealing gold from their land. A garrison of soldiers was established to protect the Indians, but they were ineffective. By the late 1820s, hundreds of white men were seeking their fortunes in the hills around Coker Creek. The most active years for gold mining in Coker Creek were between 1831 and 1860. At least eighty thousand dollars in gold was mined from Coker Creek during this period. Most of the gold was sent to the United States Mint in Dahlonega, Georgia.

One local legend claims that Coker Creek received its name from a Cherokee warrior named Coqua. (See the Coker Creek Falls legend in the introduction to this chapter.) Another legend says that the name came from a Cherokee princess, Coco Bell, who died trying to make peace between whites and the Cherokees. Historian James Mooney suggests that Coker Creek is from *kuku'*, the Cherokee name for jigger weed or pleurisy root. Today we know this beautiful orange flower as butterfly weed (*Asclepias tuberosa*). However, 1820s land acquisition records show the creek was called "Toquoa." This name was probably changed to "Coco" then "Coker."

To reach Coker Creek Falls, take Tn. 68 north from U.S. 64 at Ducktown. Continue on Tn. 68 through the communities of Turtletown and Farner. Past Farner, the road will parallel the Hiwassee River for about a mile. Approximately 5.8 miles from the point where Tn. 68 turns away from the river you will find the Calvary Baptist Church on the left and Ironsburg Methodist Church on the right. Near the churches, there will be a sign for a left turn to Coker Creek Falls. The sign indicates the falls are 4 miles from Tn. 68, but the distance is actually 4.6 miles. Turn left at the sign and drive past a little hollow where a llama farm is located. At 0.8 mile from Tn. 68, turn left at the cemetery. At 1.4 miles from Tn. 68, turn right at the fork in the road. At 3.6 miles from Tn. 68, turn left at the sign for Forest Service Road (F.R.) 2138. The unpaved road is very rough, especially the last mile before the parking lot for the falls. At the parking lot, there are two picnic tables and a short trail to the falls, which will be on your left. Once you reach the falls, you may wish to scramble down the side of the hill to get a better view.

From the falls, return to Tn. 68 and go north 2 miles to Coker Creek Village. The United States Forest Service rents a space inside the store where they have an information desk and sell books on the natural and local history of the area. You can also rent a pan from the store's proprietors and try your luck at the village's gold sluice.

WACHESA TRAIL

Coker Creek

The Joe Brown Highway is a largely unpaved road that closely follows portions of the ancient Wachesa Trail. The Wachesa Trail was the main path from the Great Indian War Trail and the Overhill Towns to the Valley and Lower towns. In North Carolina and Georgia, it hooked up with major trade paths, including those to Charleston, South Carolina. According to James Mooney, the name came from an Indian, Watsi'a or Wachesa, who lived on the trail near present-day Murphy.

The Wachesa Trail was the route used by Sir Alexander Cuming in 1730, when he visited Moytoy at Tellico. The soldiers who garrisoned Fort Loudoun also followed the Wachesa Trail to reach the fort from Fort Prince George.

From 1813 to 1816, a major road called the Unicoi Turnpike was built. The Unicoi

Turnpike closely followed the Indian trail. Thomas Jefferson promoted its development as early as 1805. Permission for the construction of the road was granted by the Cherokees at the Hiwassee Garrison in March 1813. The turnpike ran from Chota, through Cane Creek, Tellico Plains, Coker Creek, and Unicoi Gap in Tennessee, to Unaka and Hayesville in North Carolina. In Georgia, the road went to Hiwassee, the Unicoi Gap of Georgia, the Nacoochee Valley, Toccoa, and the Tugaloo River.

The Joe Brown Highway begins at Tn. 68, just south of the community of Coker Creek, and winds many miles through the Unicoi Mountains and around Lake Hiwassee, before it ends in Murphy. On the Tennessee side, it is F.R. 40; on the North Carolina side, it is N.C. 1326.

From U.S. 64 in Ducktown, Tennessee, take Tn. 68 north to Coker Creek Village. Continue on Tn. 68 past Coker Creek Village for 1.1 miles to a sign that says "Unicoi Mountain, Cherokee National Forest." The sign is located at an otherwise unlabeled intersection, with a truck stop on either side of the road. Turn right at this intersection. In less than a quarter mile, there is a sign for F.R. 40. The sign may be partly obscured by trees. The road turns to dirt but is in good condition. The crest of Unicoi Mountain is 2.9 miles from the sign. You can turn around at the crest, or continue on to Unaka or Murphy.

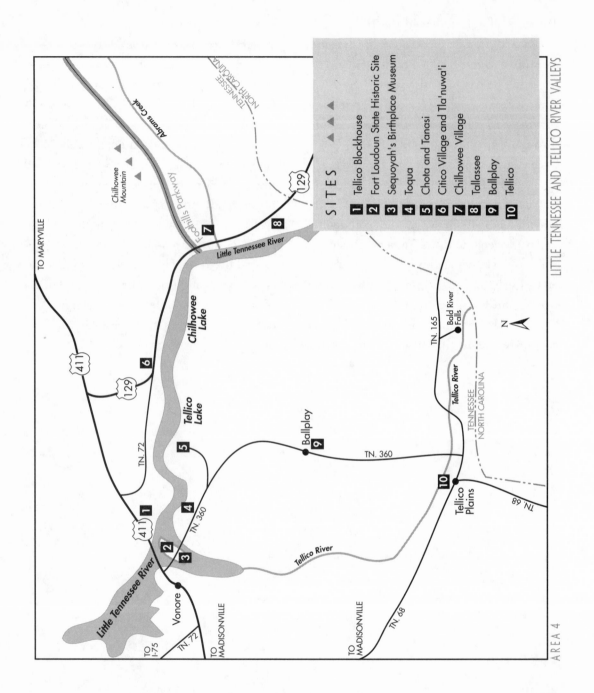

SITES

1 Tellico Blockhouse
2 Fort Loudoun State Historic Site
3 Sequoyah's Birthplace Museum
4 Toqua
5 Chota and Tanasi
6 Citico Village and Tla'nuwa'i
7 Chilhowee Village
8 Tallassee
9 Ballplay
10 Tellico

TO MARYVILLE

Abrams Creek

TENNESSEE
NORTH CAROLINA

129

Chilhowee
Mountain

Foothills Parkway

7

8

Little Tennessee River

Chilhowee
Lake

411

129

6

TN. 72

Tellico
Lake

5

1

411

4

TN. 360

2

3

Vonore

Little Tennessee River

TO
I-75

TN. 72

TO
MADISONVILLE

Tellico River

Ballplay

9

TN. 360

10

Tellico
Plains

TN. 165

Bald River
Falls

Tellico River

TENNESSEE
NORTH CAROLINA

N

TN. 68

TO
MADISONVILLE

89 .NT

AREA 4

Mouth of Abram's Creek on the Little Tennessee River

AREA 4

LITTLE TENNESSEE AND TELLICO RIVER VALLEYS

▲ ▲ ▲

Native Americans inhabited the Little Tennessee River and the Tellico River valleys as early as Archaic times. During the 1960s and 1970s, extensive excavations took place in the Tellico River Valley in an hurried effort to learn as much as possible about the history of the valley. The rush was due to the fact the valley was about to be inundated by the closing of the Tellico

Dam. Through these excavations, researchers were able to learn a great deal about the prehistoric and historic Indians who lived in the region. However, one researcher estimated that only about 20 percent of the important sites in the Tellico Reservoir area were actually excavated.

A series of reports on the excavations published by the Tennessee Valley Authority (TVA) and the University of Tennessee provide glimpses into the history of this important valley. Although the area has been flooded for over ten years, scholars are still examining the wealth of information obtained during the excavations and learning more about the peoples who lived there.

The sites of many Cherokee towns now lie underwater, but in many cases, the approximate area of the towns can be accessed by overlooks around Tellico Lake. A few isolated sites remain above water, like the Tellico Blockhouse and a small part of the town of Chota. Drives through the peaceful countryside of the Tellico Valley will take you away from the lake to the location of the Overhill Town of Tellico and other Cherokee sites in the area.

TELLICO BLOCKHOUSE

Vonore

The Tellico Blockhouse was built in 1794. It was constructed by the United States "to protect the Cherokees from continued encroachment by whites into the valley." Hanging Maw, an influential chief who lived on the Little Tennessee, upriver from Fort Loudoun, tried to establish peaceful relations with the whites. During a meeting with representatives of Governor William Blount in June 1793, a group of local militia attacked Hanging Maw's village. Governor Blount's representatives managed to escape and stop the militia from killing the rest of Hanging Maw's party, but many Overhill Cherokees who were friendly toward the United States had already been killed. Hanging Maw and his family were forced to live in the woods that winter. In the spring, Hanging Maw gave Blount a tract of land on which to build the Tellico Blockhouse, believing the blockhouse would protect his people from more attacks.

In 1795, The Factory Act was passed. This act facilitated the establishment of trading posts in Indian territory. The trading posts would also be used as centers for teaching agriculture and mechanical arts to

Tellico Blockhouse

the Cherokees. The secretary of war, Henry Knox, believed the best path toward peace with the Indians was to "civilize" them and make them knowledgeable about white industries and lifestyles. By 1796, a trading post had been added to the military garrison at the Tellico Blockhouse.

John McKee was the first Indian agent to live at the Tellico Blockhouse. He was succeeded by Silas Dinsmoor, who is credited with teaching the Cherokees how to make cloth. The blockhouse was the site used for much of the official business between the United States and the Cherokees.

Several treaties were negotiated at the site between 1794 and 1805. When the Overhill settlements along the Little Tennessee River began to disperse, and the once-thriving population moved south toward Georgia, the Cherokee Agency office was moved to the Tennessee River at the mouth of the Hiwassee River. Later it moved to Charleston, Tennessee.

While the Cherokee Agency office at the Tellico Blockhouse was active, white travelers had to stop at the blockhouse to receive a permit from the War Department that allowed them to enter Indian territory.

One of the most famous visitors was Louis Philippe, the Duke of Orleans, who later became King of France. Although traveling under the pseudonym of Mr. Orleans, the Duke's visit to the area was well-publicized. The Duke was quite taken with the Cherokees he met during his visit. He later wrote in a letter: "We have seen many Indians, and we remained several days in their country. They received us with great kindness and our national character contributed not a little to this good reception, for they love the French. After them, we found the Falls of Niagra the most interesting object of our journey."

When the TVA restored the site of the blockhouse, they decided to stabilize the actual ruins rather than build a reconstruction based on partial records. Full records of the Tellico Blockhouse were not available because many of the papers were burned during the War of 1812. Some of the foundations had disappeared due to landowner use, so authentic materials were used to fill the gaps in the reconstructed ruins. However, the stone outlines of the foundation accurately duplicate the blockhouse foundation in 1799.

A self-guided interpretive trail explains the Tellico Blockhouse ruins. If pamphlets are not available on-site, they may be picked up at the Fort Loudoun Visitor Center. (For directions and hours for the visitor center see the next section, Fort Loudoun State Historic Area and Tuskegee Site.)

To reach the site of the Tellico Blockhouse from Interstate 75, take the Loudon exit and follow Tn. 72 east to Vonore. In Vonore, turn north onto U.S. 411. A few miles north of Vonore, turn right onto Clearview Road. Take a right turn onto Blockhouse Road almost immediately after turning onto Clearview Road. Blockhouse Road dead-ends in 0.5 mile at the site of the blockhouse. The site is just across the river from Fort Loudoun and provides a scenic view of the fort and the Tellico Reservoir.

FORT LOUDOUN STATE HISTORIC AREA AND TUSKEGEE SITE

Vonore

Fort Loudoun, on the Little Tennessee River, was one of the British forts built in Cherokee territory in the mid-1750s.

The Overhill Cherokees had invited the British to build a fort in their area as early as 1747. However, due to financial and

Fort Loudoun

political delays, Governor James Glen of the colony of South Carolina, was unable to send troops to build and garrison Fort Loudoun until 1756. On September 21 of that year, an expedition of two hundred men set out from Fort Prince George. They arrived at the Cherokee town of Tomotley ten days later. Eventually, they set up the "English Camp Tennecy River" at the nearby town of Tuskegee, which was only a few hundred yards from the site where the fort would be built.

John William Gerard DeBrahm, the engineer for the expedition, argued with the military commander, Captain Raymond Demeré, over the location of the fort. Eventually a site on the side of a hill was chosen and construction of the fort commenced. The original plan for the fort was an elaborate, European-style structure, built in the shape of a diamond. A bastion was to be built at each point of the diamond. Outside of the walls, a three-foot-deep ditch would be dug. Honey locusts with long thorns would be planted in the ditch to discourage Indians "who always engaged naked."

Demeré and DeBrahm argued over every detail of the fort. Eventually DeBrahm moved to Tomotley, a nearby Cherokee village, to avoid Demeré. After some of the earthworks and one palisade had been built, DeBrahm began construction of a second palisade outside the perimeter of the first one. Demeré could see no purpose for the second palisade. He argued that the plans for the fort were too grandiose and were taking too long to complete. DeBrahm and Demeré could not reconcile their differences. DeBrahm left for Charleston on

Christmas Day, abandoning the soldiers, who completed the fort themselves.

Demeré declared the fort finished on July 30, 1757. His men had built a new palisade, torn down the first two palisades, built quarters and latrines, constructed platforms, and mounted the cannons. By this time Raymond Demeré was ill and requested a replacement. On August 14, Raymond Demeré turned over his command to his brother, Captain Paul Demeré.

The fort enjoyed only a couple of years of peace and trade with the Cherokees. Beginning in 1759, relations between the British and the Cherokees began to deteriorate. In 1760, the Cherokees held the fort under siege for seven months. Eventually, Paul Demeré surrendered the fort to the Cherokees. Demeré and many of the soldiers were massacred as they tried to leave the area.

After the siege and attack on Fort Loudoun in 1760, the Cherokees temporarily occupied the fort before it burned. Lieutenant Henry Timberlake visited the Overhills in 1762. He noted the fort's "ruins" in his journal but did not describe them. When Louis Philippe, Duke of Orleans and later King of France, visited the area in 1797, he described the Fort Loudoun site as "buried in brush now, with only a little rubble and a few irregularities of terrain to mark the fort's existence."

According to Henry Timberlake's map of 1762, Tuskegee Town (also spelled Toskegee, Taskigi, Teeskegee, and Tuscagee) was located just southeast of Fort Loudoun. At the time of Timberlake's visit, Attakullakulla was principal chief of Tuskegee. In 1776, Tuskegee was burned by Colonel William Christian's army from Virginia.

Besides serving as the base camp for the troops who built Fort Loudoun, Tuskegee is an important site in Cherokee history because it was the birthplace of Sequoyah. In 1975, archaeologists successfully located the site of Tuskegee, even though substantial erosion had lowered the surface elevation of the site several inches below that of its mid-eighteenth-century level. Cultivation of the site had destroyed features such as post molds and hearths. However, brass buttons, lead bullets, glass beads, nails, and kaolin pipestems were found at the site, which confirmed the presence of Overhill Cherokees. Other artifacts found at Tuskegee indicated that earlier tribes, dating back to the Archaic period, also lived at the site. Tuskegee now rests under the waters of the Tellico Reservoir, near the reconstructed Fort Loudoun.

Fort Loudoun has been reconstructed directly above the site of the original fort. The original site was sealed with seventeen feet of dirt after extensive excavation. The stockade walls and barracks overlook the beautiful Tellico Lake and the sites of Chota, the Tellico Blockhouse, and Tuskegee Town.

About ten weekends each year, volunteers stage a living-history encampment at the fort. Participants portray English soldiers of the Independent Company of South Carolina, who built and garrisoned the fort from 1756-60. The original daily routine within the fort, from morning prayer and musket practice to tomahawk—throwing competitions, is faithfully maintained. The uniforms, weaponry, cooking and daily utensils are all authentic. The Cherokees who traded and lived at the fort are also accurately represented.

The Fort Loudoun visitor center houses a bookstore and a small museum with a film about the fort. The park also has picnic tables and nature trails. Winter hours are 8 A.M. to 4:30 P.M. (December 1 to March 1). The hours for the rest of the year are 8 A.M. to sunset. The center is closed Thanksgiving, New Year's Day, and Christmas. Admission is free. For information, call 615-884-6217. Schedules of garrison weekends can be obtained at the visitor center or by calling the information number.

From Interstate 75, take the Loudon exit and follow Tn. 72 east to Vonore. In Vonore, turn north onto U.S. 411. A few miles north of Vonore turn right onto Tn. 360 (Citico Road). Watch for signs for Fort Loudoun, which will be on the left of the road as it crosses onto the island.

SEQUOYAH'S BIRTHPLACE MUSEUM

Vonore

Sik-wa-yi, or Sequoyah, was born around 1770 in the Overhill Town of Tuskegee. His mother was Wurteh, the sister of Chief Doublehead. His father is believed to have been Nathaniel Gist of Virginia. The talented Sequoyah had a normal Cherokee upbringing. As he grew older, Sequoyah recognized the advantages of being able to read and write. He began work on a syllabary for his own people. His system of eighty-six symbols was quickly adopted by the Cherokees, and within a few years, the nation became literate.

Burial mound at Sequoyah's Birthplace Museum

Sequoyah's Birthplace Museum is a tribally-owned museum located on a scenic island in Tellico Lake. The museum contains artifacts excavated from the Little Tennessee River Valley prior to the completion of the Tellico Reservoir. There is also a book-and-gift shop with crafts from contemporary Cherokee artists. A solemn memorial to the Cherokees is located on the grounds, along with a burial mound containing the remains of eighteenth-century Cherokees which were removed from the Tellico Reservoir prior to the inundation of the area.

The museum is open year round except for Thanksgiving, Christmas, and New Year's Day. Museum hours are 10 A.M. to 6 P.M. Monday through Saturday, and noon to 6 P.M. on Sunday. The memorial by the lake is accessible at all times. There is a small admission charge for the museum. For information, call 615-884-6264.

From Interstate 75, take the Loudon exit and follow Tn. 72 east to Vonore. Take U.S. 411 north from Vonore and turn right onto Tn. 360 (Citico Road). After crossing the bridge connecting the island to the mainland, watch for signs for Sequoyah's Birthplace Museum, which will be on the right 0.5 mile past Fort Loudoun State Historic Area.

TOQUA

Vonore

Henry Timberlake passed through the Cherokee town of Toqua briefly in 1761 and 1762, on his way to and from Toqua's neighbor, Tomotley. He describes a scene in Toqua where he saw "several Indians weeping for the death of their relations, killed in the late battle." The battle Timberlake described was a recent skirmish with the "northern Indians," the Shawnees, in which eight Cherokees were either killed or captured. According to Timberlake, the Cherokees

> attributed this loss to the want of arrows, the northern Indians having poured several vollies of arrows, and done great execution, before the Cherokees could charge again, after the first fire. This was especially disadvantageous to the Cherokees, as both parties met unexpectedly on the top of a mountain, which they were both crossing, and engaged so close, that the northern Indians availed themselves of this advantage, and the superiority of their numbers.

At the time of Timberlake's visit, Toqua was not as large as the neighboring towns of Chota or Tomotley. However, it had its own council house and a force of eighty-

Toqua Beach

two warriors. The head chief was the fierce warrior Willawanaw, who later signed the treaty at Watauga in 1775. Toqua was the town where Nancy Ward rescued Lydia Bean from burning at the stake in 1776.

Toqua was an ancient settlement and may have been a more important location in earlier days. Partial excavations were done at the site as early as the 1890s. Between the spring of 1975 and the spring of 1977, an intensive excavation was done on four acres of the site. These excavations revealed that it had been an important chiefdom in the Dallas era (a cultural phase of the late Mississippian period). The Dallas-era village was approximately five hundred thousand square feet in size and surrounded by a wooden palisade. Two large burial mounds, known as the Toco mounds, and more than

110 structures were identified. However, 68 of these structures were identified as being built by later Cherokees.

The Toco mounds were landmarks that were once visible for several miles on the flat land surrounding the area. The mounds and village now lie beneath the Tellico Reservoir, but the area where they were located can be viewed from Toqua Beach, a recreational area on Tn. 360 between the Sequoyah's Birthplace Museum and the Chota site. Facilities at Toqua Beach include picnic tables and boat ramps. There is a small admission fee.

To reach Toqua Beach from Sequoyah's Birthplace Museum, turn east on Tn. 360. Watch for the Toqua Beach sign on the left, about 5 miles from the museum.

CHOTA AND TANASI

Vonore

After the Spanish expeditions of the 1500s, the next white men known to visit the Cherokee Overhill country were two traders named James Needham and Gabriel Arthur. They arrived in the area in 1673. Needham and Arthur were sent by Abraham Wood, a Virginia trader who lived at Fort Henry (present-day Petersburg, Virginia). Wood wanted to establish a trading path between the Overhill Towns and Virginia. In a letter to John Richards of London, Abraham Wood described one of the Overhill settlements. Wood probably got the description from James Needham's journal. Tennessee historian Samuel Cole Williams suggested that the Overhill Town described by Wood may have been Chota.

> This towne is seated on ye river side, haveing ye clefts on ye river side on ye one side being very high for its defence, the other three sides trees of two foot over, pitched on end, twelve foot high, and on ye topps scafolds placed with parrapits to defend the walls and offend theire enemies which men stand on to fight, many nations of Indians inhabitt downe this river . . . which they are att warre withe and to that end keepe one hundred and fifty canoes under ye command of theire forte.

The name "Tennessee" originated from Tanasi, the name of a village next to Chota. In the 1970s, archaeological excavations were made at Tanasi and Chota. A 1986 report on these excavations discusses the relationship between Tanasi and Chota. The report points out that visitors to the area in the 1720s and 1730s consistently refer to Tanasi and its leaders, but do not mention Chota. Maps from 1725 and 1730 show Tanasi's location, but not the location of Chota. This evidence suggests that Tanasi was larger and more economically important than Chota during the first half of the eighteenth century. The report also suggests that the Chota site was not established until sometime between 1710 and 1745—possibly as a suburb of Tanasi. This evidence places in doubt Samuel Cole Williams' suggestion that Needham and Arthur visited Chota in 1673.

Nevertheless, by the mid-1700s, Chota had become one of the most important villages in the Overhill territory, surpassing Tanasi in size and importance.

Many important events in Cherokee history occurred in Chota. It is the village where Nancy Ward was born, and it played an important role in the French and Indian War from 1754 to 1763. Both the British and the French sent emissaries to Chota during the war to vie for Cherokee support. In 1754, Nathaniel Gist was sent to Chota to establish trade with the Cherokees. It is believed he later became the father of Sequoyah. In 1756, the Virginians built a small fort on the Little Tennessee River directly opposite Chota, but they never garrisoned it. The same year, the South Carolinians began construction on

Fort Loudoun, just a few miles downstream from Chota. Fort Loudoun was built to impress the Cherokees and to discourage French influence in the area.

In 1764, Henry Stuart and Alexander Cameron were sent to Chota to secure Cherokee support in the event of a war with the Creeks. As a result of the July 1777 treaty made at Long Island on the Holston River, James Robertson was sent to live at Chota to watch the Overhill Cherokees and prevent their correspondence with anyone unfriendly to the new American government. But by 1782, the Overhill Cherokees' relations with the Americans had deteriorated. In that year, forces led by John Sevier and Arthur Campbell destroyed ten Overhill Towns, including Chota.

Oconostota served for many years as the great war chief of Chota. The exact date of his resignation and death is not known. By 1782, however, it is known that Old Tassel had succeeded Oconostota as tribal chief of the Overhill Cherokees. Oconostota spent most of his final days at the home of Colonel Joseph Martin on Long Island (present-day Kingsport, Tennessee). Colonel Martin, married to Nancy Ward's daughter, felt sorry for the old chief because of the scarcity of food in the area at the time. When Oconostota sensed it was time to die, he requested that Martin take him back to Chota. Oconostota probably died sometime between 1780 and 1783. According to information written by Martin, Oconostota was buried in a coffin made from a canoe. In 1969, archaeologists working at the Chota site used this information to identify the resting place of Oconostota.

When Tellico Lake was formed in the late 1970s, the locations of most of the Overhill Towns were flooded, including the sites of Chota and Tanasi. Monuments marking the locations of these two villages were erected and are maintained by the Cherokees. A portion of Chota escaped inundation. At this site, there is a short trail with seven markers representing the seven clans of the Cherokees. A gravestone marks the burial site of Oconostota, the great war chief. The

location of Tanasi is marked with a solitary memorial. For information, contact Sequoyah's Birthplace Museum or Fort Loudoun State Historic Site.

The Chota and Tanasi sites are easily reached from Sequoyah's Birthplace Museum. From the museum, turn east on Tn. 360 (Citico Road). When Tn. 360 turns right across the bridge at Ballplay Creek (5.8 miles from the Sequoyah museum), continue straight instead of turning across the bridge. Drive another 4.9 miles and make a left turn. This road does not have a name. Drive 0.6 mile to the Tanasi monument which will be on the left. From the Tanasi monument, it is only another 0.9 mile to parking for the Chota site.

CITICO VILLAGE AND THE TLANUWAI

Tallassee

Si'tiku', better known as Citico or Settacoo, was the largest of the Overhill Towns identified by Lieutenant Henry Timberlake in his visit to the area in 1761 and 1762. It was located on the west bank of Citico Creek, near the spot where the creek empties into the Little Tennessee

Symbol of the Cherokee Nation at Tanasi Memorial

River. The site is now underwater, having been inundated when the Tellico Dam was closed.

Very little is known about the history of Citico. Excavations, completed before the site was inundated, identified a village and structural mound dating from the Mississippian period. Evidence at the excavation suggested the Cherokees may have lived at Citico for a period in the early eighteenth century. However, Citico didn't become an important Cherokee center until the second half of the eighteenth century

In 1776, Colonel William Christian was sent from Virginia to suppress the Cherokees. Christian crossed the Little Tennessee at Toqua and set up camp at Tomotley. All of the Overhill Towns Christian encountered were deserted. Christian spent twenty days in the area of the Overhill Towns. He burned five towns, including Citico, and held conferences with various Cherokee

Site of Citico Village

Tla'nuwa'i on the Little Tennessee River

representatives. Dragging Canoe was ordered to come to Christian but failed to make an appearance. Instead Dragging Canoe withdrew to the Chickamauga River and established new towns.

It is not clear if Citico was ever reoccupied after Christian burned it in November 1776. It was deserted in 1788 when an incident occurred there involving guards from Houston Station, which was located several miles north of Citico near the present-day community of Mint. The guards and some settlers stopped to gather apples in an orchard near the deserted town. They were ambushed by Cherokees who drove them into the river and killed them.

The mound and village site are now underwater, but the legendary Tla'nuwa'i still exists. Tla'nuwa'i, or "tlanuwa place," is a cliff on the north side of the Little Tennessee River that was believed to be the home of two mythic hawks—the *tlanuwas*. Halfway up the cliff is a cave where the hawks nested. According to ethnologist James Mooney, this cliff is on land formerly owned by John Lowrey, a Cherokee who served as an officer at the Battle of Horseshoe Bend. Across the river from Tla'nuwa'i are the bluffs known as U'tlunti'yi, the legendary home of Spearfinger. In Cherokee mythology,

Spearfinger was an ogress with a long bony forefinger that she used to stab anyone she met. She would then use her finger to dig out her victim's liver and eat it.

Tla'nuwa'i, U'tlunti'yi, and the location of Citico are best viewed from a boat landing on the Little Tennessee River, opposite the mouth of Citico Creek. The Tla'nuwa'i and Spearfinger's haunt can best be seen from the west end of the parking lot. Citico village lies under water, a little southeast of the parking lot.

To reach the boat landing from Interstate 75, take Tn. 68 (the Sweetwater exit) or Tn. 72 (the Loudon exit) east to U.S. 411. Take U.S. 411 north past Vonore. Just north of Vonore, take a right on Tn. 72. Tn. 72 follows the northern shore of Tellico Lake to U.S. 129. Turn right on U.S. 129 and drive 1.5 miles to the boat launch on the right side of the road, where U.S. 129 begins to parallel the river.

CHILHOWEE VILLAGE AND MOUNTAIN

Tallassee

Chilhowee comes from the Cherokee *tsu'lun'we*. This word is possibly a deriva-tive of the word *tsu'lu,* meaning kingfisher. Chilhowee was located on the south side of the Little Tennessee River, at the foot of Chilhowee Mountain near the mouth of Abrams Creek. Abrams Creek was named for the venerable chief of Chilhowee, Old Abraham or Old Abram. Old Abram led the attack on Fort Watauga in 1776, but he later became a friend of the settlers. In 1788, Old Abram and Old Tassel were killed by some of John Sevier's men while they met with Sevier's forces under a flag of truce. The family of John Kirk, Jr., had been killed in an Indian attack. Kirk, en-couraged by members of Sevier's force, murdered Old Abram and Old Tassel for revenge, even though they had nothing to do with the attack on Kirk's family.

In 1887, the ethnologist James Mooney met a Cherokee shaman named A'yun'ini, also known as Swimmer, from the Big Cove area of the Qualla reservation. Before Swimmer died in 1899, he related hundreds of Cherokee stories to Mooney, who later published them. One of Swimmer's stories was called the "False Warriors of Chilhowee." It was supposedly the story of an actual event. At some point in Chero-kee history, some Chilhowee warriors told their chief they were going north to fight the Shawnee. However, they actually at-tacked other Cherokees outside the village of Cowee, near present-day Franklin, North Carolina. They returned to their village and participated in a scalp dance. At the dance, a gunstocker from Cowee happened to recognize one of the guns taken by the warriors. The gunstocker returned to his own village and related the terrible truth to his people. Several Cowee warriors went to the next scalp dance, held the following week, and challenged the traitors. The scalp dance was considered neutral ground, so the warriors from Cowee had to return later to take their revenge. When they returned, they found Chilhowee Village deserted.

The Chilhowee Village site is now covered by Chilhowee Lake. The new mouth of Abrams Creek is upstream from its old location. To reach the approximate location of Chilhowee Village, follow the directions to U.S. 129 from Citico Village and the Tlanuwa section described above. Turn right onto U.S. 129 and drive east 7.4 miles to the bridge that crosses the mouth of Abrams Creek. The bridge is as close as you can get to the site on land.

From Abrams Creek, you may wish to take the scenic Foothills Parkway, which follows the crest of Chilhowee Mountain. From the Abrams Creek bridge, drive west 0.7 mile to the parkway entrance. It is 7 miles to Look Rock Tower, which provides a panoramic, 360-degree view of the area. Continue on the Foothills Parkway another 9.4 miles to U.S. 321 at the northern end of the mountain.

TALLASSEE

Calderwood Dam

Ta'lasi', as the Cherokees called Tallassee, was located at the Tallassee Ford on the Little Tennessee River. Situated near an Indian mound, parts of the village lay on both sides of the river.

Major Jonathan Tipton made devastating raids on the Overhill Towns in December 1780, but Tallassee was spared when Tipton's horsemen were unable to cross the river. The village was not as lucky in 1795, when Colonel Alexander Kelly and fifty soldiers attacked Tallassee. Eight Cherokees died in the battle, while Kelly's forces had no losses.

The town was abandoned when a treaty, signed in 1819, shifted the Cherokee boundaries further south. In 1820, the Calloway Turnpike was constructed. It connected Monroe County to Tallassee Ford at the old location of Tallassee. Today a town named Tallassee is located on the north side of the Little Tennessee River, but it is located several miles west of the site of the original Cherokee village. The original village was located in the valley near the present site of Calderwood Dam.

To reach the Calderwood Dam from U.S. 411, take Tn. 72 east to U.S. 129. Turn right onto U.S. 129 and drive 12.2 miles to an overlook of Calderwood Dam on the right side of the road.

BALLPLAY

Ballplay

Each year the Cherokees gathered at a natural amphitheater in this area to play an early form of the game of lacrosse. When Louis Philippe, Duke of Orleans and future king of France, traveled through the Overhill territory in 1797, he observed over six hundred Indians gathered in the amphitheater to watch the annual ball games. Louis Philippe got into the spirit of the games by promising six gallons of brandy to the winning team.

During the excitement of the games, Philippe fell off his horse. As was customary among Europeans, Philippe was treated by bleeding. The results were apparently successful since an old chief who was ill requested the bleeding treatment for himself. The chief claimed to feel better instantly. The chief rewarded Philippe with

Ballplay

the honor of sleeping between his grandmother and his great aunt, two very respected women.

While there are no remains of the natural amphitheater, it is interesting to note that this town and the town of Ball Ground, Georgia, both drew their names from the same Indian sport.

From Interstate 75, take the Sweetwater exit and drive east on Tn. 68 to Tellico Plains. In Tellico Plains, turn left (north) onto Tn. 165. Drive 1 mile through the old village of Tellico Plains to Tn. 360. Turn left (north) on Tn. 360 and drive 9 miles to the small town of Ballplay.

TELLICO

Tellico Plains

Present-day Tellico Plains is a quiet and scenic town nestled among the foothills of the Appalachians in the Tellico River Valley. It is a popular place for fishermen and hikers to obtain supplies on their way to the Tellico Wildlife Management Area. Although it has seen increased development in the last few years, one can still see the beauty that must have attracted the Cherokees to the area.

In 1799, Abraham Steiner and Frederick de Schweinitz, Moravian missionaries who came to the Overhill Towns, described the Cherokee valley named Tellico:

> We emerged in the great Tellico Plain, through which we rode some distance in the midst of high grass. . . . In this plain we came upon a small hill, on which a flock of turkeys ran before us. Here we had a fine view. Before us and to the side was the beautiful plain, entirely clear of woods. . . . The plain has very fertile land, all bottom, many miles around, through which the small Tellico flows on many windings. Around this plain the land rises gradually, on three sides in broken country and on the fourth in small hills that become larger and, at last, lose themselves in the Chilhowee Mountains, which can be seen at some distance.

In 1730, a British con man named Sir Alexander Cuming visited Tellico. Cuming arrived in Charles Towne under the false pretenses of being a wealthy aristocrat. He told the colonists he was on a scientific expedition into Cherokee territory. It is not clear that he had any authority to make agreements with the Cherokees on behalf of the British, but he managed to negotiate a number of concessions from them—partly through showmanship and bribes of rum. He gave Moytoy, the head warrior of

Tellico, the title of "Emperor of Tannassie" and presented him with a crown made of dyed possum's hair.

Another interesting visitor to Tellico was Christian Gotlieb Priber, a French Jesuit, who arrived in 1736. He stayed for several years. Eventually, he was captured by the British for being an agent of the French and sent to prison in Georgia. While he was at Tellico, Priber sought to establish a unique egalitarian government among the Cherokees. Priber wrote that the Cherokee government should be one where "all goods should be held in common, and that each should work according to his talents for the good of the republic; that the women should live there with the same freedom as the men; that there should be no marriage contract, and that they should be free to change husbands every day." Although

Priber's ideas may have seemed as strange to the Cherokees as they seem to us, Priber was well-liked by them. Long after his capture, the Cherokees' loyalty to France inspired by his influence continued to cause problems for the British.

Today, there are no monuments, markers, or mounds in present-day Tellico Plains to identify the location of the Overhill village. However, one great tribute to the memory of Tellico is in Oklahoma. The seat of government for the Western Cherokees is called Tahlequah, after Tellico.

From Interstate 75, take the Sweetwater exit and drive east on Tn. 68 to Tellico Plains. (For an interesting side trip from Tellico Plains, take Tn. 360 north to Tn. 165 East. Tn. 165 follows a wild and scenic section of the Tellico River to Bald River Falls and the Tellico Wildlife Management Area.)

Tellico Plains

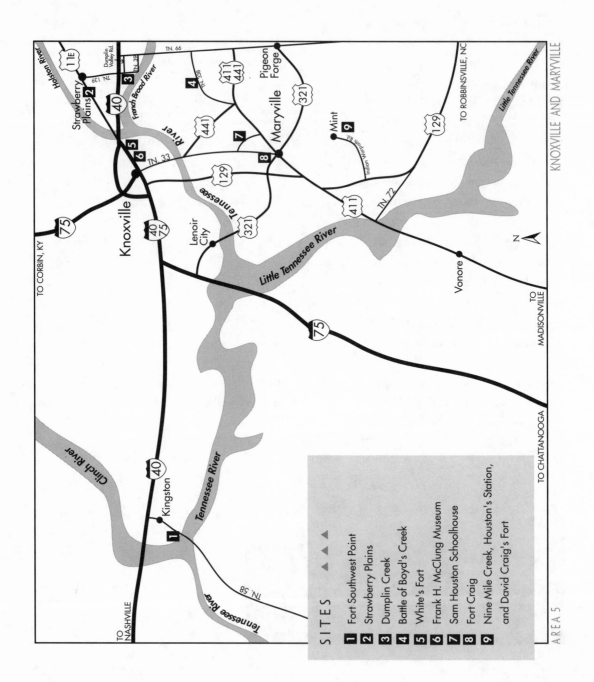

SITES

▲ ▲ ▲
▲ ▲ ▲

1 Fort Southwest Point
2 Strawberry Plains
3 Dumplin Creek
4 Battle of Boyd's Creek
5 White's Fort
6 Frank H. McClung Museum
7 Sam Houston Schoolhouse
8 Fort Craig
9 Nine Mile Creek, Houston's Station,
and David Craig's Fort

Little Tennessee River at Militia Springs,
mustering grounds for militia in the 1790's

AREA 5

KNOXVILLE
AND
MARYVILLE

▲ ▲ ▲

In 1785, a Revolutionary War veteran named James White moved his family from North Carolina and built a home on the French Broad River in eastern Tennessee. The next year he moved again to a creek near the Tennessee River, where he established a fort and a settlement. This settlement, known as White's Fort, later became Knoxville.

Many other settlers, mostly emigrants from Virginia and North Carolina, moved to sites in the Knox, Roane, and Blount county areas of Tennessee. In many cases, the settlers built forts when they arrived in the area. These forts were often subject to attacks by Indians during the last three turbulent decades of the eighteenth century. In 1788, three hundred Indians, led by Chickamaugan chief John Watts, attacked Gillespy's Fort (located near the present site of the Knoxville Airport). The Chickamaugans took twenty-eight prisoners and killed seventeen in this attack. In 1793, thirteen members of the Cavett family were killed when Cavett's Station (in Knox County, north of Sinking Creek) was attacked by another Chickamaugan, Chief Doublehead.

Several of these forts became important during the migration of settlers to the Cumberland River Valley. They served as supply depots and safe rest stops for travelers. In 1789, Fort Adair was commissioned as a commissary for the Cumberland Guard—a militia that escorted emigrant families to the Nashville area. Campbell's Station, located fifteen miles west of White's Fort, became a popular stop for hunters, traders, and travelers in the Cumberland settlements.

Knox, Blount, and Roane counties were carved out of Cherokee land—through much bloodshed on both sides. The Cherokees, led by Dragging Canoe, John Watts, and Doublehead, led many attacks against settlers who were infringing on Cherokee territory. In return, the white settlers made devastating raids on the Cherokee Overhill Towns in 1776, 1780, and 1788. These raids caused the decline of the Overhill settlements. The Cherokee capital was moved to Ustanali in Georgia, while the old capital of Chota became a shell of its former self.

Although the Cherokees ceded most of their land in northeastern Tennessee to the settlers, their claims to much of the land in the remaining portion of Tennessee still posed problems for the new state. In 1799, two Moravian missionaries, Abraham Steiner and Frederick de Schweinitz, noted the problem caused by the continued existence of the Cherokee Nation in Tennessee. The following excerpt from the missionaries' journal is taken from Samuel Cole Williams' *Early Travels in The Tennessee Country*:

> Knoxville is now the seat of the government of the State of Tennessee. The Superior Court of the eastern part of the State, also, has its sessions here. Both parts of the State, the eastern, or Washington District, and the western, or Mero District, appear to be mistrustful of each

other, and each part would be glad to have all offices within its own confines, which condition is intensified because a great part of the Cherokee country, viz., their hunting grounds, lies between the two parts and they cannot, therefore, meet without passing through great wilderness.

As white settlements in the eastern and western parts of Tennessee grew, tensions mounted between the Cherokees and settlers. The settlers viewed the Cherokee territory sandwiched between their lands as a prime area for expansion. Illegal settlements, hunting, and travel in the Cherokee Territory increased the tension between the Cherokees and their white neighbors. Misunderstandings between the two different cultures often ignited confrontations. As the white settlements grew, it became easier to push the Cherokees south toward Georgia and Alabama.

FORT SOUTHWEST POINT

Kingston

During the late-eighteenth century, Southwest Point, located on a hill above the confluence of the Clinch and Tennessee rivers, was a strategic location for control of both water and land communications. It was on the most direct route between the Washington district of eastern Tennessee and the Mero district of western Tennessee. Many settlers moving to the western settlements in the Tennessee territory passed through the area.

In 1792, John Sevier, then a leader of the Tennessee militia, took control of Southwest Point. Territorial governor William Blount called on Sevier and the militia to try to protect the Cumberland settlements in middle Tennessee. There were several fords across the Clinch and Tennessee rivers near Southwest Point, and it was a strategic location for Sevier to launch raids on Indian settlements if necessary. At the time, the Tennessee frontier was raging with hostilities. The *Knoxville Gazette* was reporting arson, horse theft, and murders almost daily.

Sevier built a blockhouse at a spring, 0.75 mile above the Tennessee River. A trench, dug from the blockhouse to the spring, was covered with logs for protection during attack. Between 1796 and 1797, the blockhouse was relocated to the present site on the hill.

The new fort, built on top of a prehistoric Indian mound, was rectangular. It measured roughly 188 feet by 308 feet. Each corner of the fort had a blockhouse,

151 ▲ ▲ ▲

Historical marker at Fort Southwest Point

In 1797, additional troops were sent to Southwest Point to aid in the removal of whites who were illegally settling on Indian land. From 1801 to 1807, the fort served as the headquarters of the Cherokee Agency. Sometime between 1798 and 1801, the Davis School for Cherokees was founded at the fort. John Ross probably received part of his education at this school. The Cherokees operated a ferry across the Clinch River at a site just above the fort. The ferry, owned commonly by the Cherokee Nation, was a very lucrative business. In 1805, the notorious Chief Doublehead managed to claim it for himself through some shady dealings. It is believed his murder in 1807 may have been ordered by other chiefs who were angry at Doublehead for this and other dishonest activities he conducted at the expense of the Cherokee Nation.

Because the Cherokees had been pushed farther south, and the frontier had changed drastically since 1792, the Cherokee Agency was moved to the Hiwassee River in June 1807. The fort at Southwest Point was closed. The Cherokee ferry was taken over by a white family named Clark, who operated it until 1898.

Southwest Point Park is maintained by the city of Kingston. It features a newly-built stockade fort with blockhouse, care-

and there was probably a fifth blockhouse in the center of the southeast wall, adjacent to the main gate.

The fort eventually became headquarters for the federal government's efforts to deal with various Indian issues in the area. Beginning in 1794, an armed escort was offered annually to the settlers journeying from Southwest Point to the Mero District.

fully reconstructed after extensive archaeological research on the site. After the grand-opening ceremonies, scheduled for the first weekend of July 1995, the fort will be open to the public with regularly scheduled hours. Southwest Point Park also has picnic tables and recreation fields. For information, call 615-376-1356.

From Knoxville, go west on Interstate 40 to Kingston. Take the exit for Tn. 58 and follow it south through town. Southwest Point Park will be 1.8 miles from Interstate 40 on the right side of Tn. 58, overlooking the Clinch River.

STRAWBERRY PLAINS

Strawberry Plains

In April 1862, Colonel William Holland Thomas's North Carolina Highland Brigade was mustered into the Confederate Army. Thomas's Legion, as they were later called, was made up of both Cherokees and whites. It included the grandson of Chief Junaluska and a young Cherokee sergeant named Swimmer. Swimmer would later help James Mooney document the Cherokee history and culture. According to Mooney, the young soldiers performed Cherokee rituals at the start of their ser-

vice for the Confederates. They consulted an oracle stone to learn if they would return from the war safely, and they celebrated the start of their service with an old-fashioned war dance.

The brigade first reported to Camp Oconostota in Knoxville. In May 1862, they were sent to Strawberry Plains to defend an important railroad bridge there. At the beginning of the war, the Confederacy didn't fully recognize the importance of this bridge, which was on the supply line from Virginia to the lower Confederate states. In November 1861, the Confederates had only one man stationed at the bridge when it was attacked by forty Union soldiers. Miraculously, the lone sentry, James Keelan, managed to defend the bridge and save it for the Confederacy.

Thomas's Legion established their first headquarters at Camp Junaluska in Strawberry Plains. During the Civil War they performed many important duties throughout the region, including defending gaps in the Cumberland and Smoky mountains, arresting deserters in Georgia, and defending the railroad lines from Bristol to Chattanooga. In September 1863, the union army captured Knoxville and forced Thomas's Legion to abandon its base at Strawberry Plains. Thomas, and part of his troops, crossed back over the mountains to

The railroad bridge at Strawberry Plains

North Carolina. The remainder of the legion stayed in northeast Tennessee under the command of General Alfred E. Jackson and eventually went on to fight several important battles in Virginia. Thomas spent several months trying to get his troops reunited. In the fall of 1864, Thomas was able to reassemble his brigade, although many members had died during the fierce fighting in Virginia.

The community of Strawberry Plains is located northeast of Knoxville on U.S. 11E and you can still see the remains of the railroad bridge that was guarded by Thomas's Legion. From Knoxville, take Interstate 40 east to Exit 394, which is the exit for U.S. 11E. Follow U.S. 11E for several miles until you reach a sign for Tn. 139 on the right. Strawberry Plains Road is directly opposite this sign. Turn left onto Strawberry Plains Road and go one block to the stop sign at Old Andrew Jackson Highway. Turn left again, drive past the school, and go 0.4 mile to Main Street. Turn right on Main Street and go one block to Big Bend Road. Turn left and follow Big Bend Road around a curve and under the railroad bridge at the Holston River. You can park on the right side of the road by one of the 1907-concrete trestles of the bridge. If you walk down the road a short distance, you can look back and see the original stone trestles to the left of the more modern ones.

DUMPLIN CREEK

Sevierville

In June 1785, John Sevier and several other representatives from the State of Franklin met with over thirty Cherokee headmen and warriors at Major Hugh Henry's station on Dumplin Creek. During this meeting, the Treaty of Dumplin Creek was negotiated, which opened additional lands for settlement by whites. Ancoo of Chota, Abram of Chilhowee, The Leach from Citico, and the other headmen received clothing and goods in return for signing the treaty. An excerpt from the Treaty of Dumplin Creek follows:

> It is agreed by us, the warriors, chiefs and representatives of the Cherokee Nation, that all the lands lying and being on the south side of Holston and French Broad rivers, as far south as the ridge that divides the waters of Little river from the waters of Tennessee, may be peaceably inhabited and cultivated, resided on, enjoyed and inhabited by our elder brothers, the white people, from this time forward and always.

The treaty was significant in that it represented the State of Franklin's independence from North Carolina. The treaty started rumors that the Frankliners planned to incorporate the Cherokees into a population count that would grant them official statehood. It also resulted in hundreds of white settlers pouring over the French Broad into the newly available territory.

To reach Henry's Station on Dumplin Creek from Interstate 40, take Tn. 66 south at the Sevierville exit. Take the first right, which is Dumplin Valley Road. Go 1.2 miles and turn left onto Tn. 139 at Kodak. A historical marker for Henry's Station will be on the right in 0.1 mile. Turn right onto Treaty Road, a gravel road off of Tn. 139 between the historical marker for Henry's

Station and an old mill. The gravel road curves past a white house on the left, then turns right up a small hill. A marker for the Treaty of Dumplin Creek will be on the left, 0.3 mile from Tn. 139.

The historical marker at Dumplin Creek

Monument marking the location of the Battle of Boyd's Creek

BATTLE OF BOYD'S CREEK

Knoxville

While John Sevier and the Watauga militia were away at the Battle of Kings Mountain, Dragging Canoe and some of the Lower Cherokee chiefs decided to attack the Nolichucky and Watauga settlements. Nancy Ward sent word to the settlements to prepare for impending attacks. Sevier, having just returned from Kings Mountain, gathered two hundred men and set out to meet the attacking Indians.

During their second night out, Sevier's party camped at Long Creek on the Nolichucky River, where they ran into a Cherokee war party and fired a few shots at the Indians. Captain William Pruett's men also arrived during the night, swelling Sevier's forces to three hundred men. The next day, the army crossed the French Broad River and made camp near Boyd's Creek. An advance guard sent out that morning discovered the Indians' camp only three miles away. The Cherokees had left their camp fires burning, hoping to draw the militia into an ambush. Sevier saw the Indians lying in wait in a halfmoon shape around the abandoned camp. Instead of falling into the trap, he set one of his own. He ordered a group of his soldiers forward to fire on the Indians and then retreat. The Indians followed the retreating men toward Sevier's main forces, who were arranged in three wings. Sevier gave the orders for the wings to swing around and enclose the Indians. The right wing closed first, followed by the left wing. Twenty-eight braves were killed and many more were wounded. The rest of the Cherokees escaped through a swampy area. During the battle, the brother of Chief John Watts was killed. Sevier was grazed by a bullet, which cut his hair but did no further damage.

The battle, which occurred on December 16, 1780, was the beginning of a long campaign against the Cherokees in which all of the Cherokee towns west of the mountains were destroyed except Tallassee and two villages near Chattanooga.

From Interstate 40, take the Sevierville exit and drive south on Tn. 66 towards Sevierville. Just north of Sevierville, take a right onto Tn. 338. This is Boyd's Creek Road. The obelisk marker honoring the Battle of Boyd's Creek will be on the right in 6.2 miles.

WHITE'S FORT

Knoxville

White's Fort was built in 1786 by the founder of Knoxville, James White. Five years later, Governor William Blount met forty-one Cherokee chiefs at White's Fort to negotiate the Treaty of Holston. Blount decided to locate the territorial capital at White's Fort. He renamed the settlement Knoxville, in honor of Secretary of War Henry Knox. White's original log fort was torn down many years ago, and the logs were used to build a house in southern Knoxville. Later, the James White Memorial Association acquired the house. The logs were moved to the present site, just a few blocks from the original site, and used in the reconstruction of the fort. Other features at the reconstructed fort are a guest house, museum, herb garden, and blacksmith shop.

Hours at the fort are 9:30 A.M. to 4:30 P.M., Monday through Saturday. It is closed Sundays. There is a small admission charge. For information, call 615-525-6514.

To reach the fort from Interstate 40, take Exit 388A (the University of Tennessee, James White Parkway exit). From the James White Parkway, turn right at the exit for U.S. 441 South. Watch for brown historical signs that will direct you to make a right turn onto State Street. From State Street, turn right onto Church Street, cross

White's Fort

the bridge, and turn right again at the Civic Auditorium and Coliseum onto Mulvaney Street. Mulvaney Street turns into Hill Street. The reconstructed fort is one block down Hill Street on the right.

FRANK H. McCLUNG MUSEUM

Knoxville

The Frank H. McClung Museum houses the most extensive collection of Indian artifacts in the Southeast. Many of the more than one million artifacts representing twelve thousand years of Native American habitation in Tennessee are on display here. The museum includes artifacts from the Archaic, Woodland, and Mississippian periods. Two of the finest pieces on display are carved sandstone figures of a man and a woman, found at an archaeological site in Wilson County. Other important artifacts include a poplar dugout canoe, believed to be of Cherokee origin and over two hundred years old, and artifacts from the Tellico Blockhouse. The museum has other major exhibits including ones on the geology and fossil history of Tennessee, Ancient Egypt, early medical practices, decorative arts, and various temporary exhibits.

Hours are 9 A.M. to 5 P.M., Monday through Friday, 10 A.M. to 3 P.M. Saturday, and 2 P.M. to 5 P.M. on Sunday. The museum is closed New Year's Day, July Fourth, Labor Day, Thanksgiving Day, Christmas Eve, and Christmas Day. Admission is free. For information, call 615-974-2144.

The museum is located on the campus of the University of Tennessee at Knoxville. From Interstate 40, take U.S. 129 (Alcoa Highway) to Cumberland Avenue following signs directing you to the campus, then turn right on Volunteer Boulevard which loops through the university campus. Watch for Circle Park Drive, whose entrance is marked by the Torchbearer statue. On weekends, parking for the museum is available on Circle Park Drive. On weekdays, obtain a parking pass from the information booth at the entrance to Circle Park Drive. Warning: Avoid football weekends at the University of Tennessee at Knoxville unless you plan to attend the game after visiting the museum.

SAM HOUSTON SCHOOLHOUSE

Maryville

Three nations have claimed Sam Houston as a favorite son: the United States, the

Frank H. McClung Museum

Sam Houston Schoolhouse

Republic of Texas, and the Cherokee Nation. Born in Virginia, Houston moved to eastern Tennessee with his family when he was thirteen. At fifteen, Houston ran away to live with Chief John Jolly and the Cherokees on Hiwassee Island. Some historians have suggested young Houston went to live with the Cherokees because he preferred wandering in the woods and reading the classics to farming. When two of his brothers finally found him on Hiwassee Island, Sam was sitting under a tree reading the *Iliad*. Houston told his brothers he preferred measuring deer tracks to measuring tape. Three years later, Houston returned to the white settlements. In 1812, he taught school at a one-room, log schoolhouse that still stands today. In his later years, Houston said his brief period of teaching was one of the most rewarding times of his life.

In 1813, Houston enlisted in the United States Army as a private. Within a year, the young Houston had risen to the rank of ensign in the Thirty-ninth Infantry Regiment under the command of Major Lemuel P. Montgomery. (The capital of Alabama would later be named for Major Montgomery.) At the Battle of Horseshoe Bend, Houston distinguished himself in the fight against the Creeks. Already suffering from an arrow wound in his leg, Houston led an attack on a band of Creeks entrenched in a ravine and was shot in both his shoulder and arm. At first, army surgeons ignored Houston and tended to the other wounded because they did not believe he could possibly recover from his wounds. However, Houston recovered, and his bravery attracted the attention of Andrew Jackson. Jackson befriended the young man and later would influence his political career.

After the Creek War, Jackson obtained an appointment for Houston as a federal agent to the Cherokees. One of Houston's assignments was to encourage the Cherokees to emigrate west. Houston did not feel this assignment was in any way disloyal to the Cherokees. Many of his Cherokee friends wanted to move west and gladly accepted the land offered to them in the Arkansas territory. During his tenure as agent to the Cherokees, Houston often appeared in Washington dressed in traditional Cherokee garments.

In 1818, after serious quarrels with John C. Calhoun, the secretary of war, Houston resigned his commission in the army. He then studied law and entered politics. His first elected office was attorney general for the Nashville District. In 1823, Houston was elected to the United States Congress, and in 1828, he was elected governor of Tennessee. However, he resigned this position only a few months later, presumably because he was upset over the breakup of his short marriage.

Houston moved to Arkansas to be with his adopted father, John Jolly. He lived with the Western Cherokees for a few years and married a Cherokee woman, Tiana Rogers, who had been a childhood sweetheart. During this period, Houston once again became active in Cherokee affairs. Houston then moved to Nacogdoches, Texas, which was still a part of Mexico. In Texas, he was caught up in the struggle for Texan independence. In 1836, after capturing General Santa Anna and gaining autonomy for Texas, Houston was elected as the first president of the new Republic of

Texas. After Texas became a state, Houston served as governor and senator. Throughout his political career, Houston was active in Cherokee affairs.

The Sam Houston Schoolhouse near Maryville is maintained by the State of Tennessee and the Sam Houston Association Board of Directors. Because the Houston schoolhouse—the oldest extant schoolhouse in Tennessee—was in significant disrepair, it was rebuilt by a local contractor in 1954. In 1973, test excavations were made to see if changes made during the restoration were historically accurate. Results showed the chimney was placed on the original hearth, and the dimensions of the original structure were closely followed. Artifacts found near the excavation indicated the site, which is located next to a quiet stream, was also used by prehistoric Indians long before the schoolhouse was built.

The Houston Schoolhouse, museum, and gift shop are open 10 A.M. to 5 P.M., Monday through Saturday, and from 1 P.M. to 5 P.M. on Sunday. There is a small admission charge. For information, call 615-983-1550.

From Interstate 75, take the Lenoir City exit and follow U.S. 321 east to Maryville. In Maryville, watch for brown-and-white signs for the Houston Schoolhouse. Follow the signs to U.S. 411 North. From U.S. 411 North, turn left on Peppermint Road, then turn right onto Wildwood Road. Watch for Sam Houston Schoolhouse Road, which will be almost immediately after the turn onto Wildwood, and take a left onto Sam Houston Schoolhouse Road. The entrance to the schoolhouse and museum will be on the right (north) side of Sam Houston Schoolhouse Road.

FORT CRAIG

Maryville

In 1785, John Craig erected a large log fort on Pistol Creek to protect himself and his neighbors from Indians. The fort had walls fifteen feet high. It encompassed 2.2 acres and had a spring within its walls. During periods of hostility, as many as 280 people would take refuge in the fort—sometimes for periods of several months.

In July 1795, the General Assembly of the Territory South of the Ohio River carved a new county out of the existing Knox County. The new county was named Blount County, after Governor William Blount. The county seat was named Maryville for Blount's wife, Mary. The town, with streets and 120 lots, was laid out on 50 acres belonging to John Craig.

Fort Craig

Fort Craig became the heart of Maryville. Today, the town has recognized its roots by erecting a monument to the fort in Greenbelt Park. Greenbelt Park is a 2.5-mile walking trail and fitness course that follows Pistol Creek.

From Interstate 75, take U.S. 321 to Maryville. In Maryville, take U.S. 411 North to the center of town. In town, U.S. 411 North (also known as Sevierville Road) climbs a hill. On the left side of U.S. 411, just before the top of the hill, there will be a historical marker for Fort Craig in the corner of the Union Planters Bank parking lot. On the right is the Blount County Chamber of Commerce. Park in the lower parking lot behind the Chamber of Commerce and take the Greenbelt walkway under Sevierville Road to the monument for Fort Craig.

NINE MILE CREEK, HOUSTON'S STATION, AND DAVID CRAIG'S FORT

Mint

Houston's Station was established in 1785 by a settler named James Houston. It was a single, one-story cabin with portholes, located on Little Nine Mile Creek. Houston's Station was adjacent to the Great Indian War Trail, which made it susceptible to Indian raids. In 1786, after Cherokees attacked a house near Beaver Creek in what is now Knox County, John Sevier gathered 160 horsemen at Houston's Station and launched raids against the Cherokees. In 1788, Indians attacked the John Kirk family who lived on Nine Mile Creek, just three miles from Houston's Station. To revenge the eleven settlers who were killed in the Kirk massacre, Sevier assembled a force at the fort of David Craig, the brother of John Craig. (See the Fort Craig section above for more information on John Craig.) David Craig's fort was located on Nine Mile Creek, several miles southwest of Houston's Station. From David Craig's Fort, Sevier and his men marched to the Hiwassee River, where they re-torched a Cherokee town they had burned in an earlier raid. Then Sevier attacked Tallassee on the Little Tennessee River, before stopping at Chilhowee. The Cherokees in the town of Chilhowee were friendly with the settlers. However, John Kirk, Jr., was encouraged by some of John Sevier's men to murder Chief Abram and Old Tassel in Chilhowee to avenge the death of his family members.

In 1790, violence erupted again along

Nine Mile Creek. Houston's Station was attacked by two or three hundred Cherokees. The fort was sparsely defended so the settlers had to fool the Cherokees into believing there was a larger force inside. The settlers withheld fire until the Cherokees were very close, and then all fired at once. The ruse worked, and the Cherokees retreated.

In 1794, the general assembly, meeting in Knoxville, recommended that additional measures be taken to protect the settlers on the frontier. They cited the "two hundred people dead, one thousand horses stolen valued at $100,000, besides malicious destruction of property and livestock" as the reason for these measures. They also recommended a chain of blockhouses be built in the area. These blockhouses would be located on Nine Mile Creek, Coyatee Ford, at Tuckaleechee Cove, at the head of Crooked Creek, and on the Tennessee River.

While the general assembly was meeting, skirmishes between settlers and Indians continued. Much of the trouble on the frontier was caused by whites or Indians, mostly Cherokees and Creeks, who did not live in the area. Many of the Overhill chiefs were attempting to make peace and even offered their help in trying to stop the raids. In 1794, eight Creeks were spotted below the Hiwassee River on their way to the white settlements south of the French Broad River. Believing the Creeks were in the area to stir up trouble, federal troops and a number of Cherokees caught up with them near David Craig's fort. In the fight, the Cherokees killed and scalped one Creek, wounded another, and captured a few supplies.

Today Nine Mile Creek and Little Nine Mile Creek meander peacefully through the beautiful farm land south of Maryville. The valley parallels Chilhowee Mountain and can be seen from the Look Rock Tower on the Foothills Parkway.

To reach the area where David Craig's fort was located from Maryville, take U.S. 411 south. Take a left turn onto Trigonia Road, just north of the intersection of U.S. 411 and Tn. 72. The beginning of Trigonia Road curves uphill around Militia Springs, which was a mustering grounds for militia in the 1790s. Follow Trigonia Road to its junction with Howard's Mill Road and take a left. David Craig's fort was located on the northeast side of Nine Mile Creek, near the junction of these two roads.

To continue to the site of Houston's Station, retrace your steps to U.S. 411. Take U.S. 411 south to Tn. 72 East. Go east on Tn. 72 to the intersection of U.S. 129, and turn left (north). Go north on U.S. 129 to Indian Warpath Road, which is unlabeled and may be difficult to identify. Indian Warpath Road is located on U.S. 129, 4.8 miles from the junction on Tn. 72 and U.S. 129. Turn right onto Indian Warpath Road.

Indian Warpath Road parallels Nine Mile Creek for several miles to the community of Mint. There are several turnoffs from Indian Warpath Road which will lead you to Nine Mile Creek. From the junction of U.S. 129, it is only 0.8 mile on Indian Warpath Road to a right-hand turn onto Reagan's Mill Road, which crosses the creek. From the intersection with Reagan's Mill Road, it is 1.9 miles on Indian Warpath Road to Chota Road, which also crosses the creek.

Continue north on Indian Warpath Road past Mint to reach the area where Houston's Station was located. On the north side of Mint, watch for Baumgardner Road, which comes in from the left, then watch for Knob Road, which comes in from the right. Houston's Station was located on Little Nine Mile Creek in the vicinity of these two roads. The Kirk massacre, which was mentioned earlier, also occurred near here.

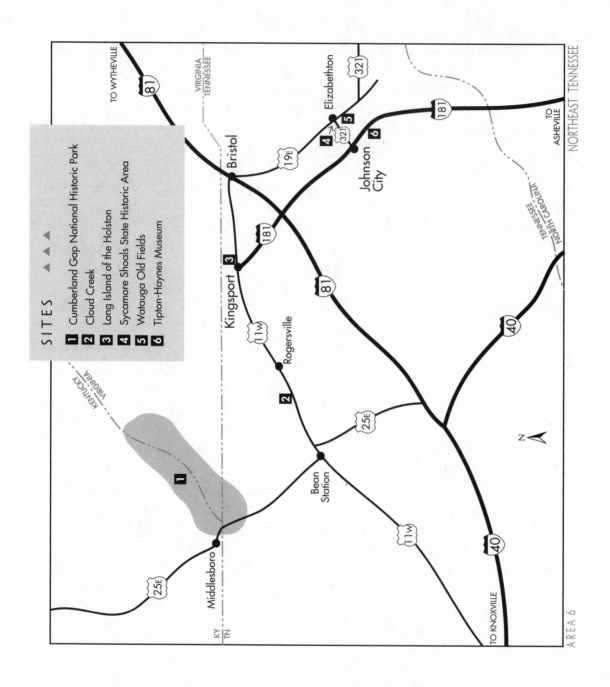

SITES ▲▲▲

1 Cumberland Gap National Historic Park
2 Cloud Creek
3 Long Island of the Holston
4 Sycamore Shoals State Historic Area
5 Watauga Old Fields
6 Tipton-Haynes Museum

TO WYTHEVILLE

81

VIRGINIA
TENNESSEE

Elizabethton
321

181

TO ASHEVILLE

5

4 321

6

Johnson City

19E

Bristol

181

TENNESSEE
NORTH CAROLINA

3

Kingsport

81

11W

Rogersville

2

40

25E

Bean Station

25E

11W

40

KENTUCKY
VIRGINIA

1

Middlesboro

25E

KY
TN

N

TO KNOXVILLE

NORTHEAST TENNESSEE

AREA 6

The Wilderness Road,
Cumberland Gap National Historical Park

AREA 6

NORTHEAST
TENNESSEE

▲ ▲ ▲

In 1609, King James issued a charter that made present-day Tennessee part of the Virginia territory. Twenty years later, King Charles I gave all the lands in the territory of "Carolana" to his attorney general, Sir Robert Heath. At that time, the territory extended from the "ocean on the east side and soe to the west and soe fare as the

Continent extends itselfe," with its boundaries at the 31st and 36th parallels. The boundaries of Carolina changed several more times before North and South Carolina were divided at the 35th parallel in 1719. The 35th parallel also became the southern boundary of the territory that would become Tennessee.

By the time the first permanent white settlers arrived in Tennessee in the late 1700s, title to the territory had belonged to several different people who had never seen the country. Ironically, none of these "title" holders included the Cherokees, Choctaws, Chickasaws, and Yuchis who had been living there for hundreds of years. On October 7, 1763, King George II issued a proclamation that sought to stop encroachment of white settlers onto Indian lands west of the Blue Ridge, but the proclamation still reserved the land for the king.

The proclamation line did not slow the emigration of the Scots-Irish and English settlers who poured into northeast Tennessee. Within a few years, hundreds of families had settled in the Watauga, Nolichucky, Carter, and Holston valleys. Forts or stations, built for trade and protection from the Indians, sprang up everywhere. Names like Bean, Rice, Henderson, Shelby, and Eaton—families who established these

settlements along the frontier—would be etched permanently in the history of northeast Tennessee.

The settlers, isolated from their government in North Carolina, drew up a document called the "Written Articles of Association," which established their own government, known today as the Watauga Association. Later, John Sevier and other settlers in the area established the independent State of Franklin. Sevier led raids on, and made treaties with, the Cherokees in the name of this independent state. Support for the independent State of Franklin eventually dissolved and the area was ceded by North Carolina to the United States in 1789. The area soon had enough citizens to warrant statehood, and on June 1, 1796, Congress admitted the state of Tennessee into the Union. By this time, northeast Tennessee had become relatively peaceful. The great Cherokee war chief, Dragging Canoe, was dead, and the Revolutionary War hero and general, "Mad Anthony" Wayne, had defeated a confederation of northwestern tribes, including the Shawnees, in Ohio. The Indians no longer posed a threat to the settlements of northeast Tennessee. But, for the rest of Tennessee, peace and the question of sovereignty was still not resolved. The Cherokees still claimed ownership of much of the state, and it would be many years before they were finally forced out.

CUMBERLAND GAP NATIONAL HISTORICAL PARK

Cumberland Gap

For hundreds of years, buffalo and elk migrated through the Cumberland Gap in the Appalachian Mountains. Indians, following the buffaloes on hunting parties into Kentucky, knew the route well. They established a great trail through the gap. Called the Warrior's Path, it led from the Potomac River to the Ohio River. Archaeologists have found relatively few sites of ancient Indian settlements within the boundaries of the Cumberland Gap National Historical Park, which indicates the gap was used primarily for travel and temporary camp sites.

The Cherokees frequently attacked travelers on the Warrior's Path, but they had no permanent settlements in the Cumberland Gap area. Other tribes in Kentucky and eastern Tennessee included the Shawnee, Iroquois, Delaware, Miami, Chickasaw, and the Tomahitan and Rickohokan Yuchis. All these tribes probably used the Warrior's Path through the Cumberland Gap at one time or another. After years of war with the Shawnees and other neighboring tribes, the Cherokees claimed the entire Kentucky area as their hunting ground.

In the 1750s, Thomas Walker became the first white man to discover the gap, but its importance wasn't recognized until 1775. In that year, Daniel Boone left Sycamore Shoals with a party of axemen and blazed a trail through the Cumberland Gap. Settlers soon followed and founded Boonesborough on the banks of the Kentucky River. Since the Cherokees claimed the entire Kentucky area, the settlers had to negotiate a settlement with them. At the Treaty of Sycamore Shoals in March 1775, the Cherokees forfeited the entire Cumberland River watershed, plus the southern half of the Kentucky River watershed—an area of 20 million acres—in the largest corporate land deal in United States history.

Cumberland Gap National Historical Park contains over twenty thousand acres in Kentucky, Tennessee, and Virginia. There are over fifty miles of hiking trails in the park, as well as picnic and camping facilities, and several interpretive programs.

The National Park Service has restored several farmsteads in the Hensley Settlement on Brush Mountain. In 1996, a new tunnel through the Cumberland Mountains will be completed as part of an ambitious restoration program, which will reroute U.S. 25E through the mountains instead of through the gap. In the 1920s and 1930s, the Cumberland Mountains were blasted, allowing the building of U.S. 25E fifty feet lower than the original Wilderness Road. Dirt from the new tunnel will be used to raise the Cumberland Gap back to the elevation of Daniel Boone's time, and native trees and wildflowers will replace miles of pavement. Cudjo's Cave, a five-tier cave system located near the present road, has been acquired by the National Park Service. They will remove the electric lighting system in the caverns, allowing park visitors to tour the cave using lanterns.

A visitor center for the park with film, museum, and sales area is located on U.S. 25E at Middlesboro, Kentucky. The visitor center is open daily, except Christmas. Summer hours are 8 A.M. to 6 P.M., and winter hours are 9 A.M. to 5 P.M. The park gates are open year-round from 8 A.M. until dusk. For information, call 606-248-2817.

From Interstate 81, take U.S. 25E to the southeast entrance of the park. From Knoxville, take Interstate 75 north to U.S. 25W. Take U.S. 25W to Tn. 63 and follow it to the park.

CLOUD CREEK

Rogersville

Cloud Creek, near the town of Rogersville, was an important landmark in many agreements between the whites and the Cherokees. In July 1777, Cherokees met at a site at present-day Kingsport to negotiate the Treaty of Long Island with representatives from the Virginia, North Carolina, and Watauga settlements. After several days of raucous merriment, a murder, and earnest diplomacy, the Cherokees agreed to cede land in northeast Tennessee. They reluctantly agreed to extend the western boundary line down the Holston River to the mouth of Cloud Creek. From there it ran to the highest point in the Clinch Mountains. The southern boundary was extended to the Nolichucky River.

The treaty opened additional land to white settlement. It also made it easier for settlers to access the land acquired in the earlier Treaty of Sycamore Shoals. John

Near the mouth of Cloud Creek

Donelson, who had visited the area in 1771 while surveying a boundary of Cherokee lands, attended the treaty meeting at Long Island in 1777. Shortly after this visit, Donelson and Indian agent James Robertson began to make plans for a settlement at a place called French Lick on the Cumberland River. In 1779, Robertson left for French Lick, but he arranged for his family to travel with Donelson later in the year.

In December 1779, John Donelson's party of thirty boats set out from Fort Patrick Henry for Big Salt Lick (near present-day Nashville). They made several extended stops on the way. The first was a two-month stop at the mouth of Reedy Creek, near the northwestern end of Long Island. Their second stop was a seven-day layover at the mouth of Cloud Creek. The Donelson party endured many incidents on the way to their destination, including battles with the Chickamaugans.

Cloud Creek was designated as a boundary in both the Treaty of Long Island of 1777 and the Sycamore Shoals Treaty in 1775. In 1783, the North Carolina General Assembly used Cloud Creek as a landmark when they extended the western boundary of the Tennessee territory, in order to open more lands for sale. This was done without any agreement with the Cherokees.

That same year, Cloud Creek was also used to divide Greene and Washington counties in the Tennessee territory.

The opening of Cherokee Dam, and the creation of Cherokee Lake, has altered the location of the confluence of Cloud Creek and the Holston River. U.S. 11W crosses Cloud Creek near its new mouth, southwest of Rogersville. From Interstate 81, take U.S. 11E to Bulls Gap. Then take Tn. 66 to Rogersville and turn south (left) on U.S. 11W. Drive 4.8 miles to the bridge over Cloud Creek.

LONG ISLAND OF THE HOLSTON

Kingsport

Long Island, situated in the Holston River at present-day Kingsport, was a favorite hunting and trading spot for the Cherokees. It lay on the Great Indian War Trail, which ran from Virginia to the Overhill settlements. Its strategic location allowed the Cherokees to control nearly all the trade and travel from east of the mountains to Kentucky and Tennessee.

The Cherokees allowed traders to camp on the island as early as the 1750s. One of

Footbridge leading to the Long Island of the Holston

these traders was Nathaniel Gist, who would become a great friend of the Cherokees. He was probably the father of George Gist, better known as Sequoyah. Nathaniel Gist would later claim that the Cherokees gave him Long Island, but he eventually lost an eighteen-year battle to gain legal title to the land.

After the massacre at Fort Loudoun, a road was cut through the wilderness from the site of present-day Chilhowie, Virginia, to Long Island. The Island Road, completed in September 1761, enabled the building of Fort Robinson. The fort was located on the north bank opposite the eastern end of the island. The river bank was so high at this spot that only three sides of the fort had to be enclosed. Later in 1761, Fort Robinson was the site of a peace treaty with the Cherokees. This treaty produced a period of quiet on the frontier that enabled the western expansion of the settlers.

After the treaty of 1761, Long Island became a layover point for travelers going west. They would stop at Long Island to rest and replenish supplies before continuing their long journey. Many settlers either obtained or built a boat at Long Island so they could continue their journey by water. An area known as "The Boatyard" grew up along the north bank of the Holston River, opposite the island.

As settlers poured into Cherokee territory, tensions increased. In 1776, the Cherokees attacked the Holston, Watauga, and Nolichucky settlements. The Cherokee forces divided into three parts, with Dragging Canoe leading his warriors toward Long Island and the Holston River settlements. As he approached the settlements, Dragging Canoe was met at Long Island by Tennessee and Virginia militias. During the ensuing battle, known as the Battle of Long Island Flats, Dragging Canoe was wounded in the thigh, and his forces were driven back.

In September 1776, Fort Patrick Henry was completed on the same site as Fort Robinson. A few days later, Colonel William Christian launched devastating attacks on the Overhill Towns from the fort. In 1781, the Treaty of Long Island was negotiated—one of the few peace treaties between the Cherokees and the whites where no land cessions were made by the Cherokees.

The Cherokees finally ceded Long Island to the settlers in a treaty concluded in Washington on January 7, 1806. In this treaty, the Cherokees gave away nearly seven thousand square miles in Tennessee and Alabama. In return, they received ten thousand dollars, a grist mill, a cotton gin, and a lifetime annuity for the aging chief, Black Fox. In 1976, the Cherokees gained part of their beloved island back when the Mead Corporation gave the northwestern end of the island to the City of Kingsport. A condition of the gift was the city must give a small portion of the land to the Cherokees.

To reach Long Island from Interstate 81, take Interstate 181 north to Kingsport. Cross the Holston River and take the exit for U.S. 11W. Turn left (west) on U.S. 11W, and go 2.0 miles to a major intersection with Netherland Inn Road. (At 0.6 mile from Interstate 181 on U.S. 11W you will pass a stone historical marker for the Indian War Path on the left side of the road in front of the fire station.) At Netherland Inn Road, turn left and cross the bridge over the north fork of the Holston River. After you cross the bridge, you will enter the historic Boatyard District, which is a city park stretching for several miles along the Holston River. At 1.6 miles from U.S. 11W, the Netherland Inn will be on the left. This is a good spot to stop and explore the Boatyard District. Park on the right side of the road in the park across from the Netherland Inn. Long Island may be reached from here by walking east a short distance along the waterfront to a footbridge across the river. On the other side is a monument to the Cherokees.

SYCAMORE SHOALS
STATE HISTORIC AREA

Elizabethton

In the early 1770s, Sycamore Shoals became a rendezvous point for settlers moving into northeast Tennessee. In March 1775, the biggest corporate land deal in American history was negotiated at Sycamore Shoals between the Cherokees and the Transylvania Company. In this treaty, known as the Treaty of Sycamore Shoals, the Cherokees sold twenty million acres of land. Dragging Canoe was upset over the treaty because it was negotiated by the older chiefs. In response, he led attacks on the Wataugan settlements. The settlers responded to these attacks by building a fort at Sycamore Shoals.

Sycamore Shoals State Historic Area and the reconstructed fort are located at the site of the Wataugan mustering grounds. The original fort was actually located about 1 mile west of the park. In addition to the reconstructed fort, the state historic area has a museum, bookstore, film on the Wataugans, a walking trail, and picnic grounds. Each June, the park hosts an Indian Festival that features Cherokee craftsmen, dancers, and programs on Cherokee culture. In July, the outdoor drama *The Wataugans* is presented. In September, the park hosts the Overmountain Victory Trail Celebration.

Sycamore Shoals Visitor Center is open Monday through Saturday from 8 A.M. to 4:30 P.M., and Sunday from 1 P.M. to 4:30 P.M. The grounds are open from 8 A.M. to dusk. Admission is free. For information, call 615-543-5808.

From Interstate 181 in Johnson City, take Exit 31 for Elizabethton and drive 5.8 miles on U.S. 321. The park entrance will be on the left. Across U.S. 321 from the park is a small road named Parkway. You can take Parkway 0.2 mile and turn right

Sycamore Shoals State Historic Area

on West G Street, then drive 0.9 mile to the original location of the fort. The site, marked by a stone monument to the Wataugans, will be on the left.

WATAUGA OLD FIELDS

Elizabethton

Elizabethton was founded at the site of an old Cherokee village called Wata'gi, at the junction of the Doe and Watauga rivers—an area the Cherokees called Watauga Old Fields. Wata'gi may have come from the Creek word *wetoga*, meaning broken waters, which described the shoals on the Watauga River. The phrase "Old Fields" was probably used because the Cherokees found graves and other signs of earlier Indian occupation in the area.

In the 1750s, white hunters and traders moved into the area and established hunting camps. Settlers soon followed. They found an area of open fields which had been cleared by the Indians. In 1770, James Robertson, who helped found Nash-

*Monument commemorating the Watauga
Old Fields at the Carter County Courthouse
in Elizabethton*

ville and became known as the "Father of
Middle Tennessee," moved to the area. He
described the Watauga Old Fields as the
"Promised Land," because the fields were
more easily cleared for farming than the
surrounding, old-growth forests. Robertson
returned temporarily to North Carolina and
brought back several families who established the first permanent white settlement
west of the Appalachians. These early pioneers organized a government which became known as the Wataugan Association.
The "Watauga Articles of Association" was
the first constitution written by native-born
Americans.

To reach the Watauga Old Fields from
Interstate 181 in Johnson City, take
Exit 31 and follow U.S. 321 to
Elizabethton. On the east side of
Elizabethton, U.S. 321 turns right. Shortly
after this turn, watch for a sign indicating
the Elizabethton Business District. Turn
right at this sign onto East Elk Street. Follow East Elk Street to the courthouse
square. The courthouse will be on the right.
In front of it is a stone with a plaque for
the Watauga Old Fields. From East Elk
Street at the Courthouse Square, turn right
onto North Main Street. North Main Street
ends at Watauga Street next to the
confluence of the Doe and Watauga rivers,
the site of Wata'gi village.

TIPTON-HAYNES MUSEUM

Johnson City

The Tipton-Haynes farm was purchased in 1784 by Colonel John Tipton, a signer of the constitutions of Virginia and Tennessee. Tipton also served as a delegate to the constitutional conventions of the State of Franklin and the United States. John Tipton built his log cabin on a stage road, which had been an old buffalo trail and Indian path. His son, John Tipton, Jr., inherited the farm in 1813. In 1839, the Tipton farm was purchased by David Haynes and given to his son, Landon Carter Haynes, as a wedding present. Several members of both the Tipton and Haynes families were active in Tennessee politics. Landon Haynes also served in the Confederate senate.

The farm is best known as the site of the Battle of the State of Franklin. In the 1780s, John Tipton and John Sevier, two of the most powerful men on the eastern Tennessee frontier, were involved in a dispute. In the winter of 1788, a North Carolina court ordered the seizure of slaves and other property belonging to John Sevier as payment for North Carolina taxes. The sheriff, Jonathan Pugh, took the slaves to Tipton's farm for protection. Tipton was a

North Carolina magistrate as well as one of Pugh's friends. Sevier was away from his home when the slaves and property were confiscated. When he returned and discovered Pugh had taken his possessions, he was furious. He raised a force of between 50 and 150 men and marched to the Tipton farm where about 45 men were assembled to guard the slaves. A battle between the two leaders was inevitable.

Sevier ordered the surrender of Tipton's men. Tipton and Pugh refused and sent for reinforcements. A group of men from Sullivan County who arrived to help Tipton, attacked the Sevier camp while John Sevier was on a scouting party. The forces in Tipton's house joined in the battle. The scouting party, hearing the guns from a distance, returned to the scene and also joined in the battle. During the fight, two of Sevier's sons were captured by Tipton's forces. There were casualties on both sides, including Sheriff Pugh who died several days later. Tipton wanted to hang Sevier's sons, but was dissuaded by Thomas Love, a mutual friend of Sevier and Tipton. The sons were eventually released. This incident between the two powerful leaders of the Tennessee frontier would become known as The Battle of the State of Franklin.

The Tipton-Haynes farm is located next to a spring and a cave. Native American

Tipton-Haynes Museum

Historical Association. From April 1 to October 31, the site is open Monday through Saturday from 10 A.M. to 5 P.M., and Sunday from 2 P.M. to 5 P.M. From November 1 to March 31, hours are 10 A.M. to 4:30 P.M., weekdays only. The museum is closed on Thanksgiving and the day after Thanksgiving, and from December 21 to January 8. For information, call 615-926-3631. There is an admission charge.

From Interstate 181 south of Johnson City, take Exit 31, which is the exit for University Parkway and U.S. 321/Tn. 67. Go west 0.25 mile and turn left (south) onto South Roan Street, which is also Tn. 36. The museum entrance will be on the right in a little less than a mile.

artifacts dating back to the Woodland period have been found at the cave, indicating the site was probably used as a hunting camp by the Indians for hundreds of years. The first white men to visit the Cherokee Overhill country, Gabriel Arthur and James Needham, are believed to have camped by the spring.

The Tipton-Haynes Museum and gift shop are operated by the Tipton-Haynes

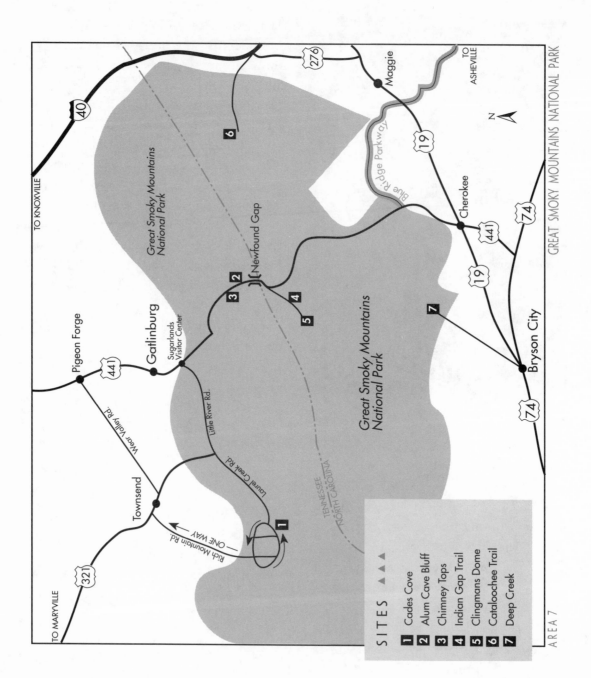

SITES ▲▲▲

1	Cades Cove
2	Alum Cave Bluff
3	Chimney Tops
4	Indian Gap Trail
5	Clingmans Dome
6	Cataloochee Trail
7	Deep Creek

AREA 7

TO KNOXVILLE

TO MARYVILLE

40

321

441

Pigeon Forge

Gatlinburg

Townsend

Sugarlands Visitor Center

Wear Valley Rd.

Little River Rd.

Laurel Creek Rd.

Rich Mountain Rd. — ONE WAY

Newfound Gap

Great Smoky Mountains National Park

Great Smoky Mountains National Park

TENNESSEE / NORTH CAROLINA

276

Maggie

TO ASHEVILLE

19

Blue Ridge Parkway

Cherokee

441

74

Bryson City

19

74

N

Abrams Creek in Cades Cove

GREAT SMOKY MOUNTAINS NATIONAL PARK

▲ ▲ ▲

The Cherokee word for the Great Smoky Mountains was Shaconage, "mountains of the blue smoke." The mountains were a rich habitat for many species of fish and animals, making the Smokies an abundant hunting ground for the Cherokees living in the nearby foothills. The Cherokees also used the craggy balds and secret valleys of the mountains to hide from hostile tribes. Later, the Cherokees used the Smoky

Mountains as a refuge from the white settlers, who found the terrain inhospitable. The eastern slopes of the Smokies, considered by early whites to be too wild for habitation, eventually became the permanent home of the Eastern Band of the Cherokee Nation when the Qualla Boundary was established on the North Carolina side of the Great Smoky Mountains.

The Great Smoky Mountains were a place of mystery and legend for the Cherokees. Somewhere in the remotest parts of the mountains lay the enchanted lake of Ataga'hi, or the "Gall Place." This was the "medicine lake" for the animals, where a wounded bear or animal could bathe to heal its wounds. Gregory Bald, or Tsistu'yi, near the North Carolina/Tennessee state line in the southwest end of the park, was the home of the Great Rabbit, the chief of the rabbit tribe. The rabbits and the bears each had a council house beneath Gregory Bald, and the bald was one of four places the bears would dance before hibernating for the winter.

Whites were slower to appreciate the mysterious and wild beauty of the mountains. However, in September 1940, President Franklin D. Roosevelt dedicated the Great Smoky Mountains National Park, and visitors from all over the world began swarming to the area. Each year, millions come to enjoy the majestic vistas, peaceful trails, and the diversity of the flora and fauna. Horace Kephart, one of the founders of the park, said: "Here today is the last stand of primeval American forest at its best. If saved—and if saved at all it must be done at once—it will be a joy and a wonder to our people for all time. The nation is summoned by a solemn duty to preserve it."

The most popular road in the national park is the thirty-three-mile Newfound Gap Road, which runs from the Sugarlands Visitor Center on the northern side of the park near Gatlinburg, Tennessee, to the Oconaluftee Visitor Center on the southern side near Cherokee, North Carolina. The Newfound Gap Road is the name of U.S. 441 inside the park. The old Newfound Gap Road, which was very steep, was rebuilt in 1964. On the northern side, Newfound Gap Road parallels the Little Pigeon River (named for the flocks of carrier pigeons that once lived in the mountains). On the southern side of Newfound Gap, the road follows Thomas Ridge, named for the Cherokee leader William Thomas. It parallels the Oconaluftee River (from the Cherokee word *egwanul'ti*, meaning "by the river").

Another major road in the park is the Little River Road. It is an eighteen-mile drive between Sugarlands Visitor Center and the park entrance at Townsend, Tennessee. The Little River Road is a low elevation, stream-side drive leading motorists to Cades Cove which is a scenic and historical valley.

While the park is open year-round, the Newfound Gap Road is frequently closed in winter and spring due to snow. Other roads within the park, such as the Roaring Fork Motor Nature Trail and Clingmans Dome Road, are also closed in winter and early spring. For information, contact the park at 615-436-1200. Park maps and brochures can be obtained at the park's three visitor centers. Sugarlands Visitor Center near Gatlinburg and the Oconaluftee Visitor Center near Cherokee are open daily year round except Christmas Day. The visitor center at Cades Cove closes for the winter season on Thanksgiving weekend and reopens in mid-March.

CADES COVE

Cades Cove was known by the Cherokees as Tsiya'hi, or "Otter Place." Lieutenant Henry Timberlake wrote in his memoirs that he had seen many brooks that were well-stocked with otters, beaver, and fish in Cherokee country. But by 1818, the time the first permanent white settlers arrived in Cades Cove, the otters in the cove had been hunted to extinction.

James Mooney identifies Tsiya'hi as a Cherokee settlement on Cove Creek in Cades Cove. It is unclear how large this settlement was. It may have been nothing more than a popular campsite for hunting. There were Cherokee villages in neighboring Tuckaleechee Cove at one time, but they had apparently been abandoned by the time Tuckaleechee Cove was settled by whites in the 1790s.

Cades Cove was named for Chief Kade. Very little is known of this Cherokee chief, except that he traded with Peter Snider in nearby Tuckaleechee Cove. The beautiful Abrams Creek, which runs the entire length of the cove before emptying into the Little Tennessee River, was named for Chief Abram, also known as Old Abraham, of Chilhowee.

In 1818, John and Lucretia Oliver used an Indian path to cross over Rich Mountain to settle in Cades Cove. At the time, there were still many Indians in the area. The Indians even provided the Olivers with pumpkins to prevent them from starving during their first winter in the cove.

When the Olivers settled in the cove in 1818, it was still Cherokee land. An 1819 treaty ceded the cove to the United States, and more settlers soon ventured into the area.

Today, Cades Cove looks much like it did in the 1930s, when the national park was established. Several log cabins, barns, churches, and other buildings have been preserved in the area, including the cabin of the first white settlers, John and Lucretia Oliver. These buildings are scattered throughout Cades Cove and are easily accessible from the eleven-mile, one-way loop road which circles the perimeter of the cove. At the western end of the cove is a trail to Abrams Falls, a five-mile-round-trip walk. The trailhead for Abrams Falls is reached from a short spur road off of the Cades Cove Loop Road, located about halfway around the loop. The Cable Mill area is just past the spur road to the Abrams Falls trailhead. Pioneer buildings and the Cable Mill are located here, as well as a visitor center with a small bookstore and rest rooms.

On the northern side of the cove is Rich Mountain Road, which closely follows an Indian trail. The one-way road exits Cades Cove to travel to Tuckaleechee Cove and on to the town of Townsend. Rich Mountain Road is a right turn from the loop road, just past the Missionary Baptist Church. The Rich Mountain Road is closed in winter and when the loop road is closed.

Other facilities in Cades Cove include a campground, picnic area, small store, and horse stables. These are reached by turning left onto a short side road located near the entrance to Cades Cove before the beginning of the Cades Cove Loop Road. The road to the campground and picnic area is open twenty-four hours, year round. The scenic loop road is open daily from dawn to dusk—except on Saturday mornings when it is closed to cars for the use of bicyclists and walkers.

From Cherokee, North Carolina, take U.S. 441 north through the Great Smoky Mountains National Park to the Sugarlands Visitor Center near Gatlinburg, then turn left onto the Little River Road. Or from Gatlinburg, Tennessee, take U.S. 441 south to the Sugarlands Visitor Center and turn right onto the Little River Road. Take the Little River Road to its junction with Tn. 73 near Townsend. Here the road changes names to Laurel Creek Road. Continue straight on Laurel Creek Road for 7 miles to the Cades Cove Loop Road.

ALUM CAVE BLUFF

Yonaguska, also known as Yanugun'ski or Drowning Bear, was the peace chief of the village of Kituwah, and later of Oconaluftee. He is credited with the discovery of Alum Cave, which he supposedly found in his youth while tracking a bear.

For many years, the cave was mined for saltpeter, which provided nitrates for gunpowder production. Alum, epsom salts, magnesia, and copperas were also found in the cave. The salts, known for their purity, were hauled over Indian Gap Road to Knoxville. William Thomas's Confederate Legion guarded the cave during the Civil War.

The hike to Alum Cave Bluff is 5 miles round-trip. The trail first crosses Little Pigeon River, then passes Arch Rock and Inspiration Point, before reaching the cave. The trail continues another 2.8 miles to the top of Mount LeConte. This is one of the most popular hikes in Great Smoky Mountains National Park, and on weekends in summer and October you may wish to claim a spot in the parking lot before 9 A.M.

To reach the trail, take Newfound Gap Road from the Sugarlands Visitor Center. The Alum Cave Bluff trail parking lot is on the left of Newfound Gap Road, 8.4 miles from the visitor center. From Cherokee, North Carolina, take U.S. 441 to the

Little Pigeon River at trailhead for Alum Cave Bluff

Great Smoky Mountains National Park, then follow Newfound Gap Road across the mountains to the Alum Cave Bluff parking lot on the right.

CHIMNEY TOPS

According to Cherokee legend, the *uktena* was a large, monster snake who hid in isolated passes in the high mountains or in deep pools in rivers. The *uktena* had horns and a bright crystal in its forehead called the *ulunsu'ti*. Anyone who was brave enough to kill the *uktena* and take the *ulunsu'ti* would have success in hunting, love, and making rain.

The legend continues with the tale of Aganuni'tsi, "The Groundhog's Mother," who was a Shawnee magician captured by the Cherokees. Aganuni'tsi was able to bargain for his life and secure his release by promising to kill the *uktena* and bring the *ulunsu'ti* to the Cherokees. Aganuni'tsi knew that the *uktena* liked to wait for unsuspecting travelers in the remote passes of the Great Smoky Mountains, so he concentrated his search in these gaps. He searched several passes in the north end of the Smokies where he found monster snakes, but not the great *uktena*. Moving south, he stopped at Walasi'yi, the Frog Place, near Mount LeConte (this is a different Walasi'yi from the better-known one at Neel's Gap in north Georgia), at the enchanted lake Ataga'hi, and at Duniskwa'lgun'yi, the Gap of the Forked Antler. At each of these places he found monster reptiles. He eventually found the *uktena* at Gahu'ti Mountain (Cohutta Mountain, Georgia) where he killed it and captured the *ulunsu'ti*.

Today, Duniskwa'lgun'yi, the Gap of the Forked Antler from the legend, is the double-peak known as the Chimney Tops. The name Duniskwa'lgun'yi implies that the antler is still attached to the deer that lies below the mountain. While the twin peaks reminded the Cherokees of deer antlers, the white settlers were reminded of a pair of stone chimneys, similar to those on their log cabins.

The Chimney Tops are visible from several points along Newfound Gap Road. Approximately 5.5 miles from Sugarlands Visitors Center are several pull-offs on the right side of Newfound Gap Road that provide excellent views of the Chimney Tops. There is also a trail that leads to the Chimney Tops. The trailhead for the Chimney Tops is located 7 miles from the visitor center on Newfound Gap Road. This hike is 2 miles one-way through a cove hardwood forest. There is also a picnic area named for the Chimney Tops, located on the

Chimney Tops

187 ▲ ▲ ▲

Newfound Gap Road about 2.5 miles below the trailhead parking lot. If approaching from Cherokee, North Carolina, take U.S. 441 north to the park and follow Newfound Gap Road across the mountains. The Chimney Tops trailhead will be on the left about 5.6 miles north of Newfound Gap and the intersection with Clingmans Dome Road.

INDIAN GAP TRAIL

When the Shawnee Indian Aganuni'tsi, "The Groundhog's Mother," was searching for the *uktena*, he passed through Indian Gap. Many Cherokees also passed through this gap since it was along the route of an ancient Indian trail.

In 1832, the North Carolina legislature chartered the Oconaluftee Turnpike Company to build a road from Whittier, North Carolina, over the mountains at Indian Gap to Sugarlands in Tennessee. Completed in 1839, the road closely followed the old Indian trail and was the first wagon road to breach the Smokies. The toll road was narrow, steep, and rocky but served as the primary road through the mountains until the Newfound Gap Road was opened in 1933.

Indian Gap on Clingmans Dome Road

To reach Indian Gap from the Sugarlands Visitor Center near Gatlinburg, take Newfound Gap Road south to Clingmans Dome Road which will be on the right. Or from the Oconaluftee Visitor Center near Cherokee, take Newfound Gap Road north to the left turn for Clingmans Dome Road. Indian Gap is located on Clingmans Dome Road, 1.2 miles from the junction of Clingmans Dome Road and Newfound Gap Road. There is a pull-off at Indian Gap where you can park and view the North Carolina side of the Smokies, or hike part of the old wagon road. This trail is known as the Road Prong and is a 3.5-mile, moderate descent from the Indian Gap parking lot to the Chimney Tops parking lot. The Appalachian Trail also passes through the Indian Gap.

CLINGMANS DOME

Clingmans Dome was originally called Kuwa'hi, the "Mulberry Place," by the Cherokees. Cherokee legend says that the chief of the bears, the White Bear, lives at

Clingmans Dome

Clingmans Dome, and that the bears have town houses under Clingmans Dome where they dance every fall before hibernating for the winter. The Cherokees believed that bears were really humans who were transformed into bears. Therefore, the bears could talk, although they seldom did. However, a hunter once heard a mother bear singing to her cub using human words.

At 6,643 feet above sea-level, Clingmans Dome is the second-highest peak east of the Mississippi. It is second only to Mount Mitchell in North Carolina, which is 43 feet higher. An observation tower has been constructed at the crest of Clingmans Dome. On clear days it provides 360-degree views of the mountains. The hike to the tower is 0.5 mile, but it is steep and may be difficult for those who have not adjusted to the thin mountain air.

To reach Clingmans Dome from the Sugarlands Visitor Center, take Newfound Gap Road south 12.6 miles to Clingmans Dome Road and turn right. To reach Clingmans Dome from the Oconaluftee Visitor Center near Cherokee, take Newfound Gap Road north to the left turn on Clingmans Dome Road. The parking lot for Clingmans Dome is located at the end of the 7-mile Clingmans Dome Road. Clingmans Dome Road opens in late spring and closes in late fall due to snow and ice.

Check for openings and closings of the road at the Sugarlands Visitor Center.

CATALOOCHEE TRAIL

The Cherokees actively hunted and fished in the creeks and valleys around the eastern end of the park. They established the Cataloochee Trail, connecting the Overhill Towns with Indian settlements along the upper French Broad River in North Carolina. The trail ran from Cove Creek on the northeast end of the park to the present-day community of Cosby, Tennessee. Eventually, the entire area was known as Cataloochee. The Cherokees surrendered the Cataloochee area in the 1791 Treaty of Holston. The name Cataloochee comes from the word *gadalu'tsi*, which means "standing up in ranks" or "fringe standing erect." The name probably referred to a thin stand of timber at the top of the Balsam Mountain range along the Haywood and Swain county line in North Carolina. These mountains are in the heart of the Great Smoky Mountains National Park and can be seen from Cove Creek Gap on the eastern end of the Cataloochee Valley.

In 1771, Bishop Francis Asbury emigrated to America and began his work as a missionary. In 1788, he made his first visit

Cataloochee Valley, Great Smoky Mountains National Park

into the remotest parts of Tennessee, where he preached the gospel to a sometimes-reluctant audience of settlers. "I reflect that not one in a hundred came here to get religion," he wrote, "but rather to get plenty of good land, I think it will be well if some or many do not eventually lose their souls." Asbury crossed the mountains in several different places, and in 1810, he used the Indians' Cataloochee Trail: "At Catahouche I walked over a log. But O the mountain height after height, and five miles over!

After crossing other streams, and losing ourselves in the woods, we came in, about nine o'clock at night. . . . What an awful day!"

In 1846, the Jonathan Creek and Tennessee Mountain Turnpike Company was established to build a toll road along the Cataloochee Trail. The road was to have a width of twelve feet and to have a grade no steeper than 12 percent. It was one of the first wagon roads in the Smoky Mountains, and it opened the Cataloochee Cove

Cataloochee Valley, Great Smoky Mountains National Park

to additional settlement. The first settlers had arrived in the cove in the 1830s, but until the road was built it remained isolated. By 1900, the population of the cove had grown to over seven hundred.

This scenic little cove is now nearly deserted except for fishermen, campers, and wildlife. Several of the buildings, including two churches and a schoolhouse, still stand by the small Cataloochee Creek, which runs through the heart of the cove. The cove is reminiscent of the better-known Cades Cove, but its remote location on the northeastern end of the park has protected it from the string of cars and traffic jams which often plague Cades Cove. In addition to camping, there are hiking trails, a ranger station, and historical exhibits in Cataloochee Cove. The road into the cove, the Cove Creek Road, is partly unpaved, sometimes steep, and very curvy, much as it has been since the Indian trail was widened for wagons.

To reach Cataloochee Cove from Asheville, take Interstate 40 west to Exit 20 for U.S. 276. Drive a short distance south on U.S. 276 and turn right onto the first road on the right, which is Cove Creek Road. From Maggie Valley, take U.S. 276 north 5.3 miles and watch for a historical marker for the Cataloochee Trail on the right. Cove Creek Road, which follows the old Cataloochee Trail across the mountains to Cosby, is unlabeled. It is located opposite the historical marker for Cataloochee Trail. Turn onto Cove Creek Road. In 3.4 miles the pavement will end, and at 7.2 miles there will be a fork in the road. The left fork is a paved road which leads into Big Cataloochee Valley. The right fork is Cove Creek Road which follows the old Cataloochee Trail to Cosby.

DEEP CREEK

Tikwali'tsi town was located on the Tuckasegee River next to the village of Kituwah, near the mouth of Deep Creek at present-day Bryson City. Sometime in the mid- to late-1700s, the people of Tikwali'tsi learned that a party of Shawnees had come from the north and were hiding nearby. A Cherokee conjurer used his magic to learn that the Shawnees were waiting in ambush along a trail, a short distance above the town. One party of Cherokees was ordered to quietly approach the Shawnees from the rear. However, a second party, against the conjurer's advice, made a foolish attack on the Shawnees at Deep Creek. The Shawnees had been hiding at a ford and took them "like fish in a

193 ▲ ▲ ▲

Indian Creek Falls near Deep Creek Campground

trap," killing nearly all of the Cherokee warriors.

The more cautious party of Cherokee warriors crossed the Tuckasegee River above Deep Creek and attacked the Shawnees from behind. The Shawnees were forced to retreat up Deep Creek into the mountains, where they were pursued by the Cherokees. In the mountains, the Shawnees killed two Cherokee captives who were slowing their escape and threw them over a cliff. An elderly Shawnee conjurer, who was also having difficulty keeping up, sat down against a tree to wait for death. The Cherokees obliged by splitting his head with a tomahawk and throwing him over the same cliff where the Shawnees had thrown the two murdered Cherokees. The defenders of Tikwali'tsi finally gave up their pursuit at Duniua'talun'yi, a gap just below Clingmans Dome, near the headwaters of Noland Creek.

The best way to enjoy Deep Creek is to hike the Deep Creek Trail. To reach the trail take U.S. 441 to Cherokee, North Carolina, and then take either U.S. 19 or U.S. 74 to Bryson City. Near the gold-domed courthouse, watch for the national park signs, which will direct you across the Tuckasegee River. Turn right on Bryson Road and drive 0.15 mile to Everett Street. Turn right on Everett Street and then left onto Depot Street. From this point, you should be able to follow signs to Deep Creek. The signs will direct you down Depot Street to a left turn on Ramseur Street. After rounding a curve to the right, the road changes its name to Deep Creek Road. Follow Deep Creek Road about 3 miles to the parking lot for Deep Creek Trail. Park and walk past the gate. You can follow the Deep Creek Trail 0.25 mile to a small falls named Toms Branch, or continue to the more-striking Indian Creek Falls. Indian Creek Trail connects with the Deep Creek Trail 0.75 miles past Toms Branch Falls. Turn right onto Indian Creek Trail and Indian Creek Falls will be just a few hundred feet more on your left.

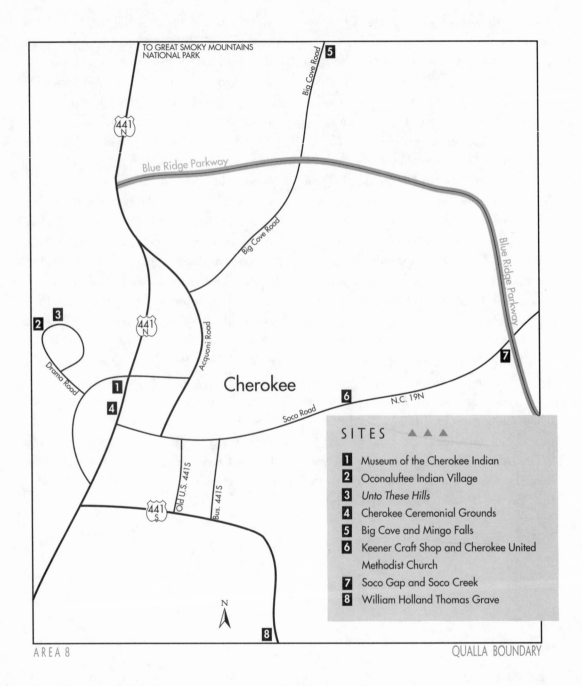

TO GREAT SMOKY MOUNTAINS
NATIONAL PARK

441 N

Big Cove Road

5

Blue Ridge Parkway

Big Cove Road

Blue Ridge Parkway

2 **3**

441 N

Drama Road

Acquoni Road

Cherokee

7

1

4

6 N.C. 19N

Soco Road

Old U.S. 441 S

Bus. 441 S

441 S

N

8

SITES ▲ ▲ ▲

1 Museum of the Cherokee Indian
2 Oconaluftee Indian Village
3 *Unto These Hills*
4 Cherokee Ceremonial Grounds
5 Big Cove and Mingo Falls
6 Keener Craft Shop and Cherokee United
Methodist Church
7 Soco Gap and Soco Creek
8 William Holland Thomas Grave

AREA 8   QUALLA BOUNDARY

Canoe maker at Oconaluftee Indian Village
Courtesy of Cherokee Historical Association

AREA 8

QUALLA BOUNDARY

▲ ▲ ▲

The Qualla Boundary is a large tract of land on the Oconaluftee River which serves as the main home of the Eastern Cherokee tribe. The town of Cherokee is also located within this tract. Since the Great Smoky Mountains National Park was dedicated in 1940, tourism has been the chief economy of the Qualla Boundary. About 75 percent of the tribe's revenue comes from the tourist industry. There are over fifty-five motels on the reservation and numerous campgrounds, shops, and restaurants. Visitors to the town of Cherokee can choose from a wide variety of attractions, including several excellent galleries that feature Cherokee and other Native American art.

What visitors don't have the opportunity to see are two of the ancestral villages of the Upper Towns, Nununyi and Tsiskwaki. While Kituwah, located several miles west of the Qualla Boundary on the Tuckasegee River (see the Kituwah Mound section in Area 10), is considered to be the original, or "mother," village for the entire Cherokee tribe, Nununyi and Tsiskwaki were the two oldest Cherokee villages on the Oconaluftee River. Although the villages were destroyed, they remain the two most important archaeological sites on the Qualla Boundary and provide much information on the development of the Cherokee culture.

Nununyi, or "potato place," was a Cherokee village with mound which was occupied in the 1700s. On a map made in 1730, the village was identified as Newni. In 1776, the naturalist William Bartram referred to it as Nuanhi. Nununyi was destroyed in October 1776, by Colonel William Moore. A second nearby village, Tsiskwaki, or "bird place," was also destroyed by Moore's North Carolina militia during the Revolutionary War. This town was also known as Oconaluftee or Egwanul'ti, meaning "beside the river." The site of Tsiskwaki is in Birdtown, an area in the eastern section of the Qualla Boundary. There was a mound here until it was excavated by representatives of the Valentine Museum in 1883. The Nununyi Mound is still largely intact, but part of the large village site and midden around Nununyi has been damaged. The Nununyi mound is located on private property near Cherokee High School. At least one proposal has been made to restore the Nununyi mound and village site to its pre-1776 condition and open it for visitation as a complement to the Oconaluftee Village.

In the early 1800s, the area near the confluence of Soco Creek and the Oconaluftee River was known as Indiantown. In 1839, when the first post office was established, Indiantown was renamed Quallatown in honor of Kwali, an old Indian woman who lived nearby.

William Holland Thomas was a white trader who operated a store at Quallatown and owned several other enterprises in the area. As a boy, he was adopted by the

Cherokee chief Yonaguska. He later became a spokesman for the Cherokees living in the Quallatown area. Thomas lobbied the federal government for several years to obtain permission for the Oconaluftee Cherokees to remain in their homelands. The foundation for his argument was that the Oconaluftee Cherokees were North Carolina citizens, unlike the Cherokees living inside the Cherokee Nation. Under the Treaty of 1819, many of the Oconaluftee Indians had chosen to accept 640-acre reserves from the government and to become citizens of the United States and North Carolina. In addition, there was an unusual clause in the 1835 Treaty of New Echota which allowed certain Cherokees to remain in the east, yet still collect the same payment as those who were being removed. Thomas argued that this clause applied to his people. While Cherokees in other parts of the Southeast were being rounded up for the removal in 1838, the Oconaluftee Cherokees waited for the outcome of Thomas's efforts. Finally, the Oconaluftee Cherokees were granted permission to stay. During the removal, Thomas cooperated with the federal forces in the capture and execution of the family of Tsali, a Cherokee who had killed a soldier during the round up. Although Thomas had already received permission for the Oconaluftee Cherokees to remain, he cooperated in the effort to capture Tsali to avoid jeopardizing the Oconaluftee Cherokees' tenuous position with the government.

After the removal, nearly all of the eleven hundred remaining North Carolina Cherokees gave William Thomas their power of attorney. He represented them in efforts to collect the money the government owed them from the Treaty of New Echota. When Chief Yonaguska lay dying in 1839, he named Thomas as his successor. Because Thomas was the official Cherokee chief and had become a respected businessman and prominent citizen of western North Carolina, he was appointed agent and trustee of the Oconaluftee Cherokees by the federal and North Carolina governments. This gave him control of all the Cherokee funds. During the years leading up to the Civil War, Thomas bought parcels of land for the Oconaluftee Cherokees, holding their lands in trust in his own name. The largest tract was called the Qualla Boundary.

Today, the Cherokee Indian Reservation consists of about fifty-six thousand acres of small reserves, scattered across western North Carolina. However, the entire reservation is often referred to by the name of the largest reserve, the Qualla Boundary.

(For more information on the Qualla Boundary, see "The Eastern Cherokees Rebuild" section in the Overview.)

MUSEUM OF THE CHEROKEE INDIAN

Cherokee

The story of the Eastern Cherokees is told through a variety of media at the Museum of the Cherokee Indian. The museum includes exhibits on the Cherokee belief system; the famous Cherokee legion of William Thomas that fought for the Confederacy in the Civil War; profiles of the principal chiefs of the Eastern Band; and an extensive collection of Mississippian pottery, shell gorgets, arrowheads, and tools. A film about the Qualla reservation and the Eastern Band of the Cherokees runs continuously. The museum also features a bookstore, gift shop, frame shop, and a gallery that sells quality Cherokee art and crafts. The museum houses an extensive library and archives that are open for research only by appointment. Users of the archives must have permission from the museum.

The museum is open daily from 9 A.M. to 8 P.M. from mid-June through August, and from 9 A.M. to 5 P.M. the rest of the year. There is a small admission charge. For information, call 704-497-3481.

The museum is located in the heart of Cherokee at the intersection of U.S. 441 and Drama Road. If coming from the Great Smoky Mountains National Park, the museum is on U.S. 441 at the second traffic light on the right. From Bryson City or Maggie Valley, take U.S. 441 north and watch for signs for the museum. The museum will be on the left, just past the Bureau of Indian Affairs and the Ceremonial Grounds.

OCONALUFTEE INDIAN VILLAGE

Cherokee

Nestled in a forest of rhododendron on the side of a mountain, Oconaluftee Indian Village is a re-created Cherokee village of the 1750s. Operated by the Cherokee Historical Association of the Eastern Band of Cherokee Indians, this realistic village features an authentic seven-sided council house, sweat house, and rustic log cabins. Traditional Cherokee crafts such as weaving, flint-chipping, mask-carving, and canoe-making are demonstrated by colorfully-dressed Cherokee artists. Indian

Museum of the Cherokee Indian

guides explain the Cherokee culture, history, and rituals as they lead the visitor through the village and a small botanical garden.

Oconaluftee Village is open each year from May 15 through October 25. Hours are from 9 A.M. to 5:30 P.M. There is an admission charge. For information, call 704-497-2315 or 704-497-2111.

Oconaluftee Village is located next to the mountainside theater home of *Unto These Hills* on Drama Road. If arriving in Cherokee from Great Smoky Mountains National Park, follow U.S. 441 south to the second traffic light and turn right. If entering Cherokee from Bryson City on N.C. 19, turn left (north) on U.S. 441, then turn left onto Drama Road.

UNTO THESE HILLS

Cherokee

For over forty years, the Eastern Band of the Cherokees has presented the outdoor drama, *Unto These Hills*. This play dramatizes the history of the Eastern Band. The play centers around the story of Tsali and his family, who hid in the North Carolina mountains to escape federal troops. The play's interpretation of Tsali's dramatic story

differs from the version found in military records, but there is no doubt that the deaths of Tsali and his family helped secure the right for a handful of Cherokees to remain in North Carolina. The version of Tsali's story that follows is the romanticized version as related in the play.

Tsali was an old man. His family included his wife, two sons, Ridges and Wasituna, and a brother-in-law, Lowney. In May 1838, when two of General Winfield Scott's soldiers came to Tsali's small farm to take him to the removal stockade, Tsali initially offered no resistance. Somewhere along the trail to the stockade, a soldier prodded Tsali's aging wife with a bayonet after she stumbled and fell. Tsali could not tolerate such an indignity. He and his sons plotted to overpower the soldiers and escape. In the scuffle, one of the soldiers was accidentally killed and the other ran away. Tsali's family hid in the mountains for several months. After most of the Cherokees had been removed from North Carolina, General Scott wanted to move his men out of the area. However, he could not let the "murderers" of his soldier go unpunished. Scott devised a plan which he took to William Holland Thomas. Scott said the Oconaluftee Cherokees, and other Cherokees still hiding in the mountains, could remain in their homes. However, in return,

Tsali and his family would have to turn themselves in. Thomas found Tsali's hiding place and explained the offer from General Scott. To save the rest of his people, Tsali's family surrendered. Tsali, Ridges, and Lowney were executed by a firing squad. Tsali's wife and young son, Wasituna, were spared.

Several important points in this tale are disputed by historians. For example, records indicate that Tsali and his family did not surrender themselves voluntarily. It is also doubtful that William Holland Thomas personally visited Tsali at his hideout in the mountains. Thomas had already received permission for the Oconaluftee Cherokees to remain in North Carolina before Tsali was arrested and executed. Thomas cooperated with General Scott in order not to jeopardize the Oconaluftee Cherokees' position. The Cherokees who found Tsali's hiding place in the mountains were led by Euchella. Euchella and his people were subject to removal because they lived on lands within the Cherokee Nation. By cooperating with Scott's soldiers, Euchella helped secure permission for his small band to remain in the east. Whatever the truth, the story of Tsali and his family has become a symbol of the Oconaluftee Cherokees' long struggle to retain their homelands in the East.

The story of Tsali, and other important stories in the history of the Eastern Cherokees, are depicted in *Unto These Hills*. Performances are held nightly, except Sundays, from mid-June through late-August. Tickets may be purchased in advance or at the box office. For information, call 704-497-2111.

From the Great Smoky Mountains National Park, take U.S. 441 to the second traffic light in Cherokee. The box office is located on U.S. 441, across from the Museum of the Cherokee Indian. The theater is on Drama Road, which is opposite the box office. From Bryson City, take N.C. 19 to Cherokee and turn left (north) onto U.S. 441.

CHEROKEE CEREMONIAL GROUNDS

Cherokee

The Cherokee Ceremonial Grounds are housed in a large building next to the ball ground in the heart of the Cherokee community. Several times each year, the ceremonial grounds host powwows that attract Native American dancers and musicians from all over the United States. Annual events include the Ramp Festival, held the first week of April in honor of the small wild onion called the ramp, and the Cherokee Indian Fall Festival, held the first week of October. Many of these events are open to the public, but photographs should be taken only with permission of the subjects. For information and dates, call 704-497-3028.

From the Great Smoky Mountains National Park, take U.S. 441 into Cherokee. The Ceremonial Grounds will be on the right side of U.S. 441, after the second traffic light and past the Museum of the Cherokee Indian. From Bryson City, take N.C. 19 to Cherokee and turn left (north) onto U.S. 441. The Ceremonial Grounds will be on the left, a little past the Bureau of Indian Affairs.

BIG COVE AND MINGO FALLS

Cherokee

Big Cove is one of the largest voting precincts in the Qualla Boundary. The Qualla Boundary has five other voting precincts: Yellowhill, Birdtown, Painttown, Cheroah, and Wolftown. Each of these voting precincts elects two representatives to the tribal council every two years. Since much of Big Cove lies within the Great Smoky Mountains National Park, and the rest is somewhat isolated from the tourist center of Cherokee, Big Cove remains one of the prettiest areas in the Qualla Boundary.

There are several campgrounds in the Big Cove area and Raven Fork Creek is popular for fishing. Qualla Boundary's most accessible and popular waterfall, Mingo Falls, is located in Big Cove.

To reach Big Cove and Mingo Falls from the Great Smoky Mountains National Park, take U.S. 441 to Cherokee. At the first light, turn left onto Acquoni Road and cross the river to Saunook Village. Coming from U.S. 74, take U.S. 441 through Cherokee. Acquoni Road will be the last traffic light before the Great Smoky Mountains National Park. From Acquoni Road, take the first left onto Big Cove Road. Mingo Falls Campground will be on the right, 4.9 miles from Acquoni Road. Turn right and cross the wooden bridge at the campground. Park in the spots which have been designated for falls parking. The trail to Mingo Falls is only about 0.25 mile one-way. The first section is a little steep, but it is worth the trip. After viewing the falls, you can return to Big Cove Road and drive several more miles into Big Cove to enjoy the scenic beauty of this area.

Mingo Falls

Keener Craft Shop

KEENER CRAFT SHOP AND CHEROKEE UNITED METHODIST CHURCH

Cherokee

Ever since the first missions in Cherokee country were established in the early 1800s, Christianity has played an important part in the religious and social structure of the Cherokee Nation. Several small churches of varying denominations are located in the Qualla Boundary. One of the oldest churches, originally established in 1830 as the Echota Mission, is the Cherokee United Methodist Church. Today, the church is a large, modern, stone structure located on the site of the original mission. The first resident missionary to the Qualla Cherokees was the Reverend Horace Ulrich Keener. His parsonage still stands adjacent to the modern church. The parsonage was built in the mid-1840s and later served as a school and then a craft shop. It still stands adjacent to the church.

The parsonage and church are located on U.S. 19 on the east side of Cherokee. From the Great Smoky Mountains National Park, take U.S. 441 to Cherokee. In Cherokee, turn left at the traffic light at the intersection of U.S. 19 and U.S. 441. Drive past the Cherokee Visitor Center on Soco Road. The parsonage and church will be on the left in a few miles.

SOCO GAP AND SOCO CREEK

Soco Gap was known to the Cherokees as Ahalunun'yi, "ambush place," or Uni'halu'na, "where they ambushed." It received its name when the Cherokees ambushed a party of invading Shawnees on the northeast (Haywood County, North Carolina) side of the gap. All of the Shawnees were killed, except one who was sent back to tell his people of the Cherokee victory at the gap.

The gap, which marks the eastern point of the Qualla Boundary, has always played an important role in defense of the Oconaluftee and Tuckasegee villages. The Cherokees often kept lookouts posted there to watch for enemies from the north. The headwaters of Soco Creek originate near the gap and the creek flows southwest into the Oconaluftee River. Soco Creek was called Sagwa'hi or Sagwun'yi by the Cherokees, meaning "one place." It was at Soco Creek that the legendary Shawnee chief Tecumseh appealed to the Cherokees to join forces with his band of confederated tribes.

207 ▲ ▲ ▲

Qualla Boundary marker at Soco Gap

THE WILLIAM HOLLAND THOMAS GRAVE

Cherokee

Although William Holland Thomas was not Cherokee, he is one of the most important figures in the history of the Eastern Band of the Cherokee Indians. Adopted by Chief Yonaguska as a young boy, he went on to become a spokesman for Oconaluftee Cherokees in Washington, D.C. As their spokesman, he was instrumental in gaining permission for the Oconaluftees to stay in western North Carolina after the removal of 1838. Thomas served in the North Carolina senate, built the first wagon road across the Smokies, built railroads, and led the famous legion of Cherokees that served in the Confederate Army. In 1839, Thomas became Principal Chief of the Eastern Cherokees and served in that capacity until he resigned in 1867. The friend and advocate of the Eastern Cherokees is buried in Campground Cemetery, which was established in 1856.

The Cherokees refused. The creek was also the location of a Civil War battle. After burning Waynesville, North Carolina, in February 1865, Colonel George Kirk's Union detachment of six hundred was defeated on Soco Creek by Thomas's Legion.

Soco Gap is located at the junction of U.S. 19 and the Blue Ridge Parkway. From the entrance to the parkway at Great Smoky Mountains National Park, take the parkway 13.5 miles to the gap. From Cherokee, take U.S. 19 east past the Cherokee Visitor Center. U.S. 19 follows Soco Creek up the gap.

From U.S. 74 take U.S. 441 north toward Cherokee. From Cherokee, take U.S. 441 south. The cemetery is on a hill on the west side of U.S. 441, 2.7 miles south of the junction of U.S. 441 and U.S. 19 in Cherokee.

WILLIAM HOLLAND
THOMAS
ᏫᎵ Ꮻ Ꮃ
1805 ⸺ 1893

BUSINESSMAN PLANTER AND AUTHOR
AGENT AND ATTORNEY FOR THE EASTERN CHEROKEES
MEMBER OF THE NORTH CAROLINA STATE SENATE AND
CHAIRMAN OF ITS COMMITTEE ON INTERNAL
IMPROVEMENTS
EARLY RAILROAD BUILDER IN WESTERN NORTH
CAROLINA
BUILDER OF THE FIRST WAGON ROAD ACROSS THE
GREAT SMOKIES
COLONEL OF THE 69TH N.C. REGIMENT
COMMANDER OF THE THOMAS LEGION, C.S.A.
FRIEND AND BENEFACTOR OF THE CHEROKEE PEOPLE

William Holland Thomas grave at Campground Cemetery

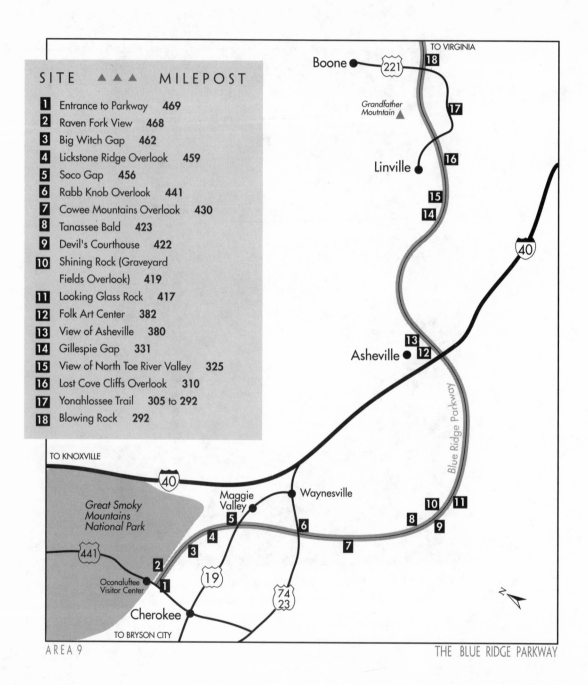

SITE ▲▲▲ MILEPOST

1 Entrance to Parkway **469**
2 Raven Fork View **468**
3 Big Witch Gap **462**
4 Lickstone Ridge Overlook **459**
5 Soco Gap **456**
6 Rabb Knob Overlook **441**
7 Cowee Mountains Overlook **430**
8 Tanassee Bald **423**
9 Devil's Courthouse **422**
10 Shining Rock (Graveyard Fields Overlook) **419**
11 Looking Glass Rock **417**
12 Folk Art Center **382**
13 View of Asheville **380**
14 Gillespie Gap **331**
15 View of North Toe River Valley **325**
16 Lost Cove Cliffs Overlook **310**
17 Yonahlossee Trail **305 to 292**
18 Blowing Rock **292**

TO VIRGINIA

Boone
221
Grandfather Mountain ▲
Linville

TO KNOXVILLE
40
Great Smoky Mountains National Park
441
Oconaluftee Visitor Center
Cherokee
TO BRYSON CITY
19
74 23
Maggie Valley
Waynesville
Blue Ridge Parkway
Asheville

AREA 9   THE BLUE RIDGE PARKWAY

Big Witch Gap

AREA 9

BLUE RIDGE PARKWAY

▲ ▲ ▲

The Blue Ridge Mountains, named for their blue appearance when seen from a distance, are a range of the Appalachian Mountain system which extends from southern Pennsylvania to northern Georgia. The Blue Ridge Parkway, established by an act of Congress in 1936, is a scenic drive covering 469 miles of the majestic range, from Virginia to North Carolina. The parkway begins near Waynesboro, Virginia, and ends near Cherokee, North Carolina. It connects the Shenandoah National Park in the north with the Great Smoky Mountains National Park in the south. Each year, nearly twenty million visitors drive a portion of the Blue Ridge Parkway, or enjoy its facilities. Several campgrounds, restaurants, and lodges are located along the drive. There are many historic, scenic, and tourist attractions accessible from the parkway.

The Blue Ridge Mountains played an important role in Cherokee mythology. Many areas along the parkway take their names from Cherokee legends and stories. One of the most prominent legends in the area involved *Tsul'kalu'*, also called Judaculla, who was a slant-eyed giant who roamed the mountains.

The first twelve miles of the parkway cross the Qualla Boundary, exiting the Cherokee reservation at historic Soco Gap. Just a few miles outside the Qualla Boundary, the parkway rapidly gains elevation.

The Blue Ridge Parkway has many entrances along its 469 miles, and most portions are open year-round. However, sections may be closed in winter or early spring due to snow, ice, or occasional landslides. If traveling in the winter season, it is advisable to allow extra time for a possible detour.

The parkway mileposts are numbered, beginning at the northern end in Virginia. Since the scenic drive described below starts at the southern end of the parkway, the first milepost will be 469, and subsequent mileposts will be in descending order. The sites in this section will end at milepost 292, near Blowing Rock, North Carolina, which is close to the northern boundary of the traditional Cherokee homelands. For information about the Blue Ridge Parkway and road closings, call 704-298-0398.

ENTRANCE TO BLUE RIDGE PARKWAY

Milepost 469

The southern entrance to the Blue Ridge Parkway is located on U.S. 441, between the town of Cherokee and the Oconaluftee Visitor Center of the Great Smoky Mountains National Park. After turning on the parkway and crossing the Oconaluftee River, stop at the kiosks, which have general information about the Blue Ridge Mountains, including the geology and the people who lived there.

RAVEN FORK VIEW

Milepost 468

The Raven Fork River runs through the heart of Big Cove, a section of the Qualla Boundary. The area was originally known as Ka'lanun'yi for "raven place." A view of the area can be seen from this milepost.

The raven is one of several birds that is featured in Cherokee stories. One such legend is the story of how the Cherokees acquired fire. It was the raven who volunteered to be the first animal to try to bring back fire from the bottom of a hollow tree which grew on an island. He flew to the island and perched on the tree, but while he was deciding what to do, the fire scorched his wings. That is why the raven is black. When the raven came back without the fire, the screech owl, hoot owl, and horned owl each tried to bring back the fire, but the smoke scorched their eyes. To this day the screech owl has red eyes from the smoke, and the hoot and horned owls have white rings around their eyes from the ashes that blew in their face. Next, the black racer snake and the great blacksnake tried to bring back the fire, but failed. Like the raven, they were scorched black and remain that color forever. At last, the small water spider volunteered to try. She could

run on top of water so she had no problem reaching the island. Once there, she spun a thread from her body and wove it into a bowl. She then placed a burning coal into the bowl which she fastened to her back. She then crossed the water, bringing the first fire back to the Cherokees.

BIG WITCH GAP

Milepost 462

Tskile'gwa was the oldest man in the Eastern Cherokee tribe when he died in an influenza epidemic in 1896. Known as Big Witch by the white settlers, Tskile'gwa lived in the valley that can be seen from this milepost. He was known for his skill as an eagle-killer, a profession reserved only for those with knowledge of the rituals which must be performed when the sacred bird was killed.

The eagle-killer was hired by the tribe to obtain feathers in preparation for an eagle dance, an important Cherokee ceremony. To prepare for the hunt, the eagle-killer would fast and pray for several days. Then, he would kill a deer and place the carcass on a high cliff. The eagle-killer would position himself nearby and wait for the eagle to arrive. Songs were used to bring the eagle down from the sky. After the bird was shot, another prayer was said to beg the spirit of the bird not to seek vengeance on the Cherokees.

LICKSTONE RIDGE OVERLOOK

Milepost 459

A panoramic view of the Qualla Boundary can be seen from the overlook at milepost 459. Qualla took its name from Kwali, the site of an old trading post and former post office located on a branch of Soco Creek. Kwali, the Cherokee name for Polly, was the name of an old Indian woman who lived nearby, so the area became known as Kwalun'yi, "Polly's Place." (For more information on the Qualla Boundary, see "The Eastern Cherokees Rebuild" section in the Overview, and Area 8, Qualla Boundary.)

SOCO GAP

Milepost 456

The Cherokees had several names for the areas near Soco Gap. Soco Gap was named Ahalunun'yi which means "ambush place." The gap received its name when the Cherokees ambushed a large party of invading Shawnees on the northern side of Soco Gap. The head of Soco Creek begins near the gap and was called Skwan'digu'gun'yi, for "where the Spaniard is in the water." This name referred to a story about a party of Spaniards who were attacked by the Cherokees. In the battle, the Cherokees threw one of the Spanish soldiers into the stream. Soco Creek was called Sagwa'hi or Sagwun'yi, meaning "one place."

At Soco Gap, the parkway crosses U.S. 19. To the north is Maggie Valley. To the south is the Qualla Boundary and the town of Cherokee. (For more information on Soco Gap, see the Soco Gap and Soco Creek section in Area 8.)

RABB KNOB OVERLOOK

Milepost 441

During the American Revolution, the Cherokees allied with the British. Encouraged by British agents like Alexander Cameron and strong leaders like Dragging Canoe, the Cherokees made several attacks on white settlements in bordering states. Realizing the threat to their settlements, the

Americans planned four expeditions against the Cherokees in 1776. General Griffith Rutherford launched an expeditionary force from Davidson's Fort, which was located at the present-day town of Old Fort, North Carolina. During this expedition, he led twenty-four hundred men through the valley of Richland Creek which can be seen from this milepost. After crossing Balsam Gap (which can be viewed at milepost 443), they proceeded down Scott and Savannah creeks to the Middle and Valley settlements, where they destroyed many Cherokee towns.

COWEE MOUNTAINS OVERLOOK

Milepost 430

The Cowee Mountain range and the valley of the Little Tennessee River can be seen from this point on the parkway. The Cherokee town of Cowee, one of the oldest and largest of the Cherokee towns, was located in the Little Tennessee River Valley. A mixed-blood named James D. Wafford, who was born in the Cherokee Nation in

Rabb Knob Overlook

Cowee Mountains Overlook

1806, told a story about a Shawnee Indian who was kept prisoner in Cowee until he escaped. During a period of peace between the two tribes, this Shawnee prisoner wandered back to the area. As he stood on a hill overlooking the valley where Cowee was located, he noticed several Cherokees on the opposite hill. He shouted to them, "Do you still own Cowee?"

The Cherokees replied, "Yes; we own it yet."

The Shawnee, who wanted to encourage the Cherokees not to sell any more land shouted back, "Well, it's the best town of the Cherokee. It's a good country; hold on to it."

TANASSEE BALD

Milepost 423

The Tanassee Bald was known to the Cherokees as Tsunegun'yi, "the white place," because of a bald spot on top of the mountain. Supposedly *Tsul'kalu'*, the slant-eyed giant, cleared this bald for his farm. In Cherokee legend, *Tsul'kalu'* was considered the lord of game, and his name was frequently invoked in Cherokee hunting formulas—prayers or chants that were often accompanied by medicinal treatments or rituals such as dances or fasting.

Tanassee Bald

Tsul'kalu' made his home on Tanassee Bald, but as the lord of game, he traveled all over the Blue Ridge Mountains. Marks left by the giant could be found at such places as Judaculla Rock and Shining Rock Mountain.

Tanassee Bald can be seen from the Devil's Courthouse and several places along the Blue Ridge Parkway. The closest turn-off is the Courthouse Valley Overlook at Milepost 423, where N.C. 215 meets the parkway at Beech Gap. There is a trail that leads to Tanassee Bald at this overlook.

DEVIL'S COURTHOUSE

Milepost 422

In 1838, when Wilbur Zeigler and Ben Grosscup wrote *The Heart of the Alleghanies or Western North Carolina*, they reported a slightly different take on the slant-eyed giant Tsul'kalu'. White settlers told the writers that the Cherokees regarded the area around Tanassee Bald as the special abode of an Indian satan. *Tsul'kalu'* supposedly slept in a cave underneath a massive over-hanging rock, which became known as the Devil's Courthouse.

While you can view Devil's Courthouse from the parking lot at Milepost 422, the short walk from the parking lot to the summit is worth the reward. From the top are panoramic views of the surrounding mountains, including an excellent view of Tanassee Bald where the legendary *Tsul'kalu'* lived. The top of Devil's Courthouse is at an elevation of 5,720 feet, while the parking lot is at 5,462 feet.

SHINING ROCK MOUNTAIN (GRAVEYARD FIELDS OVERLOOK)

Milepost 419

Shining Rock Mountain, located in the Shining Rock Wilderness Area, is the legendary dwelling place of invisible spirits. It was called Datsu'nalasgun'yi, "where their tracks are this way," referring to a rock at the base of the mountain that has markings believed to be the tracks left by *Tsul'kalu'*.

There are several trails leading to Shining Rock Mountain. One of the trails leaves from the Graveyard Fields parking lot and is a little over 4 miles one-way. This route takes the hiker through the eerie Graveyard Fields and Ridge, which received their names because the gray spruce trunks and

View from Devil's Courthouse

▲ ▲ ▲

stumps reminded the locals of a graveyard. The trail is accessible from the Graveyard Fields Overlook at Milepost 419.

LOOKING GLASS ROCK

Milepost 417

Looking Glass Rock received its name from the way light reflects off its surface when the rock is wet. The Cherokees called it the Devil's Looking Glass because it is close to Tanassee Bald and the Devil's Courthouse, both associated with the legend of *Tsul'kalu'*. The rock is whiteside granite, which has been exposed by erosion. The overlook at Milepost 417 provides an excellent view of Looking Glass Rock, and there are several other good viewpoints for the next 3 miles on the parkway.

SOUTHERN HIGHLAND CRAFT GUILD/FOLK ART CENTER

Milepost 382

The Folk Art Center, located in a multi-level, modern building on the Blue Ridge Parkway, features the finest work of regional craftspeople. The center contains a gallery, craft shop, museum, library, bookstore, and administrative offices for the Southern Highland Craft Guild. Changing exhibits showcase the work of guild members, including Cherokee artists from the Qualla Arts and Crafts Guild—a member of the Southern Highland Craft Guild since 1949. The works of individual Cherokee artists are included in the permanent collection at the Folk Art Center.

The Folk Art Center is open daily from 9 A.M. to 5 P.M., January 1 through March 31. Closing hour is extended to 6 P.M. from April 1 to December 31. The center is closed on Thanksgiving, Christmas, and New Year's Day. The museum, gallery, and craft shop are closed periodically for inventory and exhibition changes. Admission is free. For information, call 704-298-7928.

VIEW OF ASHEVILLE

Milepost 380

A view of the city of Asheville can be seen from Milepost 380. Asheville's name comes from the Cherokee name Kasdu'yi, or "ashes place." The area was originally called Unta' kiyasti' yi, "where they race," because the Cherokees held foot races here.

▲ ▲ ▲ 220 *Blue Ridge Parkway*

The third weekend of each September the High Country Art & Craft Guild of Asheville sponsors "Kituwah: The American Indian National Exhibition of Art & Education." The festival features Native American artists, dancers, storytellers, and musicians from all over the United States. Other features at the festival include Native American food, a children's art show, and special educational exhibits. For information, contact the High Country Art & Craft Guild at 704-252-3880.

GILLESPIE GAP AND THE MUSEUM OF NORTH CAROLINA MINERALS

Milepost 331

The Museum of North Carolina Minerals is located at Gillespie Gap, formerly called Etchoe Pass. The museum houses displays of North Carolina's rich mineral deposits, including precious gems, gold, and

Stone memorial at Gillespie Gap

high-quality, spruce pine quartz—which was used in the Palomar Observatory mirror. Some exhibits explain the Native Americans' use of minerals. Exhibits show how the prehistoric Indian used sheet mica for personal ornamentation and burial decorations. The museum has copies of Hopewell Mica ornaments and casts of prehistoric stone tools taken from the Sink Hole Mine at Bandana in Mitchell County.

Located behind the museum is a stone memorial commemorating two events which occurred in Etchoe Pass. The first was in 1761, when thirty men under the command of Francis Marion—who later was nicknamed the Swamp Fox for his exploits in the American Revolution—were sent to dislodge Cherokee warriors from the pass. Marion's militia battled the Cherokees in Etchoe Pass, and Marion lost twenty-one men in the battle. The second was in 1780, when troops under the command of John Sevier, Isaac Shelby, and William Campbell passed through the gap on their way to the Battle of Kings Mountain in South Carolina.

The Museum of North Carolina Minerals is open daily from 9 A.M. to 5 P.M. It is closed on Thanksgiving and the day before Thanksgiving, three days at Christmas, and on New Year's Eve and Day. It is also closed on Mondays and Tuesdays during the winter. When the museum is closed, the monument is still accessible by a walkway on the left side of the building. Admission is free. For information, call 704-765-9483.

VIEW OF
NORTH TOE RIVER VALLEY

Milepost 325

The Toe River, which can be viewed from this milepost, received its name from a Cherokee legend about a heart-broken Cherokee princess. It was originally known as the Estatoe River and was supposedly named for Estatoe, a Cherokee chief's daughter who fell in love with the son of a rival chief. Heart-broken because her father refused to let her marry the young man, Estatoe drowned herself in the river. Named in her memory, the river was later called simply the Toe. In addition to the river, Estatoe was also the name of a heavily-traveled Indian trading path, the Estatoe Trail. The Estatoe Trail connected the mountain villages with the Cherokee town of Estatoe in South Carolina. The trail crossed the North and South Carolina state lines at Rosman, North Carolina, and passed through Brevard, North Carolina.

LOST COVE CLIFFS
OVERLOOK

Milepost 310

The Lost Cove Cliffs Overlook is one of many vantage points along the Blue Ridge Parkway where you can view Brown Mountain, located approximately nine miles southwest. Brown Mountain is the home of the mysterious Brown Mountain lights— unexplainable lights that can be seen on the mountain. People who have seen the lights have given various descriptions, ranging from white, shining stars to lights that change colors before vanishing.

There have been numerous attempts at scientific or natural explanations for the lights. Explanations vary from theories that they are nitrous vapors igniting into flames, to railroad lights, to brush fires. None of these explanations have been fully accepted. The Cherokees also had a theory about the lights. They believed the lights originated from an ancient battle. The legend says that sometime around the year 1200 A.D., the Catawbas and Cherokees fought on top of Brown Mountain. According to the legend, the Brown Mountain Lights come from the Cherokee women who still search for their dead husbands on the mountain.

U.S. 221—the Yonahlossee Trail— near Grandfather Mountain

YONAHLOSSEE TRAIL

Milepost 305 to Milepost 292

The Yonahlossee Trail, a road built on an old Indian trail, received its name from the Cherokee word for Black bear, *yanu.* In 1899, the Yonahlossee Trail was built along the Indian path by Hugh McRae, who wanted to run a stagecoach from the popular tourist town of Blowing Rock to his isolated resort at Linville. The Yonahlossee Trail took two years to build and cost eigh-

223 ▲ ▲ ▲

teen thousand dollars. The present-day section of U.S. 221 between Blowing Rock and Linville is built on the original Yonahlossee Trail. For many years, the road served as the connector road for the unfinished section of the Blue Ridge Parkway at Grandfather Mountain. The parkway was finally completed with the building of the Linn Cove viaduct, and now only locals use the Yonahlossee Trail.

To reach the Yonahlossee Trail, exit the parkway at Milepost 305, the Linville and Grandfather Mountain exit, or at Milepost 292, the Boone and Blowing Rock exit. In Blowing Rock, U.S. 221 can be reached by turning right after exiting the parkway and driving through the village of Blowing Rock.

BLOWING ROCK PARK

Blowing Rock, Milepost 292

For those who are not familiar with the area, some clarification about Blowing Rock may be helpful. There are actually two locations known as Blowing Rock. A prominent rock formation which hangs over the Johns River Valley is called the Blowing Rock. This natural phenomenon is now part of Blowing Rock Park. To complicate things further, the rock and park are located in the village of Blowing Rock.

There are many legends surrounding the Blowing Rock. The legend of how this popular tourist attraction received its name begins with a Chickasaw chief and his daughter who left their homelands to live near the rock. The chief left his home because he wanted to protect his daughter from the admiration of a white man. One day, as the girl was sitting on the craggy cliff, she noticed a Cherokee brave who was traveling through the valley below and playfully shot an arrow at him. The brave acknowledged the small flirtation and eventually began to court the girl.

Several months later, as the pair sat atop the Blowing Rock, the sky darkened and turned red. The young brave recognized this as a sign that he must return to his home. Torn between duty to his people and love for his maiden, the brave threw himself over the cliff. Grief-stricken, the girl prayed to the Great Spirit to return her lover to her. Taking pity on the lovers, the Great Spirit created a powerful gust of wind that blew the young brave back up onto the rock from the valley below. Ever since, the wind has blown continuously at the site. According to the legend, objects thrown over the edge of the Blowing Rock will be returned by the wind.

Blowing Rock Park is a privately-owned attraction. The park has an observation platform, gift shop, snack shop, and of course, the Blowing Rock. The park is open daily from 8 A.M. to dark, March through November. Hours are extended to 8 P.M. in the summer. In winter, the park is open on weekends, weather permitting. There is an admission charge. For information, call 704-295-7111.

To reach Blowing Rock Park, exit the Blue Ridge Parkway near Milepost 292 onto U.S. 321 Bypass. Continue straight on U.S. 321 South when U.S. 321 Business turns off to the right. Just past the Green Park Inn, turn right at the large gray wooden sign for Blowing Rock Park.

The Blowing Rock

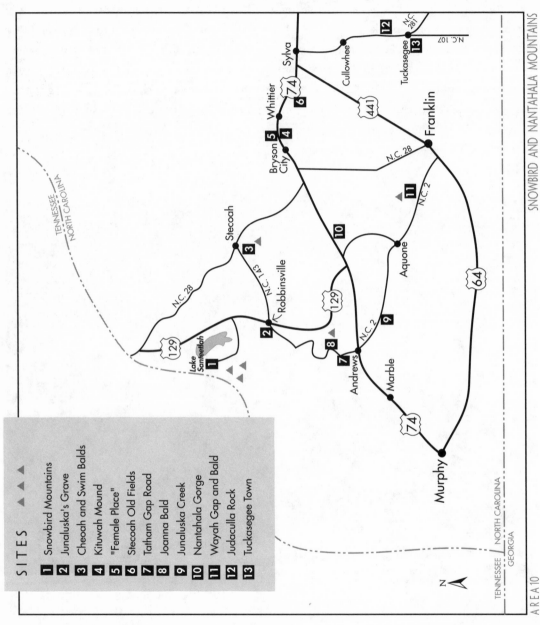

SNOWBIRD AND NANTAHALA MOUNTAINS

AREA 10

SITES ▲▲▲

1 Snowbird Mountains
2 Junaluska's Grave
3 Cheoah and Swim Balds
4 Kituwah Mound
5 "Female Place"
6 Stecoah Old Fields
7 Tatham Gap Road
8 Joanna Bald
9 Junaluska Creek
10 Nantahala Gorge
11 Wayah Gap and Bald
12 Judaculla Rock
13 Tuckasegee Town

TENNESSEE / NORTH CAROLINA

TENNESSEE / NORTH CAROLINA
GEORGIA

N

Santeetlah Lake in the Snowbird Mountains

SNOWBIRD AND NANTAHALA MOUNTAINS

▲ ▲ ▲

The Nantahala and Snowbird mountains comprise a large part of the Nantahala National Forest, which covers most of the southwestern corner of the North Carolina. The Snowbird Mountains lie in Graham and Cherokee counties, with the town of Robbinsville on their eastern edge and the town of Andrews on their southern edge. The Nantahala Mountains. located primarily in Macon County, stretch from the

Nantahala River in the north to the border of North and South Carolina. There are outlets for many recreational activities in the Nantahala and Snowbird mountains, including fishing, boating, whitewater sports, hunting, and camping. Miles of hiking trails, including the Appalachian and Bartram trail systems, crisscross these mountains.

Northeast of Robbinsville and Santeetlah Lake lies the Joyce Kilmer Memorial Forest—a protected virgin forest of immense trees, some twenty feet in diameter at the base and over one hundred feet tall. This forest is one of the few remaining remnants of wilderness that has been virtually untouched by man. Part of the fourteen-thousand-acre Joyce Kilmer-Slick Rock Wilderness Area, Joyce Kilmer Memorial Forest is dedicated to the author of the lovely poem "Trees."

Long before the white settlers arrived in the area, the Cherokees hunted in the forest, fished the abundant streams, and told stories of mythical animals who lived in the remotest parts of the Nantahala and Snowbird mountains. Legends included the tales of *Dotsi*, a water monster whose dwelling place now lies beneath Fontana Lake; of *U'lagu'*, the giant yellow jacket who carried off small animals and children. These legends live on through the many Cherokee families who still live in these mountains.

SNOWBIRD MOUNTAINS

The Snowbird Mountains received their name from the Cherokee word, Tuti'yi, meaning "Snowbird Place." Tuti'yi was the Cherokee name of Little Snowbird Creek, which empties into the Cheoah River near Robbinsville. Many Cherokee families, whose ancestors did not move west in the 1830s, still reside in these beautiful mountains.

The Snowbird community can trace its roots to the Cherokee town of Cheowa, or Tsiya'hi, meaning "otter place." The town was located on the Cheowa, now spelled Cheoah, River near the present-day town of Robbinsville. Although Cheowa was within the boundaries of the Cherokee Nation and all of its people were subject to removal, most of the Snowbird Cherokees managed to cling to their ancestral lands by purchasing the property from North Carolina. The result was several small Cherokee reserves, interspersed with white-owned land.

William Thomas had a trading post at

Fort Montgomery which was located at the town of Cheowa. The trading post was opened during the removal years and operated until the Civil War.

In several cases, the families of the Snowbird Cherokees have lived in the mountains for hundreds of years. Small Cherokee reserves, belonging to traditional Cherokee families, are scattered throughout the area near the Santeetlah and Hiwassee lakes. These reserves are part of the Cheoah Township, one of six political districts of the Eastern Band of Cherokees. The scattered arrangement of the Cheoah Township is unlike the Qualla Reservation, which is composed of two large blocks of land. Ironically, the Snowbird Cherokees of today, who have many white neighbors and are active in Graham County affairs, have remained more traditional and intermarried less with whites than the Cherokees of the Qualla Boundary. According to Sharlotte Neely, author of *Snowbird Cherokees, People of Persistence*, the first Indian-white intermarriage did not occur in the Snowbird community until around 1960.

To visit the Snowbird Mountains and community, take U.S. 129 north from U.S. 74/19 to Robbinsville. From the junction of U.S. 129 and U.S. 143 in Robbinsville, drive another 1.4 miles north

to the sign for Cheoah Ranger Office and Joyce Kilmer Memorial Forest. Turn left onto N.C. 1116 and drive approximately 3.3 miles to where N.C. 1116 ends. Turn right onto N.C. 1127, also called Kilmer Road, and drive 1.2 miles to the Snowbird Picnic Area, located where N.C. 1127 crosses Snowbird Creek. This is a scenic drive which skirts Santeetlah Lake. From the picnic area, you can explore scenic Snowbird Creek by following Kilmer Road another 0.8 mile before the road begins to climb into the mountains. Or you can decide to explore either the Snowbird community or the Snowbird Mountains.

The Snowbird community lies south and west of Santeetlah Lake. There are many small roads into the Snowbird community between the Cheoah Ranger Office and the point where Kilmer Road starts its steep ascent. It is easy to get lost on the backroads, so a stop at the Cheoah Ranger Office to purchase a map of the Nantahala National Forest might be worthwhile.

An alternative to exploring the scattered Snowbird community is to visit Joyce Kilmer Memorial Forest, which is located 7.5 miles north of the Snowbird Picnic Area. Maple Springs Observation Point, which provides magnificent views of the Snowbird Mountains and Santeetlah Lake, is also a popular destination and is only another 4.4 miles beyond the turn for Joyce Kilmer Memorial Forest. Both the Joyce Kilmer Memorial Forest and Maple Springs Observation Point are reached by following N.C. 1116 (Kilmer Road) north into the mountains.

JUNALUSKA'S GRAVE

Robbinsville

Cherokee Chief Junaluska was first known as Gul'kala'ski. According to James Mooney, *gul'kala'ski* refers to something

Grave of Chief Junaluska and wife Nicie

habitually falling from a leaning position. During the War of 1812, the Shawnee chief Tecumseh tried to persuade the Cherokees to join an Indian alliance with the British against the Americans. Junaluska, and other prominent Cherokee leaders, persuaded the Cherokees not to join Tecumseh. Instead, Junaluska raised a group of Cherokee warriors to fight with American forces in the Creek War. At some point, Junaluska boasted that he would exterminate all the Creeks. Although he distinguished himself at the Battle of Horseshoe Bend, he did not live up to his boast. Because of his failure to fulfill his prediction, he received the name Tsunu'lahun'ski, meaning "one who tries but fails."

In 1838, Junaluska, which is corrupted from Tsunu'lahun'ski, went west during the removal. He lost a wife and several members of his family on the Trail of Tears. He later returned to the East and remarried. In 1847, the North Carolina legislature awarded him citizenship and a tract of land near Robbinsville for his services during the Creek War and as restitution for the land he lost during the removal.

The graves of Chief Junaluska and his wife, Nicie, are located in the heart of Robbinsville. From U.S. 129/19, turn north at the town of Topton and take U.S. 129 to Robbinsville. Near the city limit, watch for a blue, "Drivers Licenses" sign or green, "Graham County Courthouse" sign and turn left. Go 0.25 mile to the courthouse, which will be on the right. Turn left at the courthouse onto Main Street and drive 0.1 mile to where Main Street bears right. Drive down Main Street another 0.1 mile and watch for the sign for Junaluska's grave on the left. The graves are a short walk up the hill from the sign.

CHEOAH AND SWIM BALDS

Stecoah

The two thousand-mile Appalachian Trail passes through the Snowbird Mountains just before it climbs into the Great Smoky Mountains. A popular section of the trail leads through the scenic Stecoah Gap, just north of the community of Stecoah. The community and gap were both named for the ancient Cherokee town located several miles northeast on the Tuckasegee River. (See the Stecoah Old Fields section in this chapter.)

From Stecoah Gap, it is a little over 8 miles one-way via the Appalachian Trail to Cheoah Bald. Cheoah Bald, and neighboring Swim Bald, were known as Sehwate'yi, the "hornet place." According to legend, a giant hornet had its nest here and was often seen sunning itself on the balds or flying around the mountain. The hornet was so fierce, it drove away anyone who went near the mountain.

Swim and Cheoah balds are visible from Stecoah Gap, which can be reached by taking N.C. 143 from Robbinsville through the communities of Cheoah and Stecoah. There is a parking area at Stecoah Gap for the overlook. A sign at the overlook identifies the Appalachian Trail, which passes through the gap.

The Appalachian Trail at Stecoah Gap

Kituwah Mound

KITUWAH MOUND

Bryson City

While ethnologist James Mooney was living at Qualla, many of the Cherokees he met referred to themselves as *Ani'-Kitu'hwagi*, or "people of Kitu'hwa." For this reason, Mooney believed that Kituwah was the "original nucleus" of the Cherokees. The name *Ani'-Kitu'hwagi* was usually used only on ceremonial occasions, with the name *Ani'-Yun-Wiya*, or "the Principal People," used the balance of the time when the Cherokees referred to themselves.

While it is debatable if Kituwah was the "original nucleus" of the Cherokees, the Kituwah Mound undoubtedly marks the site of one of the oldest Cherokee towns in the southern Appalachians. In the journal of his travels among the Cherokees in 1830, Alexander Cuming describes Kituwah as one of seven "Mother towns," the others being Tannassee, Ustenary, Tellico, Keowee, Noyehee, and Estootowie. According to legend, the mound at Kituwah is said to be the home of a perpetual fire, from which other Cherokee towns would draw their ceremonial fires each year for the Green Corn dance. During the Civil War, when the Cherokee soldiers were camped at Kituwah, they saw smoke

233 ▲ ▲ ▲

rising from the ancient mound. The soldiers believed this smoke came from the perpetual fire inside the mound.

From the Swain County Courthouse in Bryson City, take U.S. 19 east for 3 miles and watch for an old airplane hangar in an open field between the railroad tracks and the Tuckasegee River. The mound will be several hundred feet to the left and rear of the hangar, in the middle of the field. It may be difficult to distinguish the low rise of the mound from the rest of the field. The mound is located on private property and should be viewed from the shoulder of the road. The mound can also be reached from Cherokee by taking U.S. 19 southwest past Ela.

"FEMALE PLACE" ON TUCKASEGEE RIVER

Bryson City

Gisehun'yi, also known as Agisiyi, is a spot on the Tuckasegee River where some supernatural "white people" were seen washing their clothes and placing them on the bank to dry. The phrase "white" probably refers to magical qualities, and the women may have been from the family of the *Agis'-e'gwa*, or "Great Female," a spirit who could be invoked by conjurers.

To reach the "Female Place," take U.S. 19 east for 2.0 miles from the Swain County Courthouse in Bryson City. From Cherokee, take U.S. 19 southwest past Ela. The Female Place is located at the bridge where U.S. 19 crosses the Tuckasegee River.

STECOAH OLD FIELDS

Whittier

Stecoah was the name of a Cherokee village located in present-day Jackson, North Carolina, along the Tuckasegee River. Stecoah, whose meaning has been lost over time, was also the name of other Cherokee towns, including one located near Clayton, Georgia, and one in Graham County, North Carolina. The Stecoah village located along the Tuckasegee was one of the Middle Towns, a group of towns centered around the Tuckasegee River that spoke the Kituwah dialect. The Tuckasegee settlements are thought to be very old. The Cherokees referred to the area where the village of Stecoah was located as the Stecoah Old Fields because of its age.

During the 1750s, relations between the

Cherokees and English were strained. The leaders of the Lower Town of Keowee, one of the most influential Cherokee villages, asked the warriors from Cherokee villages to raid all the traders in Cherokee territory. The Stecoes complied with the request from Keowee, plundering traders' stores in their area. However, most of the traders escaped. When word of the Stecoah uprising spread throughout the Cherokee tribe, fear of reprisal caused other Cherokees to distance themselves from Stecoah.

During the French and Indian War (1754 to 1763), relations between the Cherokees and British were strained again and violence broke out along the frontier. In late June 1761, Colonel James Grant led an expedition against the Middle settlements, and Stecoah was destroyed. In 1776, Captain William Moore led American forces to the Tuckasegee River where they destroyed Stecoah again.

In 1819, the lands along the Tuckasegee River were sold by the Cherokees, and the site of Stecoah fell into the hands of white settlers. After the 1838 removal, William H. Thomas bought the land on the Tuckasegee River where the old town of Stecoah was located. Thomas built a home at the site, which he named Stekoa, after the town.

The site of Stecoah is located on the south bank of the Tuckasegee River, near Whittier. From Asheville or Sylva, take U.S. 74 southwest, or from Murphy, take U.S. 74 northeast. The historical marker for the William H. Thomas home is on the north side of U.S. 74, approximately halfway between Exit 72 for Whittier and Exit 74 for Cherokee. The Thomas home and Stecoah were located across the road and river from the marker. You can view the area from the marker on U.S. 74, or cross the Tuckasegee River for a better view. To cross the river, take Exit 72 for Whittier. In Whittier, take the first left and cross the Tuckasegee River. Then take another left onto Thomas Valley Road and go about 1 mile. Watch for Thomas Valley Farms and the Drexel Heritage Plant, which are in the approximate vicinity of Stecoah Old Fields.

TATHAM GAP ROAD

Andrews

Located at present-day Andrews, the Cherokee village of Valleytown was called Gu'nahitun'yi, meaning "long place," because of the long river valley where it was situated. During the removal of the Cherokees, federal troops had to devise a way to move the Cherokees from Fort Montgomery (in present-day Robbinsville) to Fort Delaney, which was located at Valleytown. There were several roads leading down the valley from Valleytown to Charleston, Tennessee, the final embarkation point for the journey west. But there was not a good road from Fort Montgomery to Valleytown.

To resolve the problem, General Winfield Scott hired James Tatham, a resident of Valleytown, to build a road across the Snowbird Mountains from Fort Montgomery to Fort Delaney. Local residents later named the road Tatham Gap Road, after the man who built it.

The winding, narrow Tatham Gap Road can still be used today. The northern end, traveling over the crest of the Snowbird Mountains, is a gravel road maintained by the U.S. Forest Service. The southern end begins in Andrews and is paved for the first mile.

When driving north on U.S. 19/74, turn right onto Business 19 and go 1.3 miles through the Andrews business district. Business 19 is also Main Street, which turns into Second Street. Watch for the Valleytown Motel on the right. Opposite the motel is Robbinsville Road. Turn left on the road and drive 0.4 mile to U.S. 19. Cross U.S. 19 and continue another 0.25 mile to Stewart Road. Turn right on Stewart, then take the first left onto F.R.

423. (This drive is a total of 0.9 mile from the Valleytown Motel.) In 0.4 mile, turn right onto a gravel road. There should be a sign for the Tatham Gap Road. From the sign and the start of the gravel road, it is 4.2 miles to a right turn for Joanna Bald. Tatham Gap Road continues straight. In 3.2 miles, Tatham Gap Road changes names to Long Creek Road and becomes paved. When Long Creek Road ends in 2.4 miles, turn right to head into Robbinsville.

JOANNA BALD

Andrews

Joanna Bald was originally named Diya'hali'yi, for "Lizard Place," because it was the legendary home of a great gray lizard with a shiny throat. On clear days, the Cherokees believed the giant lizard could be seen stretched out on the rocky slopes sunning itself.

The common gray road lizard, or *diya'hali'* (*Sceloporous undulatus*), frequently found on rocks, fences, or trees, was used by the Cherokees in a number of remedies. The Cherokees believed the way the lizard puffed out and drew its throat in represented the sucking out of poison. The name of the lizard was invoked in chants for cur-

Joanna Bald

ing snake bites. The Cherokees scratched their legs with the claws of live lizards to ward off dangerous snakes during the summer. They also lightly scratched the heads of children with these claws to help the child sleep soundly.

To reach the "Lizard Place," start in Andrews and follow the directions for Tatham Gap Road. From the sign for Tatham Gap Road at the base of the moun-

tain and the start of the gravel road, it is 4.2 miles up the mountain to a right turn for Joanna Bald. From the turn, it is another 2.9 miles to the top of the mountain where the road ends. From Joanna Bald, return to Tatham Gap Road and turn right. The road will return to pavement in 3.2 miles. When Tatham Gap Road ends in another 2.4 miles, turn right to head into Robbinsville.

JUNALUSKA CREEK

Andrews

Before Junaluska was forced to move west in 1838 with his fellow Cherokees, he had a home between Aquone and Valleytown on a small creek now known as Junaluska Creek. When he returned from the west in 1843, he tried to reclaim his land on Junaluska Creek, but the government wouldn't allow him to have it back. His old log home had been dismantled and transported down the valley. Pieces of it were used to erect the first store in the Valleytown area. Junaluska was later reimbursed for his loss and granted a new tract of land near Robbinsville. (See the section on Junaluska's grave for more on Junaluska.)

To reach Junaluska Creek when driving north on U.S. 19/74, turn right onto Business 19 and drive 1.3 miles through the Andrews business district. Business 19 is also Main Street, which eventually turns into Second Street. Drive past the

Junaluska Creek

Valleytown Motel and Robbinsville Road. The name of the road changes again at a fork in the road. Bear right on Junaluska Road and drive past the Walker Inn which is on the left. Soon you will come to the first bridge over Junaluska Creek. Junaluska was living on a farm about 0.25 mile below this bridge when he and his family were forced to move westward in 1838. The road continues to cross and parallel Junaluska Creek for several more miles.

NANTAHALA GORGE

Andrews

Nantahala is from *nundayeli*, the Cherokee word for midday sun. The name refers to the Nantahala Gorge where tall cliffs surrounding the gorge prevent sunlight from reaching the river until after the sun is high in the sky. A Cherokee settlement on the west bank of the river, near the mouth of Briertown Creek, was also sometimes referred to as Nundayeli, although the village's actual name was Kanu'gulayi, or Kanu'gulun'yi, for "brier place." The area was also well known to the Cherokees because *Uw'tsun'ta*, the great bouncing serpent, lived at the widest spot in the

Nantahala River, and the ogress Spearfinger hunted in the gorge.

In 1775, a party of Cherokees led by Attakullakulla met the naturalist William Bartram in the Nantahala Gorge. During the brief encounter, the chief asked Bartram if he was familiar with the name Attakullakulla. Bartram replied that he was. Pleased with the recognition, Attakullakulla responded, "You are welcome in our country as friend and brother." Bartram, however, was shaken by the encounter and left the area.

The Nantahala Gorge is famous for its rugged beauty and excellent whitewater sports. Each summer, thousands of rafters and kayakers journey to the cold, clear waters of the Nantahala River to enjoy a thrilling ride through the gorge. The United States Forest Service has established

Nantahala Gorge

whitewater launch sites on the river. There are many vantage points along U.S. 19 to watch the rafters.

From Bryson City, take U.S. 19 southwest to the Nantahala Gorge. About halfway down the gorge, watch for Ferebee Memorial Recreation Area, which is a good place to picnic and watch the rafters. The Nantahala River launch site is 7.9 miles south of the National Forest sign and below most of the rafting outfitters. From the launch site, take S.R. 1310 (turn left out of the launch-site parking area) and drive 9.3 miles up the Nantahala River and White Oak Creek to Aquone. This drive provides several views of waterfalls and whitewater cascades.

WAYAH GAP

Aquone

Wayah Gap receives its name from the Cherokee word for wolf, and the name probably refers to a time when wolves roamed freely in the southern Appalachians. The Cherokees had another name for Wayah Gap, A'tahi'ta, which means "place where they shouted." This name refers to the Cherokee tale of the great yellow jacket, *U'lagu'*.

In the legend, the people of the village of Briertown on the Nantahala River were plagued by a giant yellow jacket who would swoop down and carry off their children. To track the *U'lagu'*, the villagers prepared a deer with a long string attached to it. *U'lagu'* came to the village and took the deer back to his nest. The hunters of Briertown were able to follow *U'lagu'* because the weight of the deer made it fly slowly along the horizon, and the long white string was visible for miles. The hunters set out in the direction of *U'lagu'*'s path. When they came to Wayah Gap, they could see the yellow jacket's nest on the other side of the valley.

Firetower at Wayah Bald

They built fires around the mouth of the cave where *U'lagu'* made his nest. The smoke killed the giant hornet and all the smaller insects inside. However, some of the yellow jackets that lived there were not in the cave at the time. That is why, today, angry yellow jackets still haunt the woods.

In September 1776, Wayah Gap was the location of a battle between Cherokee forces and South Carolina forces who were attacking the Middle Towns. Colonel Andrew Williamson's army of South Carolinians had already attacked and burned the Lower Towns and was moving north to a prearranged rendezvous with the forces of General Rutherford. Cherokee forces, who were waiting at Wayah Gap, ambushed Williamson's army. The battle was fierce and nearly ended in defeat for Williamson, but his army was able to push on and rendezvous with Rutherford's army.

To reach Wayah Gap from Bryson City, take U.S. 19 southwest to the Nantahala Gorge. Watch for the Nantahala River launch site 7.9 miles south of the national forest sign, below most of the rafting outfitters. Turn left onto S.R. 1310, which will take you past the launch site, and drive 9.3 miles, following the Nantahala River and White Oak Creek to Aquone. From Aquone, it is another 9 miles to F.R. 69 at

Wayah Gap. Turn left onto F.R. 69, a gravel road which will lead you 4.2 miles to Wayah Bald. You can climb to the top of the old stone fire tower at Wayah Bald to get a 360-degree view of the surrounding mountains and valleys.

JUDACULLA ROCK

Cullowhee

Petroglyphs are prehistoric rock carvings, usually consisting of stylized human or animal figures, geometrical designs, or simple symbols. Pictographs have similar motifs as petroglyphs but are painted rather than carved. Petroglyphs carved in Judaculla Rock have been worn by weather and by the hands and feet of curiosity seekers, but most of the shapes on the rock are still distinguishable. Some appear to be animals and animal tracks, while others appear to be human figures, suns, and geometric figures.

The meanings of the petroglyphs at Judaculla Rock are unknown, although there have been several interesting hypotheses. According to Cherokee belief, the markings on Judaculla Rock were made by the slant-eyed giant *Tsul'kalu'*, also known

Judaculla Rock at Caney Fork Creek

as Jutaculla or Judaculla, when he leapt down from his home on Tanasee Bald to Caney Fork Creek. Another theory is that the markings represent the Cherokee victory over the Creeks at the Battle of Taliwa in Georgia.

Pottery fragments and arrowheads found on farmland in the area, and other evidence, suggests there may have been a hunting camp or village near Judaculla Rock, which may indicate why there are animal figures and tracks carved there. Today, a roof has been placed over the rock to help protect it from the weather, but pieces of the rock have been stolen.

Judaculla Rock is located in the scenic farmlands southeast of Cullowhee, North Carolina. From U.S. 74, take Exit 85, and follow Business 23 through East Sylva. In 1.3 miles, turn left onto N.C. 107 at a traffic light. Drive 5 miles to Western Carolina University, and then drive 3 more miles south on N.C. 107. Watch for a silver plaque for Judaculla Rock on the left side of N.C. 107 that directs you to turn east onto County Road (C.R.) 1737. Drive 2.5 miles down this scenic, winding road, then watch for a green sign directing you to Judaculla Rock. Turn left onto a gravel road at the sign. In 0.45 mile, watch for another green sign for Judaculla Rock.

Park on the right side of the road and walk down the gravel path to the shelter.

TUCKASEGEE TOWN

Tuckasegee

Tuckasegee comes from the Cherokee word *tsiksi'tsi*. James Mooney does not give a meaning for the word *tsiksi'tsi*, but historian Hiram C. Wilburn translates the name as "traveling terrapin." It probably refers to the slow movement of the forks of the Tuckasegee River in the vicinity of the village. Tuckasegee village was established sometime prior to 1730.

Archaeological excavations at the site of Tuckasegee revealed a structure believed to be the townhouse of the village. The structure was round and twenty-three feet in diameter. The outer wall posts were set four feet apart, and there were four sets of paired posts in the interior of the structure for support. A fire basin was located in the center of the structure and the smoke hole above the fire basin was made of clay plaster to protect the roof. Evidence that the location had been used periodically by earlier Native Americans, beginning in the Archaic period, was also found at the site.

Site of Tuckasegee Town

In 1751, angry warriors in the Cherokee village of Keowee asked the neighboring Cherokee villages to kill all of the traders in Cherokee country. Warriors from the nearby village of Stecoah heeded the call from Keowee, and attacked and plundered the traders' stores in their vicinity. However, most of the traders escaped into the mountains. Many made their way to Fort Ninety Six in South Carolina, or to Augusta, Georgia. (See the Stecoah section for more information on these events.) One white trader, Bernard Hughes, lived at Stecoah. Hughes's Indian mistress warned him of the impending attack. She also told Hughes that Slave-Catcher, one of the leaders of the Cherokee village of Kituwah, had specifically demanded Hughes's death.

Fearing the Stecoah Cherokees would carry out Slave-Catcher's demands, Hughes made his way to Tuckasegee (also known as Tsiksi'tsi). An influential white trader in Tuckasegee, Robert Bunning, demanded that the headmen of Tuckasegee protect Hughes. Then Bunting asked The Raven of Hiwassee to intervene with the Stecoah Cherokees on Hughes' behalf. When the Raven's negotiating party arrived at Stecoah, they found it deserted. Realizing they had acted alone in the failed enterprise and fearing reprisal, the Stecoah Cherokees had fled to the mountains to hide. Eventually, the Stecoah Cherokees returned from their hiding places and apologized to Hughes. They returned all of his goods except for four hundred pounds of deer skins and some damaged goods.

Tuckasegee was burned by John Sevier's Tennessee forces in 1781.

To reach the site of Tuckasegee from U.S. 74, take Exit 85, which is Business 23 through East Sylva. In 1.3 miles, turn left onto N.C. 107 at a traffic light. In 5 miles, Cullowhee and Western Carolina University will be on your left. The site of Tuckasegee is another 6.7 miles south of the university. Stop at the bridge where N.C. 107 crosses the Tuckasegee River, just south of the junction with N.C. 281. The town of Tuckasegee was located in a field on the north bank of the Tuckasegee River, to the right (west side) of the road. This is opposite the West Fork of the Tuckasegee River. The site is on private land but can be viewed from the road.

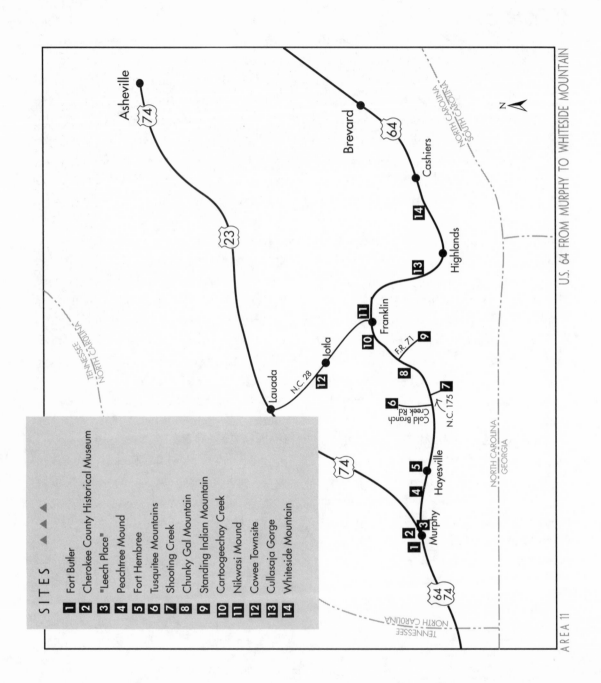

SITES ▲▲▲

▲ ▲ ▲

1 Fort Butler
2 Cherokee County Historical Museum
3 "Leech Place"
4 Peachtree Mound
5 Fort Hembree
6 Tusquitee Mountains
7 Shooting Creek
8 Chunky Gal Mountain
9 Standing Indian Mountain
10 Cartoogechay Creek
11 Nikwasi Mound
12 Cowee Townsite
13 Cullasaja Gorge
14 Whiteside Mountain

U.S. 64 FROM MURPHY TO WHITESIDE MOUNTAIN

AREA 11

Site of Fort Butler on the Hiwassee River

U.S. 64 FROM MURPHY TO WHITESIDE MOUNTAIN

▲ ▲ ▲

U.S. 64, which stretches for hundreds of miles across the United States, was once a major highway connecting east and west. Starting near the four corners area in Arizona, it passes through New Mexico, Oklahoma, Arkansas, Tennessee, and North Carolina, before finally ending on Bodie Island on the Outer Banks of North Carolina. Many sites tied to Cherokee history are located on or near the route, including

Fort Smith, Fort Gibson, and Sequoyah's Home in Oklahoma, and Nancy Ward's grave, Fort Marr, the Old Copper Road, and Ducktown in East Tennessee. The beauty of the rugged mountains and waterfalls of East Tennessee and western North Carolina make the stretch of U.S. 64 from Cleveland, Tennessee, to Hendersonville, North Carolina, one of the most scenic drives in the entire United States. The following chapter explores the western North Carolina portion of the drive, beginning in Murphy at the site of Fort Butler.

FORT BUTLER

Murphy

Fort Butler was one of several North Carolina forts built during the 1838 removal. It was located on the Valley River at present-day Murphy. In preparation for the removal, the federal government established a network of forts throughout the Cherokee territory. Other preparations included military intelligence reports. One of these reports, written from Fort Butler by Captain W.G. Williams and dated "8th of Febry 1838," was addressed to Colonel T.T.

Hubbard in Washington. It described the location of several of the forts in western North Carolina:

"Fort Lindsay is at the eastern side of the mouth of Nantayeelee. Fort Delaney is on Konchete or Valley river about 16 miles from its mouth. Fort Butler is opposite the mouth of Konchete on the south bank of the Hiwassee and Fort Hembrie is near the south bank of the Hiwassee, 16 miles from Fort Butler."

Today, we know the location of Fort Lindsay was at the eastern end of Fontana Lake. Fort Delaney was located in present-day Andrews. The Fort Butler site was in Murphy, and Fort Hembrie (also called Fort Hembree) was in present-day Hayesville.

In January 1837, William Thomas, who was serving as an Indian agent at the time (he had not yet become chief of the Eastern Cherokees), went to New Echota, Georgia, to ask General John Ellis Wool for permission to build a store near Fort Butler. Wool granted permission for the store, and in February, Thomas began construction. Three weeks after construction began, Captain Moses Cunningham, the commander at Fort Butler, stopped the work on the store. Cunningham said he was under orders from General Wool to tear down the building because it was within one mile of the fort. Thomas rented a cabin to store his goods and headed for New Echota to see General Wool. By this time, General Wool had voluntarily resigned as head of the Cherokee removal effort and had been replaced by Colonel William Lindsay. At New Echota, Thomas learned that two of his competitors had ingratiated themselves with General Wool and his associates and had built a store even closer to the fort than Thomas's planned store. Thomas appealed to both Colonel Lindsay and Edward B. Dudley, the governor of North Carolina, to let him build his store at the fort. Thomas argued that he should be allowed to open his store because he was an honest businessman, unlike his competitors. His competitors were also selling liquor to the Indians, and Thomas's store would not. Based on testimony of people who knew Thomas, Lindsay was persuaded that Thomas was a reputable merchant and allowed Thomas to build his store at Fort Butler.

Thomas owned other stores in Cherokee country. They were located at Nottely (in present-day Cherokee County), Fort Delaney at Valleytown (in present-day Andrews), Fort Montgomery at Cheoah (in present-day Robbinsville), Fort Cass at Calhoun, Tennessee, Quallatown (in present-day Cherokee), and Scott's Creek (in Jackson County). His stores at Quallatown and Scott's Creek served the Oconaluftee Indians who remained in North Carolina. The stores located near the forts primarily served the troops stationed there and the Cherokees who were being deported.

In spite of the network of forts in North Carolina and the diligence of the soldiers, many Cherokee families in the Valley River area managed to escape removal. These included at least twenty-four families from the Valley River area, six from the Hiwassee River area, and two from the Peachtree settlement. As a result, today there are several small Cherokee reserves located in Cherokee County between Murphy and Hiwassee Lake.

From Interstate 75, take U.S. 64 east to Murphy. In Murphy, watch for the Murphy Visitor Center on the right and drive 0.4 mile to Hiwassee Street, which will be a left turn at a traffic light. (If you reach the right turn for U.S. 64, then you have gone one block too far.) Take Hiwassee Street, which is Business 19, 0.4 mile to where it crosses the Hiwassee River. There will be a historical marker for Fort Butler and a small park at the river. The sign indicates that Fort Butler was located 0.25 mile southwest on the hill above the park.

Cherokee County Historical Museum

of Fort Butler. Native rocks and minerals, old weapons, and Spanish artifacts, including a sixteenth-century halbred, are also shown in the collection. In front of the museum is the large *Nuya Saligugi*, a stone turtle, which was found in a prehistoric soapstone quarry near the Nottely River west of Murphy.

The museum is open Monday through Friday from 9 A.M. to 5 P.M. For information, call 704-837-6792. From U.S. 64 in Murphy, turn north onto Peachtree Street at the red light. The museum, whose address is 205 Peachtree Street, is located at the corner of Alpine and Peachtree streets.

CHEROKEE COUNTY HISTORICAL MUSEUM

Murphy

This small museum is located on the second floor of the old Carnegie Library building, a red-brick building built in 1922 in the heart of Murphy. The museum features Cherokee artifacts, exhibits about the Peachtree Mound excavation, and a model

TLANUSI'YI

Murphy

The Cherokee name for Murphy was Tlanusi'yi, meaning "Leech Place." Other ways of spelling the Cherokee word for present-day Murphy were Quoneashee, Klausuna, and Clenuse. The Leech Place was a spot on the Valley River in Murphy, just above the junction with the Hiwassee River, where there is a deep hole in the river. The Cherokees believed a giant, red-and-white-striped leech lived in the river.

The "Leech Place" on the Valley River in Murphy

The leech sometimes made the water foam and boil. When someone came near the river, the leech would create a great wave to wash the person into the river. The victim might be lost forever or later found dead with their nose and ears eaten off. The Nottely River also contained a deep hole a few miles from the Leech Place. The Cherokees thought a subterranean waterway at these two holes connected the Nottely River with the Valley River. A marked log was supposedly dropped in the hole on the Nottely River and was later found at the deep hole on the Valley River.

The village of Tlanusi'yi was located at the junction of the Hiwassee and Valley rivers. A famous Cherokee chief, Nimrod Jarrett Smith, was born near this settlement on January 3, 1837. Smith's mother was a full-blood Cherokee, his father was part white. Smith served as a sergeant in William Thomas's Legion during the Civil War. Later, Smith served as clerk of the council that wrote a constitution for the new Eastern Cherokee government which was inaugurated on December 1, 1870. Nimrod Jarrett Smith served as principal chief of the Eastern Band from 1880 to 1891. He died in 1893 and is buried in Cherokee, North Carolina.

The Leech Place is located beneath the bridge where Tennessee Street crosses the Valley River in Murphy. From the Cherokee County Museum, go right (north) on Peachtree Street past the distinctive blue marble courthouse and the town center. The road will change names to Tennessee Street. Drive another 0.4 mile to the bridge. If coming from the site of Fort Butler, continue on Hiwassee Street to the top of the hill. Turn left at the light in the center of town onto Tennessee Street and go 0.4 mile.

PEACHTREE MOUND

Peachtree

Very little remains of the ancient Peachtree Mound. Comprehensive excavations in 1885 and 1933 dismantled the large mound, and the site is now a corn field. The Smithsonian Institution's excavation in 1933 reported that the site had been occupied continuously by Native Americans since the Archaic period. Pottery shards have confirmed the presence of Indians from the Woodland and Middle Mississippian periods. Evidence of buildings from the Middle Mississippian period, including a sweat house, were also found at the site. The site actually contained two mounds, one having been built on top of the other. On the larger, secondary mound, there was evidence of three ceremonial buildings. The mound also contained sixty-eight burial sites.

Some archaeologists have suggested that Spanish artifacts found at Peachtree Mound indicate the site was the location of Guasili, a town visited by De Soto in 1540. However, the Spanish artifacts may be from the 1567 Juan Pardo expedition, or an even later Spanish expedition.

In 1735, the French forced the Natchez Indians from their homelands on the Mississippi River. Many Natchez Indians moved to a site on Peachtree Creek north of the old mound. They established a village there and were eventually absorbed into the Cherokee Nation. In the early 1800s, a Baptist mission was founded at the Natchez village, and the vicinity is still known as the Mission Area.

Although many of the Cherokees in neighboring Valley and Middle towns managed to escape removal, the Indians at Peachtree did not fare as well. In an 1840 census of Cherokees who remained in the East, only two Cherokee families (eleven people) from Peachtree Creek were counted.

In Murphy, U.S. 64 bears right at a light at the junction with U.S. 19/74. Follow U.S. 64 south for 3.4 miles to the confluence of Peachtree Creek and the Hiwassee River on the right side of the road. There will be a historical marker for De Soto by the road, near the site of the mound. The area where the mound was located is on private property. Although the mound is now gone, the field where it once stood is easily seen from the road. To reach the Peachtree Mission area, drive another 0.7 mile and turn left (northeast) onto N.C. 141. Then drive 1.7 miles to the town of Peachtree where the mission was located.

FORT HEMBREE

Hayesville

Fort Hembree was another of the several forts used for the removal of the Cherokees in North Carolina. It was located sixteen miles east of Fort Butler, on the southern bank of the Hiwassee River. Several Cherokee villages were located in the area, including Tusquitee and Tuskeegee towns on

Tusquitee Creek, Shooting Creek and Noocoochy towns on Shooting Creek, and Spikebucktown on Persimmon Creek, making Fort Hembree a strategic position for the removal of the Cherokees.

Clay County Courthouse in Hayesville near the site of Fort Hembree

After the removal, Fort Hembree was abandoned. Charles Lanman, traveling to Murphy in 1849, described the site of the fort near the Hiwassee River:

> The only novelty that I noticed on the road to this place was the spot known as Fort Embree. The only evidences that there ever was a fortification here are a breastwork of timber, a lot of demolished pickets, and two or three block-houses, which are now in a dilapidated condition. The site is a commanding one, and takes in some of the grandest mountain outlines that I have ever seen.

The site of Fort Hembree is on a hill in the town of Hayesville. From U.S. 64, turn north onto Business 64 and go 1.1 miles to the courthouse square in Hayesville. A historical marker on the left side of the courthouse indicates that Fort Hembree was located on the hill 0.75 mile northwest (left) of the square.

TUSQUITEE MOUNTAINS

Tusquitee

The Tusquitee Mountains can be seen in the north along the portion of U.S. 64 from Hayesville to Chunky Gal Mountain. This range of mountains receives its name from the Cherokee phrase *tsuwa'-uniyetsun'yi*, "where the water dogs laughed." A Cherokee story tells of a hunter who was crossing over the Tusquitee Mountains at Tusquitee Bald during a drought. Hearing voices, the hunter crept toward the spot where he heard the voices and saw a pair of water-dogs (amphibious lizards also known as hell-benders or mud-puppies) walking on their hind legs and talking. They were on their way to the Nantahala River because their pond was dry. In the story, one water-dog said to the other, "Where's the water? I'm so thirsty that my apron (gills) hangs down," and both laughed. After the hunter told of this incident, the Cherokees referred to it as the place "where the water dogs laughed."

Tusquitee Creek flows in a southwest direction from the foot of the Tusquitee Mountains into the Hiwassee River. The Cherokees had a settlement on Tusquitee Creek known as Da'skwitun'yi, for "rafters place."

There are several roads leading from U.S. 64 to Tusquitee Creek and the foot of the Tusquitee Mountains. One road is Cold Branch Creek Road, which intersects U.S. 64, 5.5 miles east of the Business 64 turn for Hayesville. If traveling east on U.S. 64, turn left onto Cold Branch Creek Road near Chatuge Lake. For the first 1.7 miles, this is a scenic drive through open, rolling farmland. Then Cold Branch Creek Road leads into the present-day community of Tusquitee. Cold Branch Creek Road parallels Licklog Creek and then Cold Branch Creek, before ending at a junction with Woods Road. The junction of Cold Branch Creek Road and Woods Road is almost due south of Tusquitee Bald. You can turn either left or right and follow the road along Tusquitee Creek, or locate one of the many hiking trails leading to Tusquitee Bald.

SHOOTING CREEK

Chatuge Lake

According to Cherokee legend, the people who lived along the Hiwassee and Valley rivers long ago heard the voices of the *Nunnehi*, the Immortals, call to them. The voices warned them of terrible wars and misfortunes in the future. To avoid the evil to come, the *Nunnehi* invited the Cherokees to come live with them under the water.

Tusquitee Mountains

Several Cherokee villages, including the one at the mouth of Shooting Creek on the Hiwassee River, prayed and fasted for seven days. Finally, the *Nunnehi* came and took the people of these villages underwater. Legend says that those who stand and listen carefully at the mouth of Shooting Creek can hear the people talking below. When fishermen drag their nets at the river, the nets always catch on the bottom because the lost townspeople are pulling at the nets, reminding the fishermen not to forget them.

Shooting Creek was called Du'stiya'lun'yi, "where he shot," by the Cherokees. Water from several mountains to the east, including Chunky Gal, Vineyard, and Galloway, drains into Shooting Creek. Since the building of Chatuge Dam and the creation of Chatuge Lake, the mouth of Shooting Creek is now upstream of the original location of the legendary Cherokee village.

To reach the area where Shooting Creek empties into the Hiwassee, take U.S. 64 east of Hayesville for 5.5 miles and turn

Chatuge Lake, at the mouth of Shooting Creek

right opposite Cold Branch Creek Road onto an unnamed road. Drive 0.25 mile and turn left onto N.C. 175. In a little less than 0.5 mile, N.C. 175 turns right and crosses a bridge. Stop at the bridge which is located near the junction of Shooting Creek and the Hiwassee River.

where U.S. 64 parallels Shooting Creek. In another 5 miles, U.S. 64 begins to climb up the western side of Chunky Gal Mountain. At 2.3 miles up the mountain, an overlook provides views of Shooting Creek Valley and the North Georgia mountains in the distance.

CHUNKY GAL MOUNTAIN

Shooting Creek

Chunky Gal Mountain received its name from a local legend about a Cherokee girl who eloped with a Wayah brave. As the pair stopped to refresh themselves at a spring in a gap of the mountains, the maiden's angry father caught them and made the girl return home. The other girls of the village were envious of her well-endowed body and began calling her Chunky Gal. The mountain where her father caught her is supposedly named for this lovelorn Cherokee girl.

It is doubtful that this legend has its roots in traditional Cherokee lore, but the name Chunky Gal does seem appropriate for this steep and rugged mountain. The ascent up the mountain is demanding, but the views from Chunky Gal are spectacular.

From Hayesville, drive east 7.5 miles to

STANDING INDIAN MOUNTAIN

Shooting Creek

At the head of the Nantahala River is a high, bald peak called Yun'wi-tsulenun'yi, Cherokee for "where the man stood." Today the peak is known as Standing Indian Mountain. The name refers to an odd-shaped rock which once jutted out from the bald at the summit. The rock reminded the Indians of a human statue. Unfortunately, the human-shaped rock has broken off the mountain, but stories still linger of a mysterious person that can be seen standing on the bald.

From Hayesville, drive east on U.S. 64 and go to the top of Chunky Gal Mountain. Drive 3.9 miles east of the overlook on Chunky Gal Mountain to a right turn for F.R. 71. The small sign is easy to miss, so if you reach the Macon County line at the crest of the mountain, go back 0.4 mile.

The road to Deep Gap and the trailhead for Standing Indian Mountain

After turning onto F.R. 71, drive 0.7 mile and take the left fork onto a gravel road. The Deep Gap parking area is another 5 miles from the fork. From Deep Gap you can take the Appalachian Trail about 2 to 3 miles to Standing Indian Mountain.

CARTOOGEECHAY CREEK

Cartoogeechay is probably an English corruption of the Cherokee word *gatu'gitse'yi*, meaning "new settlement place." In *Myths of the Cherokees*, James Mooney wrote that Gatu'gitse'yi was a former settlement on Cartoogeechay Creek, but does not indicate when this settlement existed. In 1730 George Hunter, the surveyor-general of the Carolina colony, drew a map of Cherokee country. Hunter's map shows a town named Cuttagochi on a creek west of the village of Nikwasi. This may be the same village on Cartoogeechay Creek mentioned by Mooney. Later maps do not show settlements on Cartoogeechay Creek, and when General Griffith Rutherford marched up the creek in 1776 during his devastating attacks on the Middle and Valley settlements, he made no mention of a town on the creek. So the village on Cartoogeechay probably ceased to exist sometime in the mid-1700s.

In her book, *Touring the Western North Carolina Backroads*, Carolyn Sakowski explains how the Cherokees who lived in this area were allowed to stay in North Carolina after the removal. In 1818, a white settler named Jacob Siler moved to the area and later convinced his three brothers to join him. They settled in the Cartoogeechay Valley and became friends with the Indians. One of the brothers, William, developed a special relationship with the Indians in the area. When state law forbid land ownership by Indians, William Siler bought a tract of land on Cartoogeechay Creek, near Muskrat Creek, so his Cherokee friends could remain in their homeland after the 1838 removal. This small band of Cherokees became known as the Sand Town Cherokees. Isolated from the rest of the tribe for many years, the Sand Town Cherokees eventually joined their kinsmen on the Qualla Reservation.

Several sections of U.S. 64 west of Franklin follow Cartoogeechay Creek and its tributaries. To reach the area where the Sand Town Cherokees lived, take U.S. 64 west from the junction of U.S. 64 and U.S. 23/441 on the south side of Franklin. At 5.8 miles from the junction, U.S. 64

Cartoogeechay Creek

NIKWASI (NEQUASSEE) MOUND

Franklin

Nikwasi mound is a fifteen-foot, conical platform mound built during the late Mississippian period. It is not clear if the mound was built by ancestors of the Cherokees or by another tribe. The Cherokees did, however, build a townhouse on top of the platform. In 1732, Cherokee leaders met at the townhouse with Sir Alexander Cuming, who convinced six of the leaders to return to England with him. In 1761, the British marched through Middle settlements of the Cherokees, burning towns and destroying crops, but they spared the townhouse at Nikwasi. Nikwasi was not so lucky in 1776, when General Griffith Rutherford destroyed several settlements along the Little Tennessee River.

The Cherokees believed the *Nunnehi*, the Immortals, lived under the Nikwasi mound. In one legend, hundreds of *Nunnehi* warriors came out from under the ground at the Nikwasi mound to help the Cherokees fight off an invading tribe. The Nikwasi men rushed out to meet their attackers and fought a valiant battle, but found themselves overpowered. As the Cherokee warriors prepared to retreat, a stranger told the

crosses Cartoogeechay Creek just west of where the road narrows from four to two lanes. The bridge at Cartoogeechay Creek is wide enough for parking. From the north side of the bridge, you can view the approximate site of the Sand Town Indian settlement at the junction of the Muskrat and Cartoogeechay creeks.

Nikwasi (Nequassee) Mound

Cherokee chief to call off his forces. Then a large company of warriors marched out of the mound. As soon as these troops reached the outskirts of the settlement, they became invisible. Although the enemy saw the arrows and tomahawks, they could not see their attackers. After their enemy was defeated, the Cherokees knew the *Nunnehi* lived inside the mound.

From U.S. 64 on the southeast side of Franklin, take N.C. 28 north. After 1.3 miles, N.C. 28 veers left in Franklin and splits into two one-way streets that skirt the Nikwasi Mound. When heading north on N.C. 28, the mound will be on the left.

COWEE TOWNSITE

Iotla

Cowee was an important town in the Middle settlements in the 1700s. The town was located at the site of a large prehistoric

Indian mound, at the mouth of Cowee Creek on the Little Tennessee River. The original name of the settlement was Kawi'yi, which may be a shortened form of Ani'-Kawi'yi, "place of the Deer Clan."

In 1775, William Bartram, a naturalist from Philadelphia, visited Cowee and several other nearby towns, including Whatoga and Nikwasi. His journal provides excellent descriptions of the town of Cowee and the surrounding landscape. At the time of his visit, the town consisted of one hundred houses situated on both sides of the river and a large circular townhouse sitting on top of the ancient mound. Bartram was invited to the townhouse to attend a festival that preceded a game of stick ball. The following day, Cowee would accept another town's challenge to play a match of stick ball. The ceremonies began with a long oration by an aged chief, who recounted Cowee's past victories in stick ball. Next came music and dancing. A partial excerpt of Bartram's description follows:

> This prologue being at an end, the musicians began, both vocal and instrumental; when presently a company of girls, hand in hand, dressed in clean white robes and ornamented with beads, bracelets and a profusion of gay ribbands, entering the door, immediately began to sing their responses in a gentle, low, and sweet voice, and formed themselves in a semicircular file or line, in two ranks, back to back, facing the spectators and musicians, moving slowly round and round. This continued about a quarter of an hour, when we were surprised by a sudden very loud and shrill whoop, uttered at once by a company of young fellows, who came in briskly after one another, with rackets or hurls in one hand.

Unfortunately, Bartram left Cowee for Keowee in South Carolina early the next morning, so the results of the stick-ball game are unknown.

Cowee, like many of the Middle settlements, was attacked and destroyed by both American and British forces. Unlike some of the smaller settlements whose people moved further into the mountains or to western settlements, Cowee was rebuilt several times. In 1761, an army of twenty-eight hundred men, led by Lieutenant Colonel James Grant, occupied Cowee and used it as a base camp to destroy nearby towns before burning Cowee itself. In 1776, Cowee was destroyed during a campaign by General Griffith Rutherford. And in 1783, Major Peter Fine and Colonel William Lillard led a small group of Tennessee volunteers to Cowee and burned it again. Cowee was rebuilt and continuously occupied until the Cherokees gave away the land in 1819.

To reach the Cowee mound, take N.C. 28 north from U.S. 64 on the southeast side of Franklin. After 1.3 miles, N.C. 28 makes a left turn in Franklin and splits into two one-way streets that skirt the Nikwasi Mound. Continue past the Nikwasi Mound heading north. Drive 7.2 miles north of the Nikwasi Mound and watch for a historical marker on the left (west) side of the road titled, "Pottery Clay." This sign explains the importance of the high-quality kaolin found in the area. Continue past this sign for another 0.7 mile to the Cowee historical marker on the right (east) side of the road. The Little Tennessee River is near the west side of the road. Cowee was located just across the river on the northwest side. The mound is located on private property and is not accessible. It may be difficult to see from the road if the trees are heavily foliated, but it still exists.

CULLASAJA GORGE

Franklin

The rugged and beautiful Cullasaja Gorge lies on U.S. 64 between Franklin and Highlands. The road parallels the Cullasaja River, as it cuts through the gorge with its rushing cascades and scenic wa-

terfalls. About 8 miles from Franklin is a pull-off where the Cullasaja Falls can be viewed. Further up U.S. 64, there is a parking area for Dry Falls. A short, paved walkway takes you through mountain laurel and rhododendron to the waterfall. Near Highlands, the old road passed under Bridal Veil Falls. Today, there is a scenic turnoff allowing the modern traveler to continue the tradition of driving under the falls.

In 1776, there were at least two Cherokee villages on the Cullasaja River. One,

Cullasaja Gorge

named Kulsetsi'yi, for "honey-locust place" or "sugar place," was located at the junction of the Little Tennessee and Cullasaja rivers, very near the village of Nikwasi. Kulsetsi'yi, or Sugartown, as the local traders called it, was destroyed in September 1776 by General Griffith Rutherford's men, but only after the Cherokee defenders killed eighteen of the North Carolina forces and wounded twenty-two more. No Cherokees were killed, but at least one was taken prisoner. A letter written in 1850 by Silas McDowell of Franklin described what happened after Sugartown was destroyed:

A prisoner, whom they had taken, upon the promise of his life, proposed to lead the army to what was called the hidden town, where their women, children & a large number of cattle were collected. This was 7 miles distant from Nequassee in a narrow valley on the Sugartown river and surrounded at all points by mountains and was very difficult to approach from the fact that the mountains jutted in abruptly upon the river, in many places scarcely leaving room for a foot path. However, on reaching the town there was not an indian to be found save a few very old & decreped men and women, the other indians being discovered some hundreds of feet above them on the crests of the mountains apparently looking down & taking a calm survey of them from their secure situations. They achieved nothing but the destruction of

this town & some few beef cattle by that days adventures.

The junction of U.S. 64 and U.S. 441 on the east side of Franklin is near the confluence of the Little Tennessee and Cullasaja rivers and the former location of Sugartown. From this junction, take U.S. 64 east to the Cullasaja Gorge—the area where "the hidden town" was located.

WHITESIDE MOUNTAIN

Cashiers

Whiteside Mountain was known to the Cherokees as Sanigila'gi, meaning "the place where they took it out." The name refers to how the stone face of the mountain was created in the story of Spearfinger. Whiteside Mountain was a favorite haunt of the mythical ogress Spearfinger, who began building a bridge from the Hiwassee River to Whiteside Mountain in order to traverse the rugged Blue Ridge Mountains more easily. Lightning struck the bridge, however, and scattered the stone fragments. The sheer cliffs of Whiteside Mountain are where the stone bridge of Spearfinger was sheered off by the lightning.

The portion of U.S. 64 between Highlands and Cashiers provides a wonderful view of Whiteside Mountain. There is a small gravel pull-off 5.3 miles east of Highlands and 4.4 miles west of Cashiers. Park in the pull-off, which will be on the left side if coming from Highlands, and carefully cross the busy road for the view of the mountain on the other side.

Whiteside Mountain

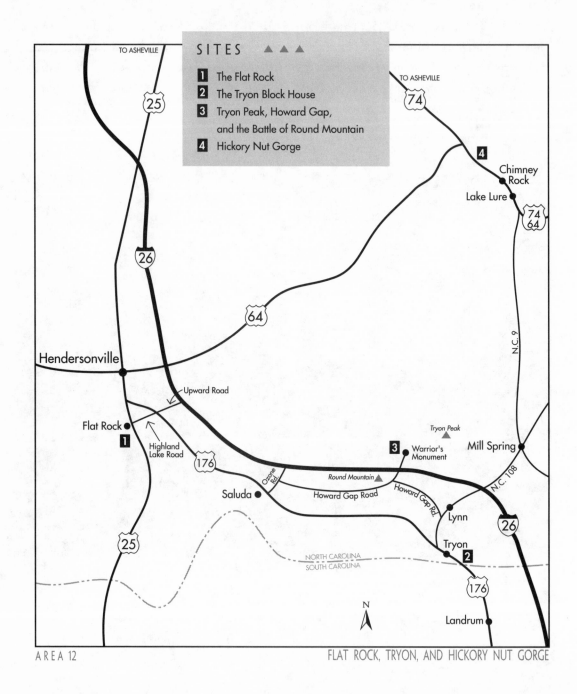

SITES ▲ ▲ ▲

1 The Flat Rock

2 The Tryon Block House

3 Tryon Peak, Howard Gap,
and the Battle of Round Mountain

4 Hickory Nut Gorge

TO ASHEVILLE

25

26

TO ASHEVILLE

74

4

Chimney
Rock

Lake Lure

74
64

64

N.C. 9

Hendersonville

Upward Road

Flat Rock

1

Highland
Lake Road

176

Ozone Rd.

Saluda

Tryon Peak

3 Warrior's
Monument

Mill Spring

Round Mountain

Howard Gap Road

Howard Gap Rd.

N.C. 108

Lynn

26

25

Tryon

2

NORTH CAROLINA
SOUTH CAROLINA

176

N

Landrum

AREA 12   FLAT ROCK, TRYON, AND HICKORY NUT GORGE

Tryon Peak

FLAT ROCK, TRYON, AND HICKORY NUT GORGE

During the seventeenth and eighteenth centuries, there were a number of well-worn trading paths leading from Charleston to Cherokee territory. One of the best known was the Cherokee Path, which led from Charleston to an area on the Congaree River south of Columbia known as the Congarees. The path then branched toward the Saluda River as it continued to Ninety Six, Keowee, and Fort Prince George. It crossed into North Carolina near the corner where Georgia, North Carolina, and South Carolina meet. Another heavily traveled, but lesser-known, route lay to the east of the Cherokee Path. It generally followed the same route as the Cherokee Path from Charleston to the Congarees. From the Congarees, it passed through the present-day South Carolina towns of Spartanburg, Campobello, and Landrum before entering North Carolina at Tryon. It then passed through Howard Gap to present-day Fletcher, near Asheville, where it joined another trading path that later became known as the Buncombe Turnpike. This was one of the most direct routes from Charleston to western North Carolina. The path encouraged trade between the Cherokees and the colonists and made it easy for white poachers to haul their bounty from Cherokee lands to trading posts in South Carolina. It also encouraged settlers to travel deeper into the wilderness seeking land on which to establish homesteads. This expansion led to conflict between the colonists and the Cherokees and set the stage for several decades of vacillating relations.

THE FLAT ROCK

Flat Rock

According to local legend, the large flat rock located in present-day Henderson County was once a gathering place for the Cherokees. Many early Indian paths converged at the Flat Rock, and it became a meeting place for hunting and raiding parties. Local legend says the Cherokees would hold hunting ceremonies at the rock, asking the spirits for good fortune as they began their hunt. Until about fifty years ago, there were reports of a dozen circular pits around the Flat Rock which supposedly contained evidence of signal fires. However, these pits have long since disappeared. Some accounts report that the Cherokees gathered at the Flat Rock before they left to attack the Block House below Tryon on the North and South Carolina state line. The warriors left their women and children at the Flat Rock then proceeded to Warrior Mountain. From Warrior Mountain, they planned to launch their attack on the Block House. (See The Block House section later in this chapter.)

The unusual, large granite outcrop was already a well-known landmark when the early settlers arrived in the area. Buncombe County court records of 1794 show that the Flat Rock was the destination of a road that was to be built in the area of present-day Henderson County from the ford at Cane Creek. In the late 1820s and 1830s, the Flat Rock area developed into a summer resort community for well-to-do families escaping the heat and sickness of Charleston. Today, Flat Rock is still a gathering place. The

The Flat Rock and Flat Rock Playhouse

state theater of North Carolina, the Flat Rock Playhouse, is located at the site of the legendary Cherokee ceremonial and meeting grounds.

To reach the Flat Rock Playhouse from Asheville, take Interstate 26 South to Exit 22, the Upward Road exit. Turn right (west) on Upward Road and go 1.3 miles to U.S. 176. At U.S. 176, Upward Road changes to Highland Lake Road. Take Highland Lake Road 1 mile until it dead-ends at Greenville Highway, which is U.S. 25. Turn left (south) on Greenville Highway and go 0.7 mile. The Flat Rock Playhouse entrance will be on the right. Turn into the parking area, and the large, flat outcrop of rock will be right in front of the playhouse.

THE BLOCK HOUSE

Tryon

In the mid-1750s, as hostilities between England and France spilled over into the colonies, tensions increased between the settlers and the Indians. The French colonial government tried to woo the Cherokees' loyalty away from the British. Meanwhile, the French encouraged the Shawnees to raid English settlements in the Carolinas. Cherokee loyalties were divided between the French and their allies, which included the Creeks and their long-time British allies. When the French and Indian War broke out and Indians started attacking upcountry settlements, several forts were built on the frontier. The forts included Young's Fort, near present-day Mill Spring in Polk County, North Carolina, Earle's Fort, near present-day Landrum, South Carolina, and the Block House, near Tryon. Tryon was located on the end of the Blackstock Road, which ran from Ninety Six across the North and South Carolina colonial line. Eventually, the Block House became a trading post between the Cherokees and the English settlers.

The violence of the French and Indian War gradually subsided. However, as white settlers continued to encroach on Cherokee lands and the American Revolution strained relations between the Cherokees and Americans, warfare again broke out on the frontier. In the spring of 1776, a group of Cherokees gathered on the side of Round Mountain and planned an attack on the Block House. After they attacked the Block House, they planned to attack Young's Fort and Earle's Fort. A Cherokee named Skyuka found his old friend, Captain Thomas Howard, who had gathered a militia of American rebels at the Block House, and warned him of the attack. Howard and his men marched out of the Block House toward a gap in the mountains. At the gap, which was later renamed for Howard, he defeated the Cherokee forces in the Battle of Round Mountain. (See the Tryon Peak, Howard Gap, and the Battle of Round Mountain section later in this chapter.)

The Block House has been renovated and moved from its original location to the countryside southwest of Tryon. It is on private property but is easily seen from the road. To reach the Block House from Interstate 26, take Exit 36. Turn right (southwest) on N.C. 108 and go 3.3 miles to Tryon. Then turn left (south) on U.S. 176. Go 0.5 mile through Tryon to New Market Road, which will be a left turn just before U.S. 176 crosses the railroad tracks. Dive 0.3 mile down New Market Road, then bear left at the fork in the road. Go another 1.5 miles on New Market Road to the stop sign and turn right. Go 0.1 mile to another stop sign and turn left. The Block House will be on your immediate left after turning at the stop sign.

The Block House

TRYON PEAK, HOWARD GAP, AND THE BATTLE OF ROUND MOUNTAIN

Tryon

A period of increased warfare between the Cherokees and the settlers on the Georgia and Carolina frontiers from the late-1750s to November 1761 is often referred to as the Cherokee War. During this period, Fort Loudoun and Fort Prince George were placed under siege by the Cherokees, and Colonel Archibald Montgomery and Colonel James Grant led devastating raids on the Cherokee Lower and Middle towns. The war was a success for the colonists, their armies having laid waste to many of the Cherokee towns of North and South Carolina and Georgia. This success encouraged settlers and traders to push more brazenly into the Cherokee territory.

In 1767, Governor William Tryon of North Carolina traveled from Salisbury to a point on Reedy River in what is now Laurens County, South Carolina, to deal with the problem of the colonists encroaching on Cherokee land. He met with the Indian agent John Stuart and representatives from the Cherokees, including Ostenaco. The purpose of the meeting was to establish a boundary line between North Carolina and Cherokee territory. According to legend, Ostenaco laid down a string of beads on the proposed boundary line. The boundary began at the Reedy River, where the South Carolina boundary was set the year before. It then ran approximately fifty-three miles north to a Spanish oak on what is now known as Tryon Peak. From Tryon Peak, it ran north to Chiswell, Virginia.

Tryon Peak is the tallest peak on White Oak Mountain, a long mountain located north of the town of Tryon. Tryon Peak is often referred to as Tryon Mountain. Other mountains or peaks that make up White Oak Mountain include Miller's Mountain and Round, or Warrior, Mountain. Near the southwest end of White Oak Mountain is a gap that divides Miller's Mountain and Round Mountain. The Indian trade path connecting Charleston and western North Carolina passed through this gap.

The establishment of the boundary line from Reedy River to Tryon Peak did not stop the problem of poaching or other encroachments on Cherokee land by the settlers. In the spring of 1776, a group of Cherokees gathered on Round Mountain and planned an attack on the Block House near Tryon and two other nearby forts. A Cherokee named Skyuka slipped away from Round Mountain and made his way to the Block House. He warned his friend, Captain Thomas Howard, who was stationed at the Block House with an American patriot militia, of the impending attack. Skyuka led Captain Howard and the militia to the gap between Miller's Mountain and Round Mountain, where they fought a decisive battle with the Cherokees that ended in victory for the patriots. This battle is referred to as the Battle of Round Mountain, or sometimes as the Battle of Warrior Mountain.

The reason for Skyuka's assistance to Howard is not clear. One legend says that Howard once saved Skyuka's life when he was bitten by a rattlesnake. Another legend says that Skyuka was in love with a settler's daughter, and he feared for her well-being if the Cherokees attacked the settlements. Skyuka's legend continued after the battle. In one version of his legend, he was captured by Cherokees and Tories after the battle and hanged for his betrayal. Other stories say he lived for many years with his family among white friends on Skyuka Creek, northeast of Tryon.

The gap between Miller's Mountain and Round Mountain is now called Howard Gap in honor of the captain who defeated the Cherokees there. The trading path through Howard Gap was eventually turned into a road. Most of this old road, known as Howard Gap Road, still exists, although it has been altered by the building of Interstate 26 through the gap. A monument commemorating the Battle of Round Mountain was placed at the gap in 1909 by the Daughters of the American Revolution. The monument had to be moved when Interstate 26 was built. It is now located on the side of Miller's Mountain, opposite Round Mountain.

The following directions lead up the old Howard Gap Road, past views of Tryon Peak, through Howard Gap, and past the Warrior Monument and Round Mountain. From Interstate 26 take Exit 36. Turn right (southwest) on N.C. 108 and go 2.4 miles to Howard Gap Road. Turn right (north) on Howard Gap Road. Tryon Peak is visible to the right for over a mile as you follow Howard Gap Road up White Oak Mountain. At 2.8 miles, turn right onto a gravel road which will loop around and cross a bridge over the interstate. As you cross the interstate, the large, stone Warrior Monument will come into view. Park at the monument to get good views of Howard Gap and Round Mountain on the

Howard Gap

other side of the interstate. Retrace your path back across the interstate, and at 0.3 mile from the monument, turn right and continue on Howard Gap Road. This section of the road circles the top of Round Mountain where the battle was fought. At 0.6 mile from the monument, Howard Gap Road returns to pavement. It is another 3.7 miles down Howard Gap Road to Ozone Road. At Ozone Road you can turn right to go to Interstate 26 or turn left and go to Saluda.

The Warrior Monument

HICKORY NUT GORGE

Chimney Rock

In 1848, a traveler by the name of Charles Lanman visited Hickory Nut Gorge while he was passing through the Asheville area. The following year, in his *Letters from the Allegheny Mountains*, Lanman described the remarkable gorge which has fascinated thousands of visitors to the area:

> From any point of view this particular spot is remarkably imposing, the gap being not more than half a mile wide, though appearing to narrow down to a few hundred yards. The highest bluff is on the south side, and, though rising to the height of full twenty-five hundred feet, it is nearly perpendicular, and midway up its front stands an isolated rock, looming against the sky, which is of circular form, and resembles the principal turret of a stupendous castle. The entire mountain is composed of granite, and a large proportion of the bluff in question positively hangs over the abyss beneath, and is as smooth as it could possibly be made by the rains of uncounted centuries. Over one portion of this superb cliff, falling far down into some undiscovered and apparently unattainable pool, is a stream of water, which seems to be the offspring of the clouds . . .

The "isolated rock, looming against the

Hickory Nut Gorge

sky" is better known as Chimney Rock. The "stream of water, which seems to be the offspring of the clouds" is called Hickory Nut Falls. Today, they are included in a popular commercial attraction, Chimney Rock Park, but can also be seen from a drive through the gorge.

Several different versions of the legend about how the Cherokees acquired tobacco, known as *tsalu* or *tso-lungh* by the Cherokees, involve Hickory Nut Gorge. Lanman's version of the legend is one of the most frequently told. He reported that he heard his version from a Cherokee chief with two names, All Bones and Flying Squirrel.

In the legend, the Cherokees had obtained some tobacco many years earlier from a visitor from the Far East. The small quantity of tobacco had long since run out, and the Cherokees wanted to obtain some more. They determined that the land where the tobacco could be found was situated on the big waters to the east. The gateway to this faraway land was the Hickory Nut Gorge and was guarded by a large number of little people, or spirits. A young warrior was sent to fetch the tobacco, but he never returned. Then a celebrated conjurer volunteered to journey to the east to fetch the tobacco. First, he turned himself into a mole and tried to pass through the gorge, but he was pursued by the little people and forced to turn back. Next, the conjurer turned himself into a hummingbird. In this shape, he was able to pass through the gateway and bring back a very small amount of tobacco. For his final attempt, the conjurer turned himself into a whirlwind and blew through the gorge, stripping the mountains of vegetation and scattering boulders as he passed. The little people were frightened away, and the conjurer was alone in the gorge and the lands where the tobacco grew to the east. The conjurer found the bones of the young warrior and brought him back to life, and the two men returned to their tribe with a large load of tobacco. Ever since, tobacco has been abundant in the land of the Cherokees.

To reach Hickory Nut Gorge from Interstate 26, take Exit 36 and follow N.C. 108 northeast to Mill Spring. At Mill Spring, turn north on N.C. 9 and go 8.6 miles to Lake Lure. At Lake Lure, N.C. 9 turns left as it joins U.S. 64 and U.S. 74A. Drive 3.9 miles northwest on U.S. 64/74A to the town of Chimney Rock. The town of Chimney Rock is near the southeast end of Hickory Nut Gorge. As you drive northwest along U.S. 64/74A, you will pass through the gorge.

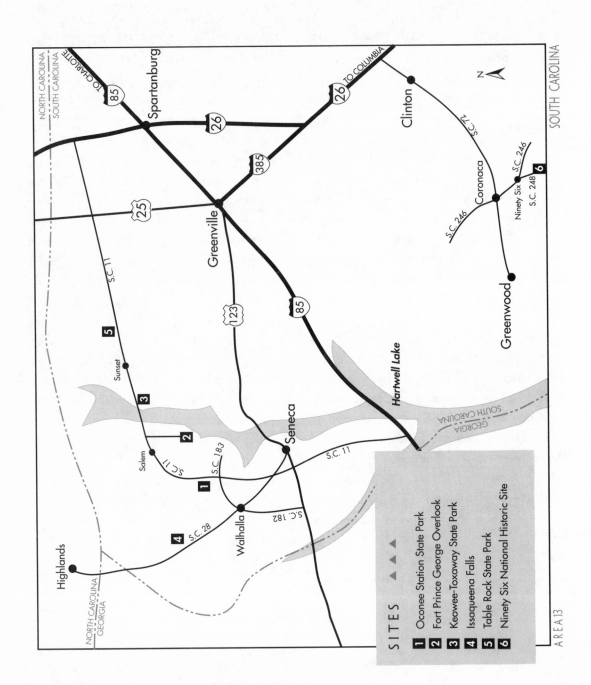

SITES ▲▲▲

1 Oconee Station State Park
2 Fort Prince George Overlook
3 Keowee-Toxaway State Park
4 Issaqueena Falls
5 Table Rock State Park
6 Ninety Six National Historic Site

AREA 13

SOUTH CAROLINA

Fort Prince George Overlook

AREA 13

SOUTH CAROLINA

▲▲▲

Trade with the Indians grew rapidly after the founding of Charles Towne (present-day Charleston, South Carolina) in the late-seventeenth century. By 1730, trade with the Creeks, Cherokees, and Chickasaws was so important to the Carolina colony that acting-governor Arthur Middleton sent the surveyor general, George Hunter, to survey the main trade path from Charles Towne to the Cherokee country. This trail, called The Cherokee Path, led to all of the Cherokee territories. It ran from Charles Towne to the colonial settlement of Ninety Six, then to Fort Prince George and the Cherokee village of Keowee. From Keowee, the principal town of the Cherokee Lower settlements, it crossed the mountains into the Middle settlements of North Carolina, then crossed the Unaka Mountains into the valley of the Little Tennessee River and the Overhill settlements. A branch of the path led to the Valley Towns, located in the area of present-day Georgia.

The Cherokees became dependent on supplies obtained from the English. These goods included guns, woolens, farm instruments, and metalware. At one point, the merchants of the Carolina colony employed three hundred traders in the Indian country, who obtained as many as seventy-five thousand deerskins each year. Because of the immense profits available through trade with the Indians, the colonists realized that it was important to maintain good relations with them. Governor James Glen of the Carolina colony carried out a series of negotiations with two of the Cherokee chiefs, Connecorte and Attakullakulla, in order to encourage loyalty to the British, rather than the French or Spanish. By 1753, Glen had received permission from the Cherokees to build forts in Cherokee territory. This permission included Fort Prince George near the principal Lower Town of Keowee. However, in 1756, William Henry Lyttleton replaced Glen as governor and relations began to break down. By 1760, the Cherokees were raiding South Carolina backcountry settlements and fighting colonial militias and British regulars at Fort Prince George and Fort Loudoun. Peaceful relations were later restored on the South Carolina frontier, but only temporarily. The next four decades were marked by constant tension between the Indians and the Carolinians.

OCONEE STATION STATE PARK

Walhalla

Oconee Station was one of several blockhouses constructed in the South Carolina back country during the 1790s. The blockhouses were constructed in response to Creek raids on Georgia frontier settlements located across the Tugaloo River. The Oconee Station blockhouse was built around 1792, and troops were posted there until 1799. The site is located at the foot of Oconee Mountain, near the former Cherokee settlements of Oconee and Tomassee.

Oconee Station

From Tomassee Bald at the top of Oconee Mountain, troops garrisoned at the blockhouse could survey the surrounding countryside.

William Richards, a native of Ireland, purchased the property around the stone blockhouse sometime after construction was completed. By 1795, Richards had established a successful trading post at Oconee Station. In 1805, he built a large brick house near the blockhouse. Richards' trading post was very successful. When he died in 1809, his inventory included 30,000 deer skins, 79 fox and cat skins, 329 bear skins, 18 wolf skins, 32 pounds of ginseng, 21 pounds of snakeroot, and many other goods including barrels of corn, gun flints, beeswax, salt, lime, and sulphur.

In addition to the blockhouse and Richards' house, Oconee Station State Park has picnic facilities, a nature trail, and interpretive programs including living history demonstrations of frontier camps and Native American programs. The park is open March through December. In January and February the park is open by appointment only. Park hours are Thursday through Sunday from 9 A.M. to 6 P.M. The historic structures are open for free tours on Saturday and Sunday afternoons from 1 P.M. to 5 P.M. For information, call 803-638-0079 or 803-638-2792.

To reach Oconee Station, take S.C. 11 north from Walhalla. From S.C. 11, take a left turn onto Oconee Station Road. Oconee Station State Park is located 2 miles down Oconee Station Road.

FORT PRINCE GEORGE AND KEOWEE OVERLOOK

Salem

During the 1740s, the South Carolina colonial government received reports that French agents were stirring up the Indians along the Carolina and Georgia frontiers. In 1746, Governor James Glen invited Connecorte of Echota and other Cherokee headmen to a conference at the settlement of Ninety Six. At the meeting, Glen requested permission to build a fort in Cherokee country, but Connecorte refused. Nevertheless, Glen showered Connecorte and the other chiefs with gifts and continued to press British interests.

Soon after the meeting, a group of French-supported Iroquois began raiding the back-country settlements. The Creeks and Cherokees followed suit. Glen implemented a trade embargo and pulled all of the traders from Cherokee country. As the trade embargo tightened, The Raven of Hiwassee requested a meeting with Governor Glen at Saluda Old Town. Glen refused to leave Charles Towne, so a delegation of more than 160 Cherokee headmen and warriors rode from Keowee to Charles Towne.

Skiagusta of Keowee spoke for the Cherokees and requested forgiveness. The Cherokees promised to return plunder from the raids and to punish the murderers. They also promised to help Glen build a fort near the principal Lower Town of Keowee. In 1753, Glen rode up the eastern side of the Keowee River and personally laid out the fort. Glen wrote in his report: "It is square with regular bastions and four ravelins. It is nearly 200 feet from salient to salient angle, and is made of earth taken out of the ditch, secured with fascines and well rammed, with banquette on the inside for the men to stand on when they fire over. The ravelins are made with posts of lightwood." The fort was christened Fort Prince George in honor of the oldest son of the Prince of Wales.

Governor Glen was replaced by William Henry Lyttleton, who was not able to maintain friendly relations with the Cherokees. In December 1759, Governor Lyttleton met with the Cherokees at Fort Prince George for peace talks. However, Lyttleton became

enraged over some recent Indian attacks and ordered the seizure of twenty-eight members of the Cherokee delegation. Among the Cherokees who were taken captive was Oconostota.

Attakullakulla came to the fort and was able to arrange the release of some of the Cherokees, including Oconostota. On February 16, 1760, Oconostota enticed Lieutenant Richard Coytmore, commander of Fort Prince George, to come outside the protective stockade of the fort for a conference. During the meeting, the Cherokees, led by Oconostota, opened fire and killed the lieutenant. Inside the fort, the English soldiers killed the remaining Cherokee captives.

Immediately after the incident that resulted in Coytmore's death, the fort fired a few cannon volleys on Keowee, but the soldiers inside could do little else. The Cherokees began a siege of the fort that would last several months. Rumors of British troops massing at Ninety Six reached the Cherokees, and they began to mass their own army at Keowee. An uneasy standoff between the town and the fort remained in effect, even though Tistoe of Keowee tried to trick the soldiers into abandoning their fort. In April, strange Indians killed several people of Keowee. Fearing the British had hired Creek or Chickasaw mercenaries and mindful of the troops concentrated at Ninety Six, the Cherokees abandoned Keowee and Toxaway and moved to settlements at Estatoe and Conasatchee. In May, Cherokee fears came true when Chickasaws and Creeks burned Keowee and Estatoe. Colonel Archibald Montgomery's army finally arrived at Fort Prince George in early June, offering the weary fort some relief.

The site of Fort Prince George is now underwater near an island in Lake Keowee. The site of Keowee is also underwater and lies near the bank of the Keowee River, southwest of the fort. To reach a view of the approximate location of Fort Prince George, take S.C. 11 northeast from Walhalla or west from Interstate 26. Follow S.C. 11 to Lake Keowee. On the west side of Lake Keowee, watch for Park Avenue, which is off of S.C. 11, 2.5 miles east from the junction of S.C. 11 and S.C. 130. Turn south on Park Avenue and drive 0.9 mile to Shallowford Road. Drive 1.3 miles on Shallowford Road to Nimmons Bridge Road and turn right. Continue south on Nimmons Bridge Road 3.2 miles as it parallels the lake, then turn left onto Road 9. Drive 1 mile to the end of Road 9 where there is a boat-launch ramp and parking area. From this small peninsula, the island visible across the lake to the northeast is located near the former site of Fort Prince

George. The former site of Keowee is also nearby on this side of the lake.

KEOWEE-TOXAWAY STATE PARK

Sunset

Keowee-Toxaway State Park is located a few miles north of the former sites of Fort Prince George and the Cherokee Lower Town of Keowee. In the 1970s, the sites of Keowee and Fort Prince George were submerged by the construction of Lake Keowee. Keowee, meaning "land of mulberry groves," was the principal town of the Lower Cherokees. It was described by William Bartram in his 1773 memoirs as "a most charming situation, and the adjacent heights are naturally so formed and disposed, as with little expense of military architecture to be rendered almost impregnable." Toxaway meaning "land of no tomahawks," was the name of another nearby Lower Cherokee Town.

The park features a museum with a nature and historical discovery trail. The trail has several unique, outdoor kiosks with displays on the Cherokees and their culture, the building of Fort Prince George and the British presence in Cherokee country, and the encroachment of white settlers into Cherokee country. The park also has a small gift shop, rental cabin, camping, hiking, and picnic facilities.

From June through August, the museum is open Wednesday through Sunday from 10 A.M. to 5 P.M. From September to May, museum hours are 11 A.M. to noon and 4 P.M. to 5 P.M. daily. The park is open daily from 9 A.M. to 9 P.M., April through October, and from 9 A.M. to 6 P.M. the rest of the year. For information, call 803-868-2605.

The park is located on S.C. 11, the Cherokee Foothills Parkway, 15 miles northwest of Pickens.

ISSAQUEENA FALLS

Walhalla

Issaqueena Falls is named for an Indian princess who is a character in many legends about this part of South Carolina. Issaqueena is usually said to be either a Creek or Choctaw princess who was captured by the Cherokees. She was supposedly living as Cherokee Chief Karuga's slave in the village of Keowee.

According to legend, Issaqueena fell in love with a white man who ran a nearby trading post. When Issaqueena learned that

Issaqueena Falls

the Cherokees planned to attack the white traders, she set out to warn her lover. Her flight is described in more detail in the section about Ninety Six National Historic Site.

With her Cherokee captors in hot pursuit, Issaqueena leaped from the falls, landed on a ledge, and hid behind the falling water until the Cherokees left. The falls which aided her escape now bear her name.

Issaqueena Falls is located on private land but is accessible from Stumphouse Tunnel Park. From Walhalla, take S.C. 28 north for 6 miles to the entrance to

Stumphouse Park on the right. From the parking lot for the picnic area, there is a trail across a small bridge which will take you to the top of the falls. The trail to the bottom of the falls is short, but steep, and requires some agility.

TABLE ROCK STATE PARK

Pickens

According to Cherokee legend, a giant chief used to dine on the top of Table Rock Mountain, sitting on the nearby mountain called The Stool. These two mountains, along with Pinnacle Mountain, lie near the head of the Saluda River, close to the east-ern boundary of the Cherokee Lower settlements. The land between the Saluda and Broad rivers was located along the boundary which separated the Cherokees and the Catawba Indians. Because the Cherokees and Catawbas didn't get along, the area was a "no man's land" and used only for hunting. Most of the land east of the Broad River belonged to the Catawbas, who were concentrated along the Catawba River. The Cherokee settlements were concentrated west of the Saluda River, on the Keowee and Tugaloo rivers and their tributaries.

One of the closest Cherokee settlements to Table Rock was Socony, or Sen-conee, which was located near present-day Pickens, South Carolina. Very little is known about Socony. Few contemporary documents or maps mention the village, so

Table Rock State Park

it may have been a short-lived or small settlement. However, it was important enough to be destroyed in 1776 by the expedition led by Major Andrew Williamson against the Lower and Middle Cherokees.

Table Rock State Park includes the southern faces of Table Rock, The Stool, and most of the south side of Pinnacle Mountain. There are several hiking trails in the area, including one that starts at Carrick's Creek Interpretive Center and goes 3.5 miles one-way to the top of Table Rock Mountain. The park also has a lodge restaurant, cabins, a picnic area with shelters, and facilities for swimming, camping, fishing, boating, and miniature golf. Several of the facilities are seasonal and may require fees. A parking fee is charged in the summer. The park is open year-round from 7 A.M. to 9 P.M., except in summer when hours are extended to 10 P.M. The restaurant is closed on Mondays and some holidays. For information, call 803-878-9813.

From Greenville, take U.S. 25 north to S.C. 11. Go west on S.C. 11 for approximately 16 miles to either the west or east entrance for the park. The main road in the park is a half circle. From the east entrance, it is 1.2 miles to an overlook for Table Rock Mountain. From the west entrance, it is 1.4 miles to the same overlook. Carrick's Creek Interpretive Center and the trailhead for Table Rock are 0.8 mile from the west entrance of the park, while the restaurant is 0.5 mile from the east entrance. The portion of the main road between the restaurant and the overlook is closed in summer and on days when the fee station is open at the west gate. The fee station is open weekends from Easter through May and in September and October. During these periods, use the west gate to reach the overlook and the interpretive center.

NINETY SIX
NATIONAL HISTORIC SITE

Ninety Six

In the eighteenth century, several trading paths that were important to the settlement of the Carolina back country met at Ninety Six, South Carolina. The Cherokee Path, one of the trails leading to Ninety Six, traveled from Charles Towne to several inland Cherokee villages. Several locations along the Cherokee Path supposedly received their names when Issaqueena followed this route on her quest to warn white settlers of an impending Indian attack. As Issaqueena rode along the path, she named various creeks and landmarks between the village of Keowee and the settlement of Ninety Six by noting the distance she had to travel. One Mile Creek, Twelve Mile River, and other towns and streams in the area received their names this way.

Other, more plausible, theories about how Ninety Six received its name are now more generally accepted. The most accepted theory is that the creeks and other landmarks received their names from traders who traveled the Cherokee Path between Keowee and Charles Towne. The names were probably given as roughly estimated mile indicators. For many years, people believed Ninety Six received its name because it was ninety-six miles from Keowee, although it is probably closer to seventy-eight miles. Recent research by local historian David P. George has suggested another plausible theory. George argues that the name Ninety Six refers to fifteen streams in the Ninety Six area that flowed in an unexpected direction. The Cherokee Path was in the valley of the Saluda River, most of whose streams all flowed in one direction. However, in the area of Ninety Six, the Cherokee Path crossed two groups of streams which flowed to the Savannah River, the opposite direction of the other streams in the valley. The early traders used the streams as landmarks and were very aware of the direction that each stream flowed. Nine of the odd-flowing streams were close together, while the other six formed a separate group. In referring to the area of the streams, the traders merged the group of nine and the group of six to form the name Ninety Six.

The hamlet of Ninety Six grew up around a trading post established by Robert Gouedy in 1751. In 1759, a ninety-square-

Ninety Six National Historic Site

foot stockade was built around Gouedy's barn in preparation for a possible attack by the Cherokees. In February 1760, Cherokees attacked Gouedy's fort. After a brief skirmish that left two Cherokees dead, the Cherokees withdrew from Gouedy's fort to make raids in other areas.

On March 3, 1760, the Cherokees returned to Gouedy's fort with two hundred warriors. The Cherokees attacked the fort for twenty-four hours. When this attack failed, the Cherokees again withdrew.

Ninety Six was soon recognized for its strategic value in controlling traffic along the Cherokee Path. It was used as a base camp for several raids into Cherokee Territory. In spite of the lawless era, the community of Ninety Six grew as settlers streamed into the South Carolina back country.

The Ninety Six National Historic Site is devoted primarily to its role in the Revolutionary War. In 1780, Americans loyal to England constructed the Star Fort and the Stockade Fort near Ninety Six. In May 1781, Nathanael Greene and his patriot forces sieged the forts. The outlines of the Star Fort and a reconstructed Stockade Fort are on a self-guided walking trail through the Ninety Six National Historic Site. The siege lines constructed by the attacking Americans, the site of a jail built in 1772, and an early pioneer road called the Island Ford Road are also included on the self-guided trail. By taking a short detour from the trail, the visitor can also see the historic Cherokee Path and the location of Gouedy's 1751 trading post. To reach these sites, continue walking straight (south) on the Charleston Road path through the old village site of Ninety Six instead of turning right onto the path for the Stockade Fort. Maps for the walking tour are available at the visitor center.

The visitor center has a ten-minute video about the fort, a museum, and a small gift shop. The park is open from 8 A.M. to 5 P.M. year-round, except Christmas Day and New Year's Day. For information, call 803-543-4068.

From Greenville, take Interstate 385 south to Exit 2 for Clinton. From the exit, travel 2.6 miles and bear right onto Business S.C. 72/56. After another 1.5 miles, bear right again onto S.C. 72 West, where S.C. 56 and S.C. 72 split. Drive 19 miles, then turn left onto S.C. 246 South. After 6.9 miles you will reach the town of Ninety Six. In Ninety Six, S.C. 246 turns left at the junction with S.C. 34 and S.C. 248. Go straight onto S.C. 248. Drive 2 miles on S.C. 248 and the park entrance will be on the left.

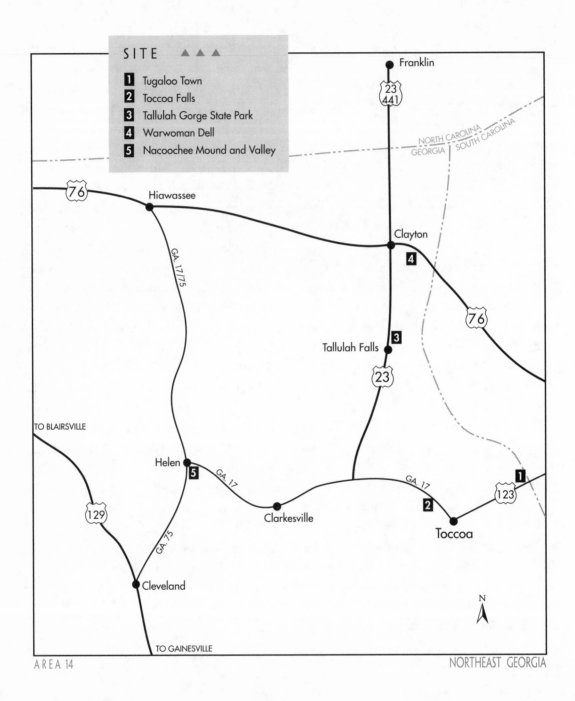

SITE ▲ ▲ ▲

1 Tugaloo Town
2 Toccoa Falls
3 Tallulah Gorge State Park
4 Warwoman Dell
5 Nacoochee Mound and Valley

Franklin

23
441

NORTH CAROLINA
GEORGIA   SOUTH CAROLINA

76

Hiawassee

Clayton

4

GA. 17/75

76

3

Tallulah Falls

23

TO BLAIRSVILLE

Helen

5

GA. 17

GA. 17

1

123

129

Clarkesville

2

Toccoa

GA. 75

Cleveland

N

TO GAINESVILLE

AREA 14

NORTHEAST GEORGIA

Site of Tugaloo Town on Hartwell Lake

AREA 14

NORTHEAST GEORGIA

▲ ▲ ▲

In the mid-1700s, there were only a few Cherokee towns in the northeast corner of Georgia. Until that time, the Creeks controlled most of central and north Georgia. They kept the Cherokee settlements confined to a small portion of land in the northeast mountains of Georgia and along the Tugaloo River.

The towns along the Tugaloo River and in the Nacoochee Valley were part of the Lower Cherokee settlements. The Georgia

Lower Towns included Chotte, Nacoochee, Sukehi, Turura, Estatoe, Tugaloo, Chauge, Tassee, and Taucoe. Further north in Georgia, near the North Carolina line, were the Middle Towns of Tuckaretchi, Old Estatoe, and Stecoe.

Between 1730 and 1761, the population of the Lower Towns decreased significantly. Several Lower Towns were destroyed by the Creeks, including Estatoe in 1750 and Tugaloo in 1752. A number of the Cherokees living in the Lower Towns fled the Creeks by going north to the Middle and Overhill settlements. In 1760, Colonel Archibald Montgomery burned most of the remaining Lower Towns. In 1761, Colonel James Grant destroyed fifteen Middle Towns, including Old Estatoe. During the American Revolution, several more attacks were launched against the Lower and Middle towns by troops from North and South Carolina. Meanwhile, the Overhill settlements were being attacked by Tennessee and North Carolina forces. After the American Revolution, with pressure from the south, north, and east increasing, many Cherokees found it necessary to move southwest into central and west Georgia, north Alabama, and southeast Tennessee.

The Cherokee census of 1835 counted 16,542 Eastern Cherokees, with 8,936 of that number residing in northwest Georgia. An estimated 5,000 Cherokees were already living west of the Mississippi. On May 28, 1830, the United States Congress passed the Indian Removal Act which provided for an exchange of Indian lands in any state east of the Mississippi River for lands west of the river. The act was aimed primarily at southern tribes, including the Creeks, Seminoles, Chickasaws, Choctaws, and Cherokees.

In 1831, Georgia sent surveyors into the Cherokee Nation to measure Cherokee land in preparation for a land lottery. The land lottery, which redistributed Cherokee lands to the citizens of Georgia, began in October 1832. Greedy whites, eager to get their hands on their winnings, often forced Cherokees off their land before the official date set by the Georgia government for removal.

The Treaty of New Echota signed in December 1835 by a minority of prominent Cherokees who favored removal, relinquished all lands in the East in exchange for land in the West and five million dollars. The United States Senate ratified the treaty by only one vote, and the deadline for final removal of the Cherokees from Georgia and other southeastern states was set for May 23, 1838.

TUGALOO TOWN

Toccoa

Tugaloo Town, along with Keowee to the east in South Carolina, was one of the most powerful and important towns of the Cherokee Lower settlements in the eighteenth century. Francis Varnod's 1721 census lists Tugaloo as having seventy men, sixty-six women, and sixty-eight children. Tugaloo, whose name comes from the word *ðugilu'yi*, referring to forks in a stream, was visited by Colonel George Chicken in 1715 and by John Herbert, South Carolina Commissioner of Indian Trade, in 1727. By the time of Herbert's visit, several white traders had established themselves near Tugaloo. One of these traders was Colonel Theophilus Hastings, who opened a trading center in 1716.

One of the leaders of Tugaloo during the early eighteenth century was the conjurer, Charity Hague. Colonel Maurice Moore, who was a member of Colonel Chicken's expedition, was visiting Tugaloo when a group of sixteen Creeks and Yamassees arrived. The Indians were sent as emissaries to persuade the Cherokees to join their forces and help the French and Spanish drive the British from the Carolinas. The Creeks and Yamassees reportedly had an army of five hundred men ready to attack all the white men in the area. However, Charity Hague had the sixteen Creeks and Yamassees killed apparently to keep the British, who supplied them with guns and ammunition, as their allies. For over sixty years, relations were strained between Tugaloo and the Creeks due to this incident.

Later leaders of Tugaloo included Skyo, who visited Charles Towne in 1749, and the Good Warrior, who signed the 1751 Treaty in Charles Towne which brought about new trade practices. By 1767, The Raven of Nikwasi had moved to Tugaloo and become chief.

In August 1776, the American commander Andrew Williamson attacked Ostatoy and Tugaloo with 640 men. Williamson wrote a description of his attack:

". . . when I arrived I found the Houses all burnt down on the other side of the River, but the corn and all the Houses on this side standing, which I entirely cut down and destroyed, and detached 100 men on Horse back who destroy another place and the corn about six miles distance, and took about 300 Raw deerskins."

Today, all that remains of the site of

Tugaloo is on a small island in the middle of Hartwell Lake on the Georgia/South Carolina state line. From Interstate 285 in South Carolina, take Exit 1 which is the exit for S.C. 11 north. Go 10 miles and turn left onto S.C. 24 towards Westminster. In 3.5 miles, turn left onto U.S. 123/U.S. 76. Go about 1 mile, then turn left again on U.S. 123 as U.S. 76 bears right. Drive 10 miles to the Georgia/South Carolina line. From Toccoa, Georgia, take U.S. 17A to U.S. 123 and go east 5.4 miles. From this point, the part of the lake to the north is where Tugaloo was located. There is a historical marker for Tugaloo on the Georgia side of the lake.

TOCCOA FALLS

Toccoa

Toccoa receives its name from the Cherokee word *tagwa hi*, meaning "Catawba Place," indicating that another tribe lived in the area before the Cherokees. The Cherokees sold the lands around Toccoa to settlers in 1738. A Cherokee legend says that when the first white men visited the falls, they saw an Indian woman walking beneath the water under the falls. On a sec-

ond look, they saw her sitting on a ledge two hundred feet in the air, dangling her feet over the edge. The Cherokees believed the woman may have been one of the *Nunnehi*, a race of invisible people.

This beautiful falls is located on the grounds of Toccoa Falls College. It is open to the public from 9 A.M. to sundown, year round. There is a small admission charge. For information, call 1-800-868-3257.

Toccoa Falls College is located a few blocks north of the town of Toccoa, on U.S. 17A.

Toccoa Falls

TALLULAH GORGE STATE PARK

Tallulah Falls

Talulu' was the name given to at least two Cherokee settlements. One settlement was located on the upper portion of Tallulah River in Rabun County, Georgia. There was also a town on Tallulah Creek, a branch of the Cheowa River, in Graham County, North Carolina. The Tallulah Falls located at Tallulah Gorge State Park were called Ugun'yi by the Cherokees, a name whose meaning has been lost.

There are several stories surrounding Tallulah Gorge and its falls. One Cherokee legend tells of a young warrior who nearly married the sister of Thunder. The young man met the maiden at a dance and fell in love with her immediately. He asked her to marry him, but she told him they must obtain her brother's consent. The young lovers, and the girl's sister, traveled down the Tallulah River to Tallulah Falls. Under the falls was a cave where the sisters lived with their brother. The warrior realized these were not ordinary women when they took off their hair and hung it on a rock to dry. The maiden asked the young man to sit beside her on a very large turtle. Then there was a loud clap of thun-

der, signaling the brother's arrival. The brother invited the young warrior to accompany him to a council and he agreed, but only if they could provide a horse. One of the sisters fetched an *uktena*, a great snake with a magic crystal in its head, for the young man to ride. Frightened almost to death, the young warrior declared he could not live in a dark place with giant snakes. Thunder became very angry. Lightning flashed from his eyes and struck the young warrior. When the young man woke, he was standing in the Tallulah River. The cave and the falls had disappeared. He returned home and told his story. But the young man only lived for seven days after his return, for anyone who visits the underworld and tells others about the visit will soon die.

In another Cherokee legend, some hunters from the West disappeared near the Tallulah River. Their concerned friends and family sent a party of medicine men to search for them. When the search party happened upon Tallulah Gorge, they found a species of little people who lived in the crevices of rocks and the caves under the falls. The medicine men decided from the shrieks of the little people that they were hostile toward men. The medicine men decided the hunting party had been lured to their deaths in the gorge by the little people.

Today the beautiful and rugged Tallulah Gorge is one of Georgia's newest state parks. It was created through a unique partnership between the Georgia Department of Natural Resources and the Georgia Power Company. Trails on both the north and south rims of the two-mile-long Tallulah Gorge provide views of the nearly thousand-foot-deep chasm, which is the home of several endangered species of plants and animals. The three-thousand-acre park has a sixty-three-acre lake with a swimming beach, over fifty campsites, tennis courts, and picnic and fishing facilities. A new visitor center, which will include historical and geological exhibits, is scheduled to open in the fall of 1995. The new building is on the north rim and overlooks the gorge. The park office hours are 8 A.M. to 5 P.M. For information, call 706-754-8257.

The town of Tallulah Falls is located on U.S. 23/U.S. 441 south of Clayton, Georgia. The entrance to Tallulah Gorge State Park is currently on the west side of U.S. 23/U.S. 441, a little north of the town of Tallulah Falls. When the new visitor center opens in the fall of 1995, the main park entrance will be moved to the east side of U.S. 23/U.S. 441, but will still be located on the north side of town.

WARWOMAN DELL

Clayton

Legend has it that an old Cherokee prophetess, known as the Warwoman, would venture out of the mountains each spring into this dell to forecast the tribe's future. She is said to have buried her divining crystals somewhere in the nearby forest when the Cherokees were removed in the 1830s.

The Warwoman Dell Recreation Area features a nature trail and picnic tables. The Bartram Trail, established in 1978 in honor of the famous naturalist and journalist, William Bartram, passes by Warwoman Dell and leads to nearby Becky Branch Falls and other waterfalls.

In Clayton, take Warwoman Road east from U.S. 23/441. After approximately 3 miles, watch for signs for the Warwoman Recreation Area or the Bartram Trail (at the time of this writing, the Warwoman Recreation Area sign was removed for road construction). The Recreation Area will be on the southern side of Warwoman Road. There is a small, dirt road leading into Warwoman Dell.

Warwoman Dell Recreation Area

Nacoochee Mound and Valley

NACOOCHEE MOUND
AND VALLEY

Helen

Legend says the Nacoochee Mound, located in the Nacoochee Valley, is the final resting place of two tragic lovers from rival Chickasaw and Cherokee tribes. However, excavations done on the site in 1915 revealed that the mound contained about seventy-five burial sites. It was probably built by Indians who lived in the area from about 1350 A.D. until the mid-1500s. It is not known whether the builders were ancestors of the Cherokees, or if the Cherokees moved into the area after the mounds were already built. It is known that the Nacoochee Valley was occupied by the Cherokees when William Bartram passed through the area and described the mound in his travel memoirs in 1776.

The Nacoochee Valley was farmed by Native Americans for centuries. The valley was the site of the Cherokee town of Little Chota, which was destroyed in 1776 by a militia of Georgia volunteers. In 1822, the first permanent white settlers arrived in the valley, and a trading post was established there. The trading post became a place where Cherokees could trade gold nuggets for merchandise. The Unicoi Trail, an old trail used by Indians and settlers, ran through the Nacoochee Valley and intersected with the nearby Coosa Trail. In 1830, the Cherokees granted permission for a company of whites and Indians to build a toll road, the Unicoi Turnpike, through the valley. The valley also served as a gathering site for the Trail of Tears.

Today, the mound is on private property and is not open to the public. However, the Nacoochee Mound is easily seen from the road that runs through the Nacoochee Valley. From Helen, take Ga. 75 south for 2 miles to the intersection of Ga. 17 and Ga. 75. The mound, which has a gazebo on top of it, is in the pasture on the east side of Ga. 75 at the intersection.

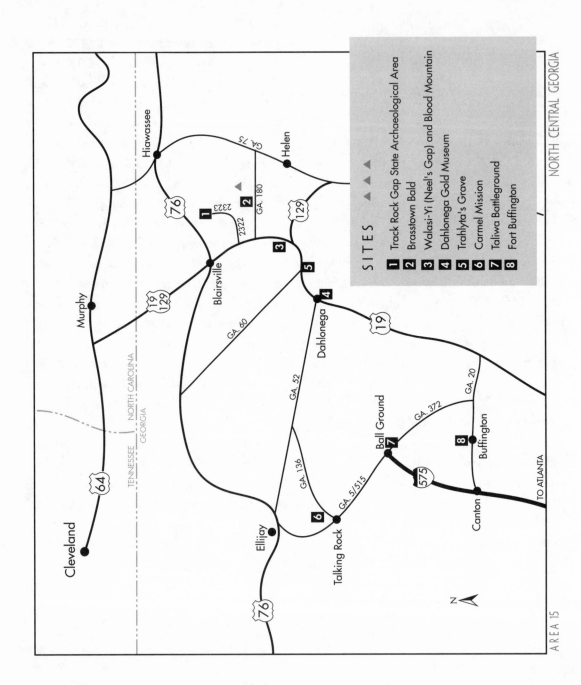

SITES ▲ ▲ ▲

1 Track Rock Gap State Archaeological Area
2 Brasstown Bald
3 Walasi-Yi (Neel's Gap) and Blood Mountain
4 Dahlonega Gold Museum
5 Trahlyta's Grave
6 Carmel Mission
7 Taliwa Battleground
8 Fort Buffington

Cleveland

Murphy

Hiawassee

Helen

Blairsville

Dahlonega

Elijay

Talking Rock

Ball Ground

Buffington

Canton

64

76

19
129

76

19
129

GA. 75

GA. 180

129

GA. 60

GA. 52

GA. 136

GA. 5/515

GA. 372

GA. 20

19

575

2323

2322

TENNESSEE
NORTH CAROLINA
GEORGIA

TO ATLANTA

N

AREA 15

Brasstown Bald

NORTH CENTRAL GEORGIA

▲ ▲ ▲

In 1799, Conrad Reed discovered a seventeen-pound gold nugget in Cabarrus County, North Carolina, setting off the first gold rush in the newly formed United States. In 1826, Coker Creek in Tennessee was the scene of another gold rush, supposedly started when an Indian maiden was seen wearing a large gold nugget around her neck.

In July 1829, events began to unravel in

the mountains of North Georgia that would make the earlier gold rushes pale in comparison—events that occurred on land owned by the Cherokee Nation. The first rumor that came out of the North Georgia mountains was that a young black slave had found a strange, yellow stone and showed it to his master. A later rumor claimed the rush was started by an Indian boy living on Ward Creek who sold a gold nugget to a Yankee trader. In actuality, the gold was discovered by a man named Benjamin Parks in Lumpkin County, Georgia. Although gold had been found in neighboring Georgia counties in the early 1800s, the discovery by Parks, and all the rumors which accompanied it, set off a new round of gold fever.

In the years following 1829, thousands of gold seekers poured into the Cherokee territory in North Georgia. New settlements sprang up at Auraria, Dahlonega, and throughout the Cherokee-owned mountains. The Cherokee lands were already threatened by politicians and land-hungry Georgians. Many Georgians felt the federal government had reneged on an 1802 agreement to remove all Indians from Georgia. The tension and conflict was intensified when the new hordes streamed into Cherokee country searching for gold. The next few years were filled with various efforts to remove the Cherokees from Georgia, and Cherokee responses to the efforts. Under pressure from Georgia, the United States Congress passed an Indian removal bill in 1830. The Cherokees opposed the bill and brought a lawsuit against it. The lawsuit eventually found its way to the United States Supreme Court. Though the Supreme Court ruled favorably for the Cherokees, this bill would become part of the foundation for the removal of the Cherokees from Georgia territory that began in April 1832.

TRACK ROCK GAP ARCHAEOLOGICAL AREA

Blairsville

The Cherokees called this gap in the mountains of North Georgia Datsu'nalasgun'yi, "where there are tracks," or Degayelun'ha, "printed place." Track Rock Gap was named for the large boulders in the area that have petroglyphs carved on them. Some Cherokees believed the carvings were tracks made when a great migration of birds and animals crossed the gap to flee danger from the west while the earth was still new and soft.

It is not known which group of Native Americans made the carvings in the gray, soapstone rock and why they were placed there. They may have marked an ancient trail that followed migrating animals, or they may have been carved by warriors relaxing after a successful hunt. Some of the petroglyphs resemble bird and animal tracks, while others resemble human footprints, crosses, and circles. The petroglyphs are gradually fading due to exposure to the elements and many years of vandalism. Iron grates have been placed over the rocks for protection against looting, but the petroglyphs are easily visible through the bars of the grate. For information, call the Brasstown Ranger District in Blairsville at 706-745-6928.

To reach Track Rock Gap, take U.S. 129/19 south from Blairsville for 3 miles, then turn left (east) on Town Creek Road (Ga. 2322). In 1 mile, turn left again onto Track Rock Gap Road (Ga. 2323) and watch for a large sign for Track Rock on the west side of the road after 3.8 miles.

Track Rock Gap Archaeological Area

BRASSTOWN BALD

Blairsville

At an elevation of 4,784 feet, Brasstown Bald is Georgia's highest peak. It offers breathtaking views of the surrounding mountains of North Georgia, North Carolina, South Carolina, and Tennessee. There is an observation deck, visitor center, and gift shop at Brasstown Bald, as well as several trails. The visitor center offers a video program on the dramatic seasonal changes of the area. There are also exhibits on the history of the mountains, including geologic history, the life of the Indians, the discovery of gold, the land lottery that distributed Cherokee land to settlers, and the Trail of Tears.

The mountain's name was adopted from a Cherokee town located on Brasstown Creek, northwest of the mountain in Towns County. The village was named Itse'yi meaning "new green place." However, it was known to the white settlers as Brasstown, probably because the settlers confused Itse'yi with the word *untsaiyi'*— the Cherokee word for brass.

Brasstown Bald is open daily from Memorial Day through October, and on weekends in spring if the weather permits. Even when the visitor center and road to the peak are closed, it is worth a trip to Brasstown Bald. A parking lot just below the peak is almost always open, and one can hike the trail to the summit or enjoy the views from the parking area. For information, call 706-896-2556 or 706-745-6928.

From Blairsville, take U.S. 129 south 8 miles and turn east on Ga. 180. From Helen, take Ga. 75 north and turn west on Ga. 180. From Ga. 180, turn north on Ga. 180 Spur and drive 2.5 miles to the parking lot. There is a $2.00 parking fee.

WALASI-YI (NEEL'S GAP) AND BLOOD MOUNTAIN

Blairsville

According to Cherokee legend, a hunter once saw a frog as big as a house at this gap in the North Georgia mountains. Therefore, the gap was named Walasi-Yi, meaning "Frog Place." In the 1930s, a road was cut through the wilderness in the area. The gap became known as Neel's Gap, named for the road's engineer. The view when you reach the top of Neel's Gap is well worth the steep climb up U.S. 129/19. The Appalachian Trail crosses the road here. The Walasi-Yi Center, a historic structure of stone and chestnut built as an inn by the Civilian Conservation Corps, is located at the top of the gap. The building is now a store and serves as a resting stop for both hikers and motorists.

About 2 miles west of Neel's Gap on the Appalachian Trail is Blood Mountain. According to Cherokee legend, Blood Mountain is one of the homes of the *Nunnehi*, a race of immortals who were invisible except when they wanted to be seen. The Cherokees believed the *Nunnehi* were their friends and would occasionally help them in battle as they did in the battle at Nikwasi Mound in North Carolina (see the Nikwasi Mound section in Area 11).

At the top of Blood Mountain is the Blood Mountain Archaeological Area. The area was designated as an "Archaeological Area" because hikers on the Appalachian Trail found many arrowheads there. According to Jack Wynn, an archaeologist for the U.S. Forest Service, there has been little significant archaeological research done at

Walasi-Yi Center at Neel's Gap

the site. Wynn reports that hikers and relic hunters have scoured the area so thoroughly there is very little left to find.

There are at least two theories about how Blood Mountain received its name and why hikers found so many arrowheads on the summit. According to local legend, the mountain received its name from a fierce battle between the Creeks and Cherokees that took place on the mountain. The legend says the battle was a great victory for the Cherokees. However, historian Robert S. Davis, Jr., has proposed another theory. He argues that Blood Mountain was the site of a battle between Cherokees and South Carolina forces under the command of Major Andrew Williamson that occurred in September 1776. Williamson and his men fought the Cherokees on Blood Mountain during an expedition to destroy the Middle settlements. The Cherokees reportedly lost three hundred men in the battle.

Neel's Gap and Walasi-Yi Center are about 13 miles south of Blairsville on U.S. 129/19. There is a parking lot and overlook for visitors to the store at the Walasi-Yi Center, but Appalachian Trail hikers should park at the Byron Reece Memorial Parking Lot a little north of the Walasi-Yi Center. From there, take the blue-blazed spur trail west about 0.5 mile to the white-blazed Appalachian Trail. Continue west on the Appalachian Trail for another 1 to 1.5 miles to the shelter which marks the summit of Blood Mountain and the battlefield.

DAHLONEGA GOLD MUSEUM STATE HISTORIC SITE
Dahlonega

Operated by the state of Georgia, the Dahlonega Gold Museum tells the history of gold mining in Georgia and the founding of the towns of Auraria and Dahlonega. The museum has displays explaining the land lottery that gave Cherokee lands to settlers and the Trail of Tears. The museum also has a small gift-and-book shop, and a film titled *Gold Fever*.

The town of Dahlonega hosts several festivals each year, the most popular of which is Gold Rush Days in October. Dahlonega is from the Cherokee word *dala'nige'i*, which means "yellow."

The museum is open Monday to Saturday from 9 A.M. to 5 P.M. and Sunday from 10 A.M. to 5 P.M. It is closed Thanksgiving, Christmas, and New Year's Day. There is an admission fee. For information, call 706-864-2257.

Dahlonega Gold Museum State Historic Site

You can approach Dahlonega via U.S. 19, Ga. 52, or Ga. 60. Regardless of what road you take, you will circle the museum located in the old Lumpkin County Courthouse in the heart of town.

TRAHLYTA'S GRAVE

Dahlonega

According to a local legend, Trahlyta was a Cherokee princess who kept her beauty and youth by drinking magic waters from a spring located near present-day Dahlonega. She was kidnapped by a re-jected suitor and taken far away from the magic spring. As soon as she was taken away from the spring, her youth started to disappear. She quickly became very old and ill. Her abductor promised to bury the dying princess near her home. Her tribe marked her grave with stones, and it is now a custom for passersby to add a stone to her grave for good luck.

There are many legends of tragic lovers in the southern Appalachians, some of which may date from Cherokee times. No doubt, many of these stories originated after the Cherokees left the area. The legend of Trahlyta's Grave may have been invented by the owners of nearby Porter Springs Hotel to attract visitors. Legend has it that

Trahlyta's Grave

Trahlyta's fountain of youth was located at the old Porter Springs resort.

Trahlyta's Grave is located 8 miles north of the Dahlonega Courthouse Square, at the intersection of U.S. 19 and Ga. 60. The large pile of stones in the center of the junction is marked by a historical sign.

CARMEL MISSION

Talking Rock

The Carmel Mission was first known as the Taloney Mission, named for the nearby Cherokee settlement of Talona. In his history of Gilmer County, George Gordon Ward explained that the village of Talona was located a few miles west of the mission, on the eastern edge of present-day Blaine. Early white pioneers found cleared land stretching from the village of Talona, up Talona Creek, to the site of present-day Whitestone. As the area near Whitestone grew, it became known as Taloney. Then a new settlement, about two miles south of Talking Rock, also became known as Taloney. This new settlement was located near the Federal Road. A post office was established there in 1820, with Reverend Moody Hall as postmaster. In 1824, the

newer Taloney settlement changed its name to Carmel.

The Taloney Mission was founded in 1819 by Reverend Hall. Moody Hall was from New Hampshire and worked for the American Board of Commissioners for Foreign Missions. Hall had worked at Brainerd Mission before being assigned the task of opening the Taloney Mission. The mission included both a school and a church, and it served Cherokees, whites, and mixed-blood families. The missionaries went to surrounding households to recruit new members. Reverend Isaac Proctor, who arrived at the mission sometime prior to May 1826, wrote in May 1828:

> We had a solemn and interesting meeting. The congregation was large. Three full Cherokees were baptized. They live about 25 miles from us in a small town very much secluded. Some of our members and Mr. Butrick have visited them. These men appeared better than any candidates (all things considered) I have ever seen. They are very anxious to have some parts of the scripture, or any Cherokee tracts.

In 1831, Reverend Proctor was arrested by the Georgia Guard for not obeying a new law that required missionaries in Cherokee territory to obtain licenses and

Georgia farm near the Carmel Mission Site

take an oath of allegiance to Georgia. Reverend Daniel S. Butrick managed to escape arrest because he was away at the time. Other Georgia missionaries were also arrested but soon released. A few months later, both Proctor and Butrick left Georgia to escape the pressure from the state. Carmel Mission struggled along as a state-supported school in the later years, until it finally closed sometime between 1836 and 1839.

From Atlanta, take Interstate 575 north to Ga. 5, the Zell Miller Parkway. Take Ga. 5 to the intersection with Ga. 136 and turn left onto the exit road for Ga. 136. After 0.2 mile, the exit road will meet Ga. 136. Turn right and go 0.1 mile to the Talking Rock "Y," which is the name for the intersection of the old Ga. 5 and Ga. 136. A historical marker for the Carmel Mission is in the center of the intersection.

TALIWA BATTLEGROUND

Ball Ground

James Mooney described the relationship between the Cherokees and their Creek neighbors to the south as "one of hostility with occasional intervals of good will."

These two enemies were constantly vying for hunting grounds and land to settle and farm. The Indian system of honor and revenge also contributed to the many years of quarrels and conflicts between the two tribes. The boundaries between the two nations were constantly shifting. During the historic period, a large part of the disputed ground was in North Georgia.

The Battle of Taliwa took place around 1755 near the Cherokee village of Long-swamp Town, at a creek called Mountain or Long-swamp Creek. The battle occurred where the Great Indian War Trail crossed the creek. The story of the battle was passed on to James Mooney from James D. Wafford, a mixed-blood who was born in the Cherokee Nation in 1806. Wafford learned it from a trader named Brian Ward, who claimed to have witnessed the battle. According to Ward, the Cherokees numbered five hundred and were at first overpowered by the estimated one thousand Creek warriors. The Cherokees fell back, regrouped, and rallied to attack, flushing the Creeks from cover and forcing them to run. Legend says that Nanyihi, later known as Nancy Ward, was responsible for rallying the Cherokees to victory after her husband Kingfisher was killed. (For more information on Nancy Ward, see the Overview section.)

Traditionally, the Battle of Taliwa was reported as a decisive victory for the Cherokees which opened up North Georgia for settlement by the Cherokees. However, historian Robert S. Davis, Jr., suggests the importance of the battle, if it actually occurred, has been exaggerated. He points to the lack of Cherokee settlements in North Georgia until after the American Revolution as evidence that the battle did not settle the boundary dispute. The two tribes continued to quarrel about ownership and boundaries in North Georgia until March 22, 1816, when a treaty with the federal government established a final boundary line between the two tribes. The boundary ran across Georgia, about 10 miles south of Atlanta to the Coosa River in Alabama, then northwest to the Alabama-Mississippi line.

The name of the present-day town of Ball Ground has traditionally been attributed to the location of a stick-ball playing field—the Cherokee game similar to modern lacrosse—in the area that was regularly used by local Indians for sport. It has also been suggested that the Cherokees and Creeks played a game of ball here to decide their claims to lands in North Georgia lands. A more-recent theory is that white settlers confused the Cherokee words for ball game with the word for battle, and that a more accurate name for Ball Ground would have been Battle Ground.

A historical marker commemorating the Battle of Taliwa is located in Ball Ground, near the place where the battle is believed to have taken place. From Interstate 75 north of Atlanta, take Interstate 575 north towards Canton. Take Exit 10 for Ga. 20E and follow it 8.7 miles through Buffington (and past the Fort Buffington Historical Marker) to Ga. 369. Turn left (northeast) on Ga. 369 and drive 2.1 miles to Ga. 372. Turn left (north) onto Ga. 372 and drive 7.5 miles to Ball Ground. The historical marker will be on the left side of the road, in a small park area by the city hall.

FORT BUFFINGTON

Buffington

Fort Buffington was one of at least thirteen removal forts in Georgia used during the Cherokee removal of 1838. By May 1838, only two thousand Cherokees had voluntarily moved west. General Winfield Scott ordered seven thousand troops into Cherokee territory to commence the roundup of the remaining Cherokees. After their initial imprisonment in the local forts or stockades, they were moved to internment camps to wait emigration to the west.

The other removal forts in Georgia, and their approximate present-day locations, were Fort Hetzel (East Ellijay), Fort Gilmer (Carters), Fort Newnan or Talking Rock Fort (Blaine), Fort Embry (Dahlonega), Fort Cumming (Lafayette), Fort Wool (New Echota), Chastain's Fort (20 miles northeast of East Ellijay in Fannin County), Fort Campbell (Dawson County), Fort Hoskins (Spring Place), Fort Means (near Kingston in Bartow County), Cedartown Fort (Cedartown), and a fort at Rome. In his book, *Cherokee Footprints,*

Charles O. Walker mentions Fort Scudders, also known as Fort Eaton, which was located at Frogtown in Forsyth County, but this fort does not appear on an 1838 map of military posts in the Cherokee Nation drawn by Lieutenant E. D. Keyes.

Fort Buffington was located in the present-day town of Buffington, which is east of Canton. From Interstate 75 north of Atlanta, take Interstate 575 north towards Canton. Take Exit 10 for Ga. 20E. Follow Ga. 20E for 3.2 miles. The historical marker for Fort Buffington will be on the right, in front of the Buffington School.

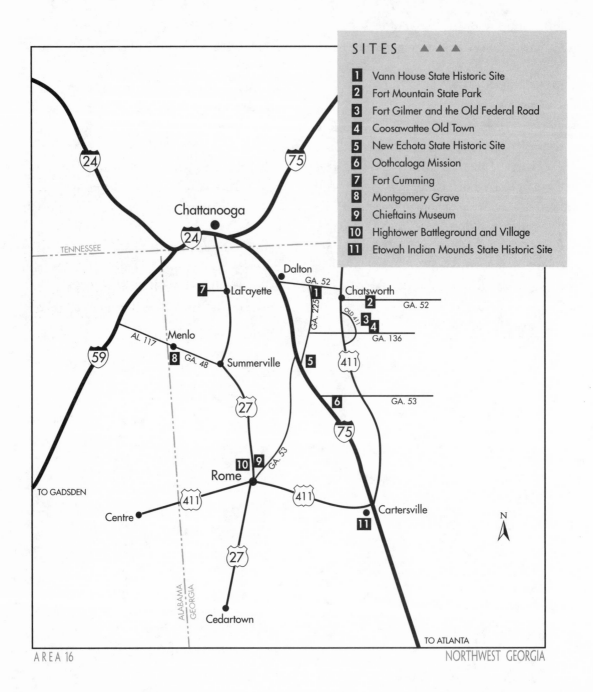

SITES ▲▲▲

1 Vann House State Historic Site
2 Fort Mountain State Park
3 Fort Gilmer and the Old Federal Road
4 Coosawattee Old Town
5 New Echota State Historic Site
6 Oothcaloga Mission
7 Fort Cumming
8 Montgomery Grave
9 Chieftains Museum
10 Hightower Battleground and Village
11 Etowah Indian Mounds State Historic Site

AREA 16

NORTHWEST GEORGIA

Carters Dam, location of Coosawattee Old Town

AREA 16

NORTHWEST GEORGIA

▲ ▲ ▲

In October 1831, Wilson Lumpkin was elected governor of Georgia on a platform that encouraged "the general emigration of the Indians to the West." Lumpkin was sworn in November 9, and he was immediately confronted with states rights issues concerning Georgia's Indian policies.

On December 2, 1831, at the request of the Georgia legislature, Governor Lumpkin addressed the subject of Georgia's Indian relations. The following excerpt from the speech appeared later in his autobiography, *The Removal of the Cherokee Indians from Georgia*:

> The unfortunate remnant of Cherokee Indians remaining in Georgia ought now to consider themselves the admitted charge of our peculiar care; and if possible we ought, as their friends and benefactors, to preserve and cherish them. They ought not forcibly to be dispossessed of their homes, or driven from the land of their fathers; they ought to be guarded and protected in the peaceable enjoyment of a sufficient portion of land to sustain them, with their families, in their present abodes, so long as they may choose to remain; and their rights and property should be as well secured from all lawless depredation as those of the white man. It would be as cruel as unjust, to compel the aborigines to abandon the graves of their fathers; but in the present extraordinary state of things it would be visionary to suppose, that the Indian claim can be allowed to this extensive tract of country—to lands on which they have neither dwelt, nor made improvements.

Lumpkin served two short terms as governor. He made his last speech to the Georgia legislature on November 3, 1835. On December 29, 1835, the Treaty of New Echota was signed at the former capital of the Cherokee Nation in northwest Georgia. In July 1836, Lumpkin was commissioned to execute the treaty which called for the forfeiture to the state and federal governments of all Cherokee lands east of the Mississippi. The treaty also forced the removal of all Cherokees to the West.

VANN HOUSE
STATE HISTORIC SITE AND
SPRING PLACE MISSION

Spring Place

Built in 1804, the two-story brick mansion at Spring Place was the home of the James Vann family, one of the most prosperous and influential families in the Cherokee Nation during the early 1800s. In 1809, James Vann was shot and killed at a nearby tavern, and his son, Joseph, inherited the property. Joseph, an astute businessman, increased the family's fortunes and became known as "Rich Joe Vann." The Vann family continued to prosper at Spring Place until 1835, when they were evicted by Georgia soldiers. They temporarily moved to a family farm on the Tennessee River (see the Vannville section in Area 2), before moving to the Cherokee lands in the west.

The house at Spring Place features

Vann House State Historic Site

an interesting, cantilevered stairway with no known means of support; hand-carved Cherokee roses; and colorfully painted rooms of sky blue, grass green, harvest yellow, and Georgia-clay red. The house contains period furnishings, artifacts found on the grounds, and personal items of Joseph Vann. The Moravian mission that James Vann helped found at Spring Place is nearby. The mission educated many Cherokee children in the area.

The Vann House State Historic Site hosts many special events each year, including living-history demonstrations during Vann House Days, held the third weekend in July, and a Moravian Christmas celebration held the second weekend in December. The house is open Tuesday through Saturday from 9 A.M. to 5 P.M. and Sunday from 2 P.M. to 5:30 P.M. It is closed Mondays, Thanksgiving, Christmas, and New Year's Day. There is a small admission fee. For information, call 706-695-2598.

To reach Vann House State Historic Site from Interstate 75, watch for signs on the interstate near Dalton for Ga. 52. The site is located on Ga. 225, about 1 mile south of the intersection of Ga. 225 and Ga. 52, on the outskirts of Chatsworth. From New Echota State Park, take Ga. 225 north. The Spring Place Mission site is nearby and is identified by a Georgia historical marker. From the Vann House parking lot, turn left (south) onto Ga. 225 (south) and take the next left (east) onto Ga. 52A. The marker is just around the corner from the Vann House, on the right side of Ga. 52A.

FORT MOUNTAIN STATE PARK

Chatsworth

The origin of the eight-hundred-fifty-five-foot-long rock wall that gives this mountain its name is clouded in mystery. One local legend says that it was built by a fair-skinned, moon-eyed race of people who once inhabited this region. (According to Cherokee legend, when the Cherokees moved into the area north of Fort Mountain between the Little Tennessee River and the Chickamauga area in Tennessee, they displaced a pale-skinned, moon-eyed race who had been living there for many years. There is some overlap in the local and Cherokee legends of a fair-skinned race, possibly European, who once lived in the southernmost Appalachians. However, most archaeologists and historians discredit these legends.) Along the east-to-west course of the wall there are twenty-nine circular pits, several feet in diameter and thirty-feet apart. It is not known if the wall was built for ceremonial, calendric, or defensive purposes, but most archaeologists agree that it was built by Native Americans—probably from the middle or late Woodland Period.

The Cherokee name for Fort Mountain, also known as Cohutta Mountain, was Gahu'ti, which comes from the Cherokee word *gahuta'yi*, meaning "a shed roof supported on poles." In Cherokee legend, Fort Mountain was the dwelling place of a great serpent called the *Ustu'tli*, which had three-cornered flat feet on each end of its body and moved in strides like an inch-worm. The local hunters were afraid to go near

the mountain. One day, a warrior from a northern settlement set a great fire around the base of the mountain. The fire climbed upward and engulfed the *Ustu'tli*. The Cherokees also believed that Gahu'ti was the place Aganuni'tsi' or Groundhog's Mother, killed the Uktena, another great serpent who carried a magical blood crystal in its forehead.

Visitors to Fort Mountain State Park can enjoy camping, picnicking, cottages, and summer recreational activities, including swimming, miniature golf, and boat rental. The park is open daily from 7 A.M. to 10 P.M. There is a parking fee. For information, call 706-695-2621.

From Interstate 75, take U.S. 76 through Dalton to Chatsworth. In Chatsworth, take Ga. 52 east for 8 miles to Fort Mountain State Park. The entrance to the park will be on the left side of Ga. 52.

The rock wall at Fort Mountain State Park

FORT GILMER
AND THE FEDERAL ROAD

Ramhurst and Carters

Fort Gilmer was built in 1838 by order of General Winfield Scott. It was used by Scott as a temporary headquarters when the removal efforts got under way in May 1838. Fort Gilmer was one of at least thirteen removal forts located in Georgia. (See the Fort Buffington section in Area 15 for the locations of the other removal forts in Georgia.) Fort Gilmer's location was probably chosen because it was on the Federal Road, near the Cherokee town of Coosawattee.

The Cherokees first gave permission to construct a road across their country in an informal agreement made in 1803. In 1805, this agreement was ratified in a treaty. The horse-and-wagon road closely followed Indian trading paths that led from Augusta, Georgia, to Lookout Mountain, Tennessee. The road then connected with trails to Nashville and north Alabama. The new twenty-four-foot-wide road was built to modernize the portion of a Cherokee trail which began near Athens, Georgia. From Athens, the new road ran northwest to Vann's Ferry near present-day Lake Lanier, then to the Cherokee villages of Hightower, Tate, and Talking Rock. From Talking Rock, it closely followed Talking Rock Creek through the settlement of Carters. Near Ramhurst, the road branched, with the right fork running through Eton and Tennga toward Knoxville, and the left branch leading to Spring Place, Rossville, and then on to Nashville.

The Cherokees benefited from the in-

creased commerce the Federal Road brought to the Cherokee Nation. They built taverns along the road, which doubled as inns, as well as stores and toll ferries. Toll roads that branched off the main road were built by enterprising locals, and stagecoach lines were later established in the area. The Federal Road became the primary postal

Fort Gilmer was located along the Federal Road.

route in Cherokee country, and it became one of the main delivery routes for the *Cherokee Phoenix*.

Unfortunately, the Federal Road, and the other roads which brought commerce to the Cherokee Nation, also brought the white settlers who eventually took the Cherokees' land. And it was the Federal Road that many of the Cherokees of Georgia would follow to Ross's Landing and Charleston in Tennessee, to begin their final exodus from their eastern homelands.

The Forks of the Federal Road is located in the town of Ramhurst. In this area, old U.S. 411 has been replaced with a newer stretch of highway to the west. U.S. 76 follows the new U.S. 411 for a short distance north of Ramhurst, then it follows the old U.S. 411 for a short distance east of Ramhurst. To reach Ramhurst and the Forks of the Federal Road, take U.S. 76 east from Dalton to Chatsworth. Then take U.S. 411 south 6 miles to where U.S. 76E and Ga. 282 turn right (east). Drive 0.1 mile to a historical marker on the right, located at the intersection of old U.S. 411 and U.S. 76/Ga. 282.

To reach the site of Fort Gilmer from the Forks of the Federal Road, take old U.S. 411 south (this is also U.S. 76E) for 2.3 miles to where U.S. 76E turns left (east) towards Ellijay. Stay straight and continue down old U.S. 411 another 0.7 mile. The marker will be on the left (east) side of the road next to a wooded area near Carters.

COOSAWATTEE OLD TOWN

Carters Lake

In the sixteenth century, most of the Indians of the Southeast were organized into several large chiefdoms. One of these chiefdoms was Coosa, whose capital town, also named Coosa, was located at the confluence of the Coosawattee River and Talking Rock Creek at present-day Carters, Georgia. In 1559, the Spanish sent Tristan de Luna to Pensacola, Florida, with supplies, soldiers, and colonists. The purpose of this mission was to establish three towns to secure the Southeast as a colony of Spain. One town would be established at the Indian capital town of Coosa, with two other towns outside the Coosa chiefdom at Ochuse (Pensacola Bay, Florida) and Punta de Santa Elena (Port Royal Sound, South Carolina).

Tristan de Luna's expedition landed at Pensacola Bay in August 1559. In February 1560, in search of food, he moved his colonists to an Indian town on the Alabama River named Nanicapana. In April, de Luna sent a detachment of one hundred infantrymen and forty cavalrymen, led by Mateo del Sauz, to the capital of Coosa. They reached Coosa on July 26, having stopped on the way at several other villages of the Coosa chiefdom on the way. They were greeted warmly by the principal chief of Coosa whom the Indians referred to as "the great lord of Coosa."

There were seven small settlements on the Coosawattee River within ten miles of the town of Coosa. The settlements, some of which were palisaded, contained both summer and winter houses. The Coosas traded food for Spanish colored beads, silk ribbon, and articles of clothing. Then the great lord of Coosa asked the Spaniards to accompany his warriors on a raid to the villages of the Napochies—a tributary society of the Coosas that were no longer under Coosa control. The population of the Coosas had diminished in recent years due to the deadly epidemics brought by De Soto's visit in 1540. However, the Napochie population had been spared from the epidemics. They revolted from Coosa control, refusing to pay tribute. The Napochies also controlled several of the routes leading northward from the Coosa chiefdom, and the Coosas wanted to regain control of those routes.

Del Sauz sent twenty-five infantrymen and twenty-five cavalrymen to accompany the Coosas' three hundred warriors on the raid. When they reached the Napochies' first village (probably the Audubon Acres site in Chattanooga, Tennessee), they found it abandoned. They pursued the Napochies to a second village on the Tennessee River (probably the site of the Citico Mound in Chattanooga, Tennessee), then to a ford across the river where the people of both villages had crossed to the other side. The Spaniards crossed to an island in the middle of the river and one of the soldiers fired, killing a Napochie. The Napochies soon surrendered, promising to pay tributes and to become loyal subjects of the great lord of Coosa once again.

When de Luna received the news that del Sauz had reached Coosa, he ordered his colonists to prepare to go there, but they refused. They had become mutinous due to starvation. Eventually, del Sauz and his men returned to Pensacola. The colonists and the soldiers were eventually evacuated, the colonial expedition having been a failure.

Recent research into this time period (the early 1500s to the early 1600s) suggests the possibility that many of the Southeastern Indians of this time were organized into large chiefdoms similar to the Coosa chiefdom. It is not clear if the Cherokees were a part of any of these large chiefdoms.

In the late 1500s to early 1600s, Coosa and other large chiefdoms began to break up. One of the primary causes was severe population loss brought on by European diseases. It is believed many of the Coosa Indians in Georgia later became associated with Creek tribes. It has also been suggested that as eastern Tennessee and northwest Georgia were depopulated, Cherokees gradually began to move into these areas.

Two hundred years after de Luna visited the village of Coosa, the site would become the Cherokee town of Coosawattee (also known as Coosawattee Old Fields, probably referring to the fact it was a very old settlement). Like many of their villages, the Cherokees built Coosawattee on a site that had been previously occupied. The town was located on the Federal Road. At the time of the removal it was one of the larger Cherokee settlements with six hundred inhabitants. In 1823, the Baptists opened a mission at Coosawattee. In 1835, Coosawattee was placed on the Baptist preaching circuit after most of the missionaries had been forced to leave Georgia. Two frequent speakers on the circuit included the Cherokee preachers Jesse Bushyhead and Evan Jones. Coosawattee was also the principal town in the Coosawattee District, one of the eight districts of the Cherokee Nation established in 1820.

The building of Carters Dam and the reregulation dam on the Coosawatee River and Talking Rock Creek have caused the sites of the Coosa and Coosawattee to be inundated, but the general area is still accessible. The area, now under the management of the United States Army Corps of Engineers, is used for power production and recreation. Recreational facilities include a marina, picnic, fishing, camping, and swimming facilities, rental cabins, nature trails, and a visitor center. The visitor center has displays explaining the construction of the dam and the recreational facilities at the reservoir, as well as exhibits on natural history, the Cherokees, and earlier Native American cultures. For information, call 706-334-2248.

To reach Carters Dam when approaching from the north on Interstate 75, take U.S. 76 east from Dalton to Chatsworth. In Chatsworth take U.S. 76/U.S. 411 south for 6 miles to where U.S. 76 turns right and separates from U.S. 411. Follow U.S. 76 and go 0.1 mile after turning right, then turn right again onto old U.S. 411 (which is also U.S. 76). Continue to follow U.S. 76/411 another 2.3 miles. When U.S. 76 turns to the left toward Ellijay, continue straight on old U.S. 411, past the site of Fort Gilmer to the Powerhouse Road. You can turn down Powerhouse Road and go 1 mile to the towering Carters Dam. Here you can see the reregulation area and approximate site of the Indian town of Coosa and the Cherokee town of Coosawattee. You can also continue down old U.S. 411 to Ga. 136, turn left (east) on Ga. 136 which follows Talking Rock Creek for 2 miles to a left turn for the visitor center. The visitor center is located on top of the mountain, overlooking Carters Lake (Coosawattee River) and the reregulation area.

If approaching from the south from Interstate 75, take Ga. 136 east from Resaca to the entrance for the visitor center, or turn (left) north on old U.S. 411 and go 2.3 miles to Powerhouse Road.

NEW ECHOTA STATE HISTORIC SITE

Calhoun

For the traveler who has time for only one stop in Georgia, New Echota is the best choice. Using Sequoyah's alphabet, Elias Boudinot printed the first issues of the *Cherokee Phoenix* in New Echota in 1828. It was here that the Cherokee legislature es-

tablished the Cherokee Nation in 1825, with New Echota as its capital. It was in New Echota that the Reverend Samuel A. Worcester, the American Board missionary at New Echota from 1827 to 1835, was arrested by the Georgia Guard—an act which resulted in a United States Supreme Court victory for the Cherokees. And it was in New Echota where the Treaty of New Echota was signed in 1835.

The New Echota site fell into great disrepair after the Cherokees left. Virtually nothing of the old town remained until the 1950s, when the people of the county began restoring the Reverend Samuel Worcester's house and established New Echota as a state historic site. Three of the buildings at New Echota State Historic Site are reconstructions, including the *Cherokee Phoenix* print shop, the Cherokee Supreme Court House, and the Cherokee Council House. Three authentic buildings have been moved to the site, including the James Vann Tavern (circa 1805), which was moved here from its original location on the Chattahoochee River when that site was doomed to be inundated by Lake Lanier. The only building originally located at the site is the Worcester house, which was built in 1828 to serve as a Presbyterian Mission Station and family home. Fort Wool was located in the woods behind the Worcester house. This fort served as a military post during the forced removal of the Cherokees in 1838.

Nearby is the small New Echota cemetery, where one of the marked graves belongs to Chief Pathkiller—the principal chief of the Cherokees before John Ross. The only other marked graves in the cemetery belong to Jerusha Worcester, the infant daughter of Reverend Samuel Worcester, and Hariett Boudinot, the Connecticut-born wife of Elias Boudinot who died due to complications in childbirth.

In addition to tours of the reconstructed town of New Echota, the park offers a museum with a fifteen-minute video about New Echota and a small gift shop. New Echota State Historic Site is open Tuesday through Saturday from 9 A.M. to 5 P.M. and on Sunday from 2 P.M. to 5:30 P.M. It is closed Mondays, Thanksgiving, Christmas, and New Year's Day. There is an admission fee. For information, call 706-629-8151.

New Echota State Historic Site is easily reached from Interstate 75. Take Exit 131 and go east about 1 mile on Ga. 225 to the entrance.

A replica of the printing press used to publish the Cherokee Phoenix *at New Echota State Historic Site*

OOTHCALOGA MISSION

Belwood

Oothcaloga, also Oochgelogy, Mission was founded in 1821 by Reverend John Gambold of the Spring Place Mission. Gambold had lost his wife, Anna Rosel, in February of that year and had buried her in the cemetery at Spring Place. In April 1821, after repeated requests by the Cherokees to establish a Moravian mission near

New Echota, Gambold resigned his post at Spring Place, took a new wife, and headed south to his new assignment. The new mission was built 4 miles south of New Echota. In 1827, Gambold died and was replaced by J. R. Schmidt. Schmidt was later replaced by Franz Eder, who was replaced by Reverend Henry Gottlieb Clauder. Clauder helped convert The Ridge to Christianity. Although both the Spring Place and Oothcaloga missions thrived in the early 1830s, their land was confiscated by the state of Georgia, and they were forced to close in January 1833. The Moravians were awarded $2,878 for the loss of their land and property at Spring Place, and $4,676.50 for their losses at Oothcaloga.

The two-story portion of an old house in the Belwood community, south of Resaca, was believed to have been part of the Oothcaloga Mission. The house recently burned and all that remains is a pile of rubble and a historical marker for Oothcaloga Mission. From Interstate 75, take Exit 129 which is the Ga. 53/Fairmount/Rome exit. Go east on Ga. 53 for 0.2 mile and turn right (south) onto Outlet Center Road. Go 0.2 mile and turn left on Belwood Road. Drive 1.6 miles south on Belwood Road and watch for the historical marker on the right.

FORT CUMMING

LaFayette

Fort Cumming, built in 1836, was one of at least thirteen forts in Georgia used during the removal of the Cherokees in 1838. It was under the command of Captain Samuel Farriss. Like many of the removal forts, it was manned by local volunteers. The fort had a stockade built of upright logs, and a rifle tower with port holes in each corner.

As the historical marker at the site suggests, the fort may have been named for a minister named David B. Cumming. In 1836, Cumming, David T. Fulton, and David King were appointed itinerant missionaries to the Cherokee Nation by the Holston Conference of the Methodist Church. Cumming took a strong interest in the Methodist Cherokees and accompanied the Cherokees to Oklahoma. In 1837, before the final removal, Cumming reported 480 Cherokee members of the Methodist Church in the entire eastern United States.

The site of Fort Cumming is in the town of LaFayette, in an area known as Big Spring. From Interstate 75 south of Chattanooga, take Ga. 2 west to U.S. 27. Turn left (south) at the traffic light in Fort Oglethorpe and drive 16 miles on U.S. 27

to LaFayette. When U.S. 27 bears left and Business 27 goes straight on the north end of LaFayette, take Business 27 for 1.6 miles to Indiana Street. (If approaching from the south on U.S. 27, take Business 27 when it turns left off of U.S. 27 and go 1.75 miles.) Turn west on Indiana Street and drive 0.5 mile. There is a historical marker for the location of Fort Cumming on the right, just past the railroad tracks. The marker is inside a fence on city property and may be difficult to see if the fence or area around the marker are overgrown.

MONTGOMERY'S GRAVE

Menlo

Colonel Hugh Montgomery served as a United States agent to the Cherokees from 1825 to 1838. He was charged with trying to convince the Indians to emigrate west voluntarily, but he was generally unsuccessful in this effort. The Cherokees did not have confidence in Montgomery and complained that he failed to keep intruders off of their lands.

Montgomery's Grave

Montgomery helped survey the state line in North Georgia and the line between Franklin County and the Cherokee Nation. He also served in the Georgia legislature and state senate. For his many services to Georgia, Montgomery was given land in Chattooga County, where he is now buried in the Alpine Community Church Cemetery.

From U.S. 27 in Summerville, take Ga. 48 west for 8 miles to Menlo. Or from Mentone, Alabama, take Al. 117 for 10.8 miles down Lookout Mountain to Menlo. (Al. 117 changes to Ga. 48 at the state line.) In Menlo, take Ga. 337 south 1.75 miles to the white-clapboard Alpine Community Church, which will be located on the left. The grave is in the church cemetery, which is open to the public.

CHIEFTAINS MUSEUM

Rome

In the early 1800s, The Ridge, one of the most prominent leaders of the Cherokee Nation, purchased a log cabin on the Oostanaula River in northwest Georgia and built a beautiful plantation. He and his family operated a small ferryboat near this plantation. His son, John Ridge, established a home about 6 miles north of The Ridge's property. John Ross settled across the river, a few miles away from The Ridge's plantation, presumably to be near The Ridge and the center of Cherokee politics. (For more on the Ridge family, see the Overview section.)

The Ridge's house is now home to the Chieftains Museum, which is owned by the Chieftains Museum Association. The museum, a National Historic Landmark, is a stately, white-frame mansion which was expanded in the early 1800s. The logs from the original 1794 structure are contained within the more recent walls, but a section has been exposed for visitors to see the original construction.

The tragic story of The Ridge, one of the signers of the Treaty of New Echota, is told at the museum. The museum also has artifacts that were excavated at the sight, information on the Mississippian-era Indians who inhabited the area at one time, and information on the history of Rome and northwest Georgia.

The museum is open Tuesday through Saturday from 10 A.M. to 4 P.M. It is closed Sundays, Mondays, and all national holidays. There is a small admission charge. For information, call 706-291-9494.

From Interstate 75, take U.S. 411 or Ga. 53 to Rome and follow the signs for

The Chieftains Museum, home of The Ridge

the museum. The museum is located north of Rome on the Riverside Parkway, between U.S. 27 and Ga. 53 Spur.

HIGHTOWER BATTLEGROUND AND VILLAGE

Rome

In September 1793, a large group of Cherokees—led by Chief Doublehead, his nephew, Chief John Watts, and a chief named The Bench—attacked Cavett's Station near Knoxville. During the attack, five Cherokees and Alexander Cavett were killed. The Bench told the survivors inside the station that if they would surrender, they would not be killed. The Cavetts agreed to the terms but were killed by an angry Doublehead, who attacked the unarmed captives when they emerged from the building. One small boy who survived was secretly carried away by John Watts. The boy was later killed by Creeks who had accompanied the Cherokees to the Knoxville area.

In retaliation for the attack on Cavett's Station, and for other depredations in East Tennessee caused by the Chickamaugans, John Sevier led a force of seven to eight hundred volunteers into Georgia in pursuit

of the raiders. On October 14, 1793, Sevier's party made camp at the Cherokee town of Ustanali, near the forks of the Conasauga and Coosawattee rivers (near present-day Resaca). He took several Cherokee prisoners at Ustanali, and he learned from them that the raiding party of Cherokees and Creeks was made up of Indians from every town in the area. Nearly every man from the villages of Sallyquoah (present-day Fairmount, Georgia), Coosawaytah (on the Coosawattee River in present-day Gordon County, Georgia), Turkeytown (present-day Centre, Alabama), and Ustanali had participated in the expedition. The prisoners also informed Sevier that the Indian forces were headed toward a town called Hightower located at the confluence of the Coosa, Etowah, and Oostanaula rivers. After resting a few days, replenishing supplies, and then burning Ustanali, Sevier marched his army toward Hightower.

The Tennesseans caught up with the band of Cherokees and Creeks at the ford on Etowah River, near where it empties into the Coosa River. The Indians, now under the command of Kingfisher, had dug in on the other side of the ford and were waiting for the militia to cross. Sevier ordered Colonel Kelly and part of his Knox County Company to find another crossing downstream. Kelly and his men found a new ford and began to swim across the river. The Indians left their entrenchments and ran downstream to meet Kelly's men. Then, Captain Evans and his mounted infantry began to cross at the original ford. Confused, most of the Indians hurried back to the upper crossing. Sevier described the encounter:

> An engagement instantly took place and became very warm; notwithstanding the enemy were at least four to one in numbers, besides the advantage of situation, Captain Evans with his heroic company put them in short time entirely to flight. They left several dead on the ground and were seen to carry others off both on foot and horse. Bark and trails of blood from the wounded were to be seen in every quarter.

After the battle, Sevier's forces pursued the Indians down the Coosa River, destroying several Creek and Cherokee towns as they went. This was the final battle campaign for both John Sevier and Kingfisher, but for different reasons. Kingfisher died bravely in the Battle of Hightower. John Sevier gave up Indian-fighting in favor of Tennessee politics.

The name of the Cherokee town of Hightower is an American corruption of the Indian word *etowah*, or *i'tawa'*, which is probably of Creek origin. After the destruction of Hightower by Sevier's forces in 1793, it was probably relocated further upstream to an area near present-day Cartersville, Georgia.

The junction of the Coosa, Etowah, and Oostanaula rivers, where the original village of Hightower was located, is in downtown Rome. If approaching from the south of Rome on U.S. 27, turn left onto Broad Street. Drive 0.65 mile through the historic section of Rome to West Second Avenue. Turn right (north) and cross the Oostanaula River. After driving about 0.5 mile, watch for the entrance to the Heritage Park and Riverview Sports Complex on the left. The entrance is under a railroad trestle. If approaching from the north side of Rome, take U.S. 27 south to the junction with Ga. 101 and Ga. 20. At the traffic light, U.S. 27 turns to the left. Keep straight, which is Ga. 101, and go about 0.25 mile to the entrance of Heritage Park which will be on the right. Inside Heritage Park, turn left toward the picnic and playground area. The forks of the rivers are visible from the gazebo, or from the foot path over the old railroad bridge. Just across the river from Heritage Park is a stone monument erected in 1901 by the Daughters of the American Revolution to commemorate the Battle of Hightower. To visit the stone marker, turn right on Ga. 101 from the Heritage Park and cross the Oostanaula River. Then turn right on Broad Street and cross the Etowah River. At the foot of Myrtle Hill Cemetery, turn right onto Branham Street and go 0.4 mile to Pennington Avenue. The stone marker is at the corner of Pennington and Branham.

ETOWAH INDIAN MOUNDS STATE HISTORIC SITE

Cartersville

The Etowah Mounds mark the site of a thriving civilization of Indians from the Mississippian period who lived in the area during the period from 1000 A.D. to 1500 A.D. Centered around three major mounds, the palisaded town of about one to two thousand inhabitants was a major center for trade, religion, and politics. The largest mound, now known as Mound A, is about 63 feet high and 335 feet by 395 feet at the base. This mound was believed to have supported religious and political structures. Mound C, one of two smaller platform mounds found at the site was a mortuary mound containing a rich deposit of Native

American artifacts—many of which are on exhibit in the museum at the state historic site.

Sometime after the Battle of Hightower in 1793, the Cherokee village of Hightower, also called Etowah, moved to the vicinity of the Etowah Mounds. Excavations on the grounds of the Etowah Mounds have found the floors of Cherokee houses, indicating that the land around the mounds was part of the Cherokee village. Several references from early visitors to the area indicate that Etowah was a thriving village. When United States Indian agent Benjamin Hawkins visited the Cherokee village of Etowah in 1796, he reported that a Cherokee woman named Sally Hughes was operating a ferry on the Etowah River, a short distance above the Etowah Mounds. In 1817, eight Cherokee chiefs escorted the Reverend Elias Cornelius of the American Board of Foreign Missions to the Etowah Mounds while he was visiting in the area. In 1823, a Cherokee mission originally called Pumpkinvine Mission—for the Pumpkinvine River which empties into the Etowah River near the mounds—was established at Etowah. The mission, later renamed the Hightower Mission, went by this name until it closed in 1831.

A self-guided trail at the Etowah Indian Mounds will take you by the three largest mounds, a defensive moat, a borrow pit (created when dirt was dug to build the mound), the central plaza, and a fish trap. A museum is also located on the grounds. Special events are held at the site throughout the year, including the annual Indian Skills Day in the fall and Artifacts Identification Days in March and October.

The Etowah Indian Mounds State Historic Site is open Tuesday through Saturday from 9 A.M. to 5 P.M. and on Sunday from 2 P.M. to 5:30 P.M.. It is closed on Mondays. However, if a legal holiday falls on Monday, the site is open. The site is open year-round except Christmas, Thanksgiving, and New Year's Day. There is an admission charge. For information, call 404-387-3747.

To reach Etowah Indian Mounds State Historic Site from Interstate 75, take Exit 124, the Main Street exit, and follow the brown signs for 6 miles. The route will take you through the town of Cartersville.

Etowah Indian Mounds State Historic Site

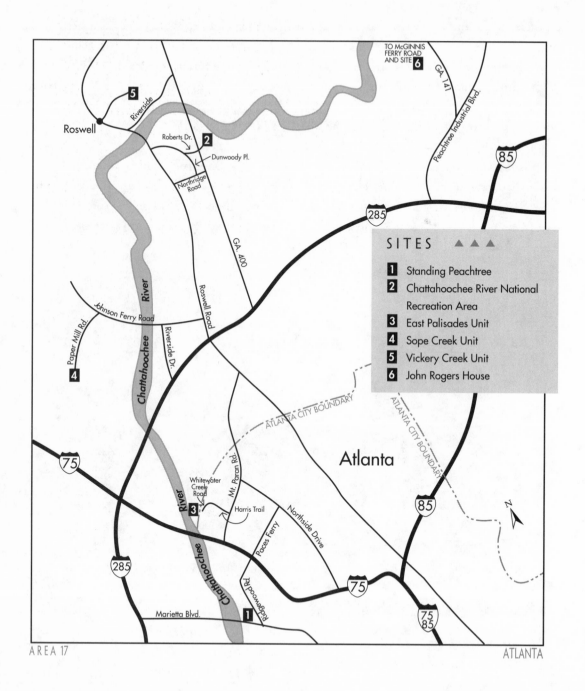

SITES ▲ ▲ ▲

1 Standing Peachtree
2 Chattahoochee River National
   Recreation Area
3 East Palisades Unit
4 Sope Creek Unit
5 Vickery Creek Unit
6 John Rogers House

TO McGINNIS
FERRY ROAD
AND SITE 6

Roswell

Riverside

Roberts Dr.

Dunwoody Pl.

Northridge
Road

GA. 141

Peachtree Industrial Blvd.

85

285

GA. 400

Roswell Road

Johnson Ferry Road

Chattahoochee River

Paper Mill Rd.

Riverside Dr.

ATLANTA CITY BOUNDARY

ATLANTA CITY BOUNDARY

Atlanta

75

Whitewater
Creek
Road

Mt. Paran Rd.

Harris Trail

River

3

Paces Ferry

Northside Drive

85

285

Chattahoochee

Ridgewood Rd.

75

Marietta Blvd.

1

75
85

N

Fort Peachtree

ATLANTA

▲ ▲ ▲

After the American Revolution, Europeans began to settle in the Indian country of Georgia. Many of these settlers entered the country as traders or soldiers and, finding the country rich and promising, decided to stay. A few of these early settlers were Tories or British refugees who were forced out of American strongholds in the East. Some of the settlers intermarried with the Cherokees and Creeks and were accepted into the tribe.

Several of the major rivers in Georgia,

like the Chattahoochee River, had unnavigable stretches that slowed European migration west. However, many of the early settlers made their way into Indian territory by way of old trade paths that usually followed the ridges of the mountains. The site of present-day Atlanta was at the junction of three ridges, which made it an important spot on transportation routes. Several Indian trails converged near Atlanta, including the Sandtown Trail, the Peachtree Trail, the Tallapoosa Trail, the Stone Mountain Trail, and the old Alabama Road. As roads and railroads were built across Georgia, many following the old trade paths, the Atlanta area developed as a major transportation hub.

STANDING PEACHTREE

Atlanta

Standing Peachtree was the English name for a Creek village that stood on both sides of the Chattahoochee River at its confluence with Peachtree Creek. The Creeks called the village Pakanahuili. The name is usually attributed to a large peach tree which stood at this location, but some historians attribute the name to an old pitch tree that stood on an Indian mound near the village.

During the War of 1812, the Cherokees sided with the Americans, and the Creeks supported the British. The Chattahoochee River was the boundary line between the Creek and Cherokee lands during this period, with the Cherokees on the northwest side of the river and the Creeks on the southeast side. Lieutenant George Gilmer, who later served two terms as governor of Georgia, was sent to Standing Peachtree to build a fort—part of a chain of forts in the area. The forts served to protect American communications and supply lines for troops moving south and west. The fort was originally named Fort Gilmer but was later called Fort Peachtree.

Fort Peachtree was built on a knoll overlooking Peachtree Creek and the Chattahoochee River. On a flat area below the fort, James McConnell Montgomery, superintendent of artificers, set up a boatyard so workmen could build flatboats used for shipping supplies to Fort Mitchell located on the Chattahoochee River near the present-day town of Fort Mitchell, Alabama.

Peachtree Road, built at a cost of $150, was one of the first roads in the Atlanta area. It connected Fort Daniel (built in 1813 on Hog Mountain in present-day Gwinnett County) with Fort Peachtree.

Peachtree was later used as the name for fifteen more roads in Atlanta.

After the Creek land cession in 1821 opened up the lands south and east of the Chattahoochee River for settlement, thousands of settlers poured into the area. James McConnell Montgomery, the young officer from Fort Peachtree, returned in 1821 and became one of the first permanent white residents in the area. Montgomery established a plantation and a ferry on the Chattahoochee River near the site of the old fort. The ferry was an important link in travel to the Cherokee Nation north of the river. Montgomery became postmaster of the new community of Standing Peachtree.

The site of Fort Peachtree and Montgomery's thousand-acre plantation is now occupied by the Atlanta Water Works. A small replica of Fort Peachtree has been constructed on the Atlanta Water Works property. There are also three historical markers near the fort—one for Standing Peachtree, one for Fort Peachtree, and one for Montgomery's Ferry—and there are excellent views of the Chattahoochee River from this area.

To reach Standing Peachtree when approaching Atlanta from the north on Interstate 75, take Interstate 285 Bypass west. Then take Exit 11, the South Atlanta Road exit. At the end of the exit ramp, turn left and go across Interstate 75. Drive 2.3 miles southeast on South Atlanta Road and cross the Chattahoochee River. Turn left on Bolton Street and drive 0.2 mile to Moore's Mill Road. Turn left on Moore's Mill Road. There will be a historical marker at the corner of Moore's Mill Road and Bolton Street indicating that Montgomery's plantation was located in the vicinity. Drive down Moore's Mill Road 0.2 mile and turn left on Ridgewood Road. Go 0.4 mile down Ridgewood Road to the entrance gates of the Atlanta Water Works River Intake Facility. Drive another 0.3 mile down the unnamed road to the fort, which will be on the right.

CHATTAHOOCHEE RIVER NATIONAL RECREATION AREA

Atlanta to Buford

In his book, *The Chattahoochee River*, P.C. King wrote that Chattahoochee was Cherokee for "river of painted rock." In *Georgia Place-Names*, Kenneth Krakow suggests other possible meanings of the name. He suggests Chattahoochee was derived from the word *uchee*, for corn, and the word *hochee*, for pounded or beaten. He thinks the name may have meant either "pounded rock," or "corn rock," or "flour rock." He points out that one of the early Indian agents in the area spelled it Chatta Ho Chee. Other spellings appearing on old maps included Catahoochee, Chattahuces, and Chatta Uchee.

P.C. King wrote about a local Towns County legend of a Cherokee warrior who wished to marry the daughter of a chief. The chief did not want the marriage to take place, so he gave the young warrior an impossible task to perform as a condition of the marriage. The chief told the young warrior he must find a river that flowed both north and south before he could marry the daughter. He was surprised when the brave returned with news of such a river. The brave had located the headwaters of both the Chattahoochee and Hiwassee rivers. The headwaters of both rivers lie in the North Georgia mountains in Towns County and are so close together they are almost as one. The waters of the Chattahoochee River flow south, while the waters of the Hiwassee River flow north.

As the Chattahoochee River winds it way down a 436-mile course to the Gulf of Mexico, it passes through some of the most varied country in the south. From scenic mountain valleys like Nacoochee, it passes through metropolitan Atlanta, the Georgia Piedmont, and the sandy plains of south Georgia. The course of the river is dotted with man-made lakes, formed by dams providing power and recreational opportunities to the area. Ironically, one of the most natural and scenic stretches of the Chattahoochee passes through the Atlanta area.

The Chattahoochee River National Recreation Area is a series of parklands located along a forty-eight mile stretch of the river beginning upstream (northeast) of Atlanta near Buford, Georgia, and ending at the northwest edge of Atlanta at a place called Paces Mill. The parklands consist of over a dozen separate units along the river and provide access to the river for fishing, picnicking, and hiking. There is a fitness trail located at one of the units, and several of the areas have historic ruins. One of the most popular activities on the river is rafting. There are several drop-in points from which to launch a raft or canoe for a leisurely float downstream. Concessionaires are on hand in summer months to help with canoe, kayak, and raft rentals, and some even provide shuttle service from three of the major take-out points back upstream to the major parking areas.

The Chattahoochee River National Recreation Area Administrative Offices are located at the Island Ford Unit of the recreation area. Park personnel are on hand weekdays to assist visitors, but the small bookstore and offices are closed on weekends. Maps of the entire park and trail maps are available everyday in the foyer of a building to the right of the main headquarters, even when the park offices are closed.

To reach the Island Ford Unit from Interstate 285 Bypass on the north side of Atlanta, take Ga. 400 north about 5 miles to the Northridge Road exit. At the end of the exit ramp, turn right (west) on Northridge Road and cross over Ga. 400. On the other side, turn right onto Dunwoody Place and go 0.5 mile. Turn right on Roberts Drive and go 0.5 mile, crossing Ga. 400 again. Then turn right onto Island Ford Parkway at the main park entrance. Drive 1.2 miles to the end of the road where the park headquarters are located.

Several of the units of the Chattahoochee River National Recreation Area are of importance in Native American history. These areas are listed below. For more information on the Chattahoochee River National Recreation Area, call 404-399-8070 or 404-952-4419.

EAST PALISADES UNIT

Atlanta

The East Palisades Unit is one of several locations along the Chattahoochee River where Native American rock shelters can be found. The large shelter at this location was probably used more heavily by prehistoric Indians, although Cherokee and Creek Indians may have used it as temporary shelter or for hunting camps. The bluff shelter is reached via the two-mile River Edge/Salamander Creek loop trail. The first part of the trail is an easy walk and parallels the Chattahoochee River. At the back end of the loop, the trail makes a steep ascent up a ridge to an overlook of the river. The bluff shelter can be reached easily from the first section of the trail. From the parking lot, the trail starts on the right near the picnic tables. You will soon cross a large wooden footbridge and then a medium one. About a half mile down the trail, you will cross two smaller footbridges. Just past the second small footbridge (the fourth bridge from the beginning of the trail), turn right onto an unmarked path. The path will take you a short distance away from the river to a ridge. From this trail, the large rock bluff shelter is easily seen on the side of the ridge.

The East Palisades Unit of the Chattahoochee River National Recreation Area is located on the northwest edge of the city of Atlanta. If traveling south on Inter-state 75, take Exit 107, the Northside Parkway and West Paces Ferry Road exit. Then take Northside Parkway east to Mount Paran Road. If traveling north on Inter-state 75, take Exit 108, the Mount Paran Road and Northside Parkway exit, to Mount Paran Road. Go east on Mount Paran Road less than 0.5 mile and turn left on Harris Trail. Follow Harris Trail to Whitewater Creek Road. Turn left on Whitewater Creek Road and drive a short distance until you see a sign on the right for the Chattahoochee River National Recreation Area. Turn right at the sign and go 0.25 mile down the road until it ends at the parking area.

Rock Shelter in East Palisades Unit of
Chattahoochee River National Recreation Area

Sope Creek

SOPE CREEK UNIT

East Marietta

Sope Creek is named for a Cherokee by the name of Chief Sope. Very little is known about Sope, except that he lived in the area where Sope Creek emptied into the Chattahoochee River. Sope somehow managed to escape the removal efforts and remain in the area after 1838. He is buried in nearby Sewell Cemetery.

Sope Creek is a beautiful, rocky creek with several small cascades that flows through a scenic hardwood forest. There are two main trails in the Sope Creek Unit.

The longer Fox Trail is a loop trail that begins at the Paper Mill Road parking lot and descends toward Fox Creek by way of Sibley Pond. The shorter Mill Trail parallels the road as it approaches the cascades at Sope Creek and the ruins of an old, 1850s paper mill.

To reach Sope Creek from Interstate 75 on the north end of Atlanta, take Interstate 285 Bypass east to Exit 17, the Roswell Road exit. Go north on Roswell Road to Johnson Ferry Road and turn left (northwest). Drive 2.5 miles, crossing the Chattahoochee River, to Paper Mill Road and turn left (west). The road crosses Sope Creek at 1.7 miles but there is no parking at this location. Proceed another 0.4 mile to a parking area on the left. From this parking area, you can hike either the Mill Trail, which will take you back to Sope Creek, or the Fox Trail.

VICKERY CREEK UNIT

Roswell

Vickery Creek receives its name from a woman named Sharlot (Charlotte) Vickery who lived near the headwaters of the creek. Sharlot was half Cherokee and half white and was married to a white man named Daren Cordery. They were part-owners of a ferry that crossed the Chattahoochee northeast of Vickery Creek in present-day Forsyth County. Soon after the 1838 Cherokee Removal, an industrialist named Roswell King began construction of a dam, sawmill, kiln, and cotton mill on Vickery Creek. Roswell King supposedly passed through the area in 1830 when a man named Charles Wofford, who was half Cherokee, was operating a gristmill on the creek. Roswell apparently remembered the potential of the site and returned immediately after the Cherokees were removed.

The Roswell Manufacturing Company experienced many years of success on Vickery Creek. Additional buildings were built on the hillside along Vickery Creek as operations expanded to include a flour mill and a woolen mill. During the Civil War, the woolen mill produced Confederate uniforms. When General Sherman discovered the uniform manufacturing business in the latter days of the war, he ordered the mill burned and the mill workers arrested. Many of those arrested were women and children who were shipped as prisoners of war to Louisville, Kentucky. The fate of most of these women and children is a mystery, but many are believed to have died in captivity.

A 4.5-mile loop trail has been established by the park service on the lower portion of Vickery Creek Unit near the Chattahoochee River. This trail passes through pine forests, skirts a meadow, and takes the hiker by an old dam on Vickery Creek that was part of the Roswell Mill complex. Access to this part of the trail system is from parking areas on Sloan Street or Riverside Road.

To reach Vickery Creek from Interstate 285 Bypass on the north side of Atlanta, take Ga. 400 north about 5 miles to the Northridge Road exit. At the end of the exit ramp, turn right (west) on Northridge Road and cross over Ga. 400. On the other side, turn right onto Dunwoody Place and go 1.4 miles to Roswell Road. Turn right on Roswell Road and cross the Chattahoochee River. As you cross the river, the mouth of Vickery Creek will be visible on the right (northeast) side of the river. As soon as you reach the other side of the river, turn right on Riverside Road. Drive across Vickery Creek and turn left at the sign for the Vickery Creek parking area. From the parking area, the trail climbs uphill before looping right (east) toward the old dam.

The trail system can also be accessed from Sloan Street near Founders Cemetery, where Roswell King is buried. Follow the directions from Interstate 285 Bypass to Roswell Road and cross the Chattahoochee River. Go past the turn for Riverside Road and drive into the town of Roswell, where Roswell Road changes names to South Atlanta Street. Turn right from South Atlanta Street onto Sloan Street and drive 0.4 mile to the small parking area at Founders Cemetery. Park on either side of the road and take the trail downhill to the old dam on Vickery Creek.

Vickery Creek

JOHN ROGERS HOUSE

Shakerag

John Rogers was born in 1774 in Burke County, Georgia. In 1803, he married a half-Cherokee girl named Sarah Cordery. Together, they had twelve children, several of whom became active in Cherokee affairs. During the Creek War, John Rogers enlisted as a private in a company of mounted Cherokees and served as a courier for General Andrew Jackson. Because Rogers had married a Cherokee woman, he was entitled to land in Cherokee country. In 1817, he applied for a 640-acre reservation on the east side of the Chattahoochee River. Around 1819, he was forced to abandon the reservation and move to the west side of the Chattahoochee River. At his new location, he established a plantation with sixteen slaves. Rogers raised cattle, pigs, and horses and built a ferry across the Chattahoochee. An 1836 assessment of his holdings, and additional claims made in 1837, placed a value of $9,044.50 on his property.

John and Sarah's children received private tutoring at home while they were young. As they grew older, they were sent to academies where they continued their education. One son, Robert, became a medical doctor, Methodist minister, and missionary to the Creek Indians. Another son, Johnson, was a lawyer and outspoken critic of Chief John Ross's policies. Both Robert and Johnson were active proponents of removal and signed the New Echota Treaty on December 29, 1835. Another son, William, was appointed a special commissioner for the Cherokee Nation by John Ross in the late 1820s. As part of his job as a special commissioner, William Rogers, along with John Ridge, son of The Ridge, took testimony from Cherokee and white settlers to help settle a boundary dispute in Georgia. Rogers also represented the Cherokees in efforts to free the missionaries, Dr. Elizur Butler and Reverend Samuel A. Worcester, when they were imprisoned in 1831. Rogers was elected clerk of the Cherokee National Committee in 1832 and traveled to Washington with other Cherokee delegates on several occasions between 1832 and 1835. By 1835, William Rogers had switched his loyalty from John Ross to The Ridge and the proponents of removal. William Rogers signed the Treaty of New Echota with his brothers in 1835.

After the removal, William traveled to Washington to arrange for the payments which were due to the Cherokees who had been forced to abandon property in the east. In 1840, William built a new home on the Chattahoochee, near his father's ferry and home. John Rogers had received permission to stay in Georgia after the removal but had lost his home in the 1832 land lottery. However, John was able to buy his property back from the lottery winner at three times its value.

John Rogers's ferry was replaced many years ago by a bridge. The bridge and the road to the bridge are now closed from Bell Road to the Chattahoochee River. However, the 1820s John Rogers house is still standing.

To reach the John Rogers House in the Shakerag community from Interstate 75, take Interstate 285 Bypass east several miles to Exit 23B. From the exit, go north on Ga. 141, the Peachtree Industrial Boulevard. At 3.9 miles, Ga. 141 N will split from Peachtree Industrial Boulevard. Bear left and take Ga. 141 N approximately 8 miles. Turn right (east) on McGinnis Ferry Road. Go 1.7 miles down McGinnis Ferry Road and turn right on Rogers Ferry Road. Take Rogers Ferry Road 0.8 mile to Bell Road. (Rogers Ferry Road will turn to gravel for a short distance but is in good condition.) Turn right on Bell Road and go about 0.25 mile to 7355 Bell Road. The John Rogers house is at this address on the left side of the road. The house is painted blue, has a tin roof, and is set in the woods. It is on private property and should be viewed from the road.

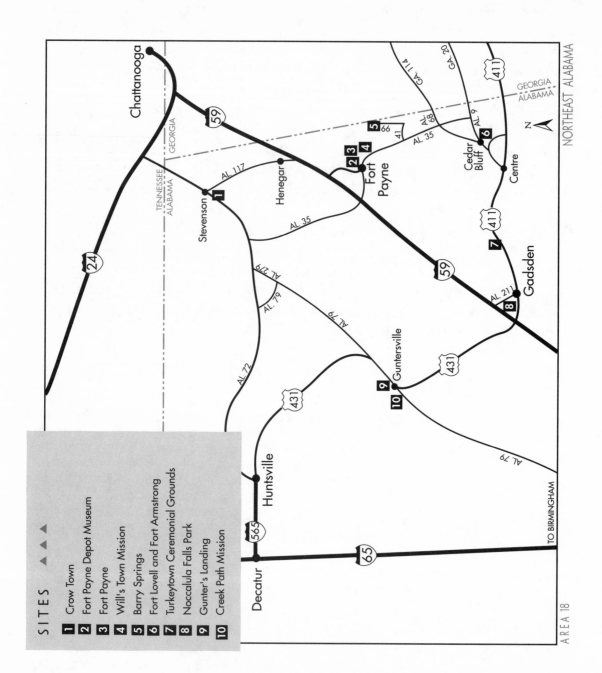

SITES ▲▲▲

1 Crow Town
2 Fort Payne Depot Museum
3 Fort Payne
4 Will's Town Mission
5 Barry Springs
6 Fort Lovell and Fort Armstrong
7 Turkeytown Ceremonial Grounds
8 Noccalula Falls Park
9 Gunter's Landing
10 Creek Path Mission

NORTHEAST ALABAMA

AREA 18

Crow Creek

AREA 18

NORTHEAST ALABAMA

▲ ▲ ▲

Northern Alabama is dominated by the Cumberland Plateau region, a wedge-shaped area that includes the Tennessee River Valley and the northern part of the Black Warrior River. To the southeast of the Cumberland Plateau region lies the Valley and Ridge Province—a geographic region whose prominent features include streams and ridges that run in a northeast to southwest direction. Weiss Lake, Lookout Mountain, and the Coosa River all lie within this province. South and east of the Valley and Ridge Province is the Piedmont region, which includes the Tallapoosa River and Mount Cheaha — Alabama's tallest mountain, standing 2,407 feet.

The natural resources found in northeast Alabama attracted many prehistoric Native Americans to the region. In his book, *Prehistoric Indians of the Southeast: Archaeology of Alabama and the Middle South*, author John A. Walthall explains that the Coosa River Valley was extensively settled by prehistoric man. Walthall goes on to explain that Indians used the Coosa River to travel from Georgia to mineral quarries in Alabama's Piedmont. The Piedmont region had many mica, steatite, graphite, and greenstone quarries, making it an important source of materials for tools and ornaments for the Indians. Because they were located near these quarries, villages on the Coosa River became part of an important Indian trade route.

The cedar glades found in parts of the Cumberland Plateau region provided wood for utensils and medicinal herbs. They also attracted concentrations of game in spring.

The rivers provided rich beds of mussels and a habitat for wildlife. For these reasons, the river valleys of the Cumberland Plateau region had the highest population density in Alabama during prehistoric times. Moundville, the largest prehistoric town in the Southeast, was located in the Black Warrior Valley, near the southern edge of the Cumberland Plateau. Hundreds of prehistoric sites, primarily from Mississippian-era cultures, have been documented in this area along the Tennessee River. In the Cumberland Plateau, Russell Cave (near present-day Bridgeport, Alabama) and the Stanfield-Worley bluff shelter (near present-day Tuscumbia, Alabama) are among the oldest-known Native American sites in the entire Southeast.

The natural riches of northern Alabama also attracted later Indians to the area, including members of the Coosa, Chickasaw, Choctaw, and Creek tribes. The Cherokees were relative latecomers to the area, in terms of establishing permanent settlements, arriving in the late 1700s. However, the Cherokees had hunted in the area for many years. Like their predecessors, they settled near streams, rivers, and springs. Both Sequoyah and John Ross lived in this area at different times during their lives.

CROW TOWN

Stevenson

Long before the Chickamaugans established Crow Town at Crow Creek in the late 1700s, the area was inhabited by an early group of Indians identified as the Crow Creek Culture. It is believed that they lived in the Guntersville Basin about the time De Soto passed through Alabama. At least two Crow Creek village sites have been found on the Tennessee River, near the mouth of Crow Creek.

The Chickamaugan village of Crow Town was also probably located near the mouth of Crow Creek. Crow Town is mentioned in the captivity narrative of Joseph Brown (see the Nickajack Cave section in Area 1 for more on the Joseph Brown captivity) as being the place where Mrs. Glass, wife of a Major Glass, and her baby were purchased from the Creek Indians. At that time, Brown wrote the Tennessee River could be forded easily at an old crossing of the Creeks. The original site was inundated when the Guntersville Basin was established.

U.S. 72 crosses Crow Creek south of Stevenson. On the southeastern end of the bridge, there is a boat ramp and parking area next to Bud's Barbecue, where you can park and view the plentiful waterfowl on Crow Creek. From the parking area at the boat ramp, the former location of the Chickamaugan Crow Town would be to the right (southeast and downstream), toward the junction of Crow Creek and the Tennessee River.

FORT PAYNE DEPOT MUSEUM

Fort Payne

Fort Payne was built on the site of Will's Town, a Cherokee settlement established about 1770. Will's Town was named for the mixed-blood chief Red Head Will. Several important Cherokees called Will's Town their home at some point in their lives. Sequoyah lived here before moving west, and John Ross's family also lived here briefly.

The town's historical museum is located in an interesting railroad building that was built in 1891. The museum features a collection of North American Indian artifacts including pieces from the Cherokee, Creek, Hopi, Apache, Pueblo, and Seminole tribes. Other exhibits include railroad memorabilia and newspaper articles from the turn of the century. The museum sponsors an annual Intertribal Powwow, usually held the third or fourth weekend in October.

Hours are 10 A.M. to 4 P.M. on Monday, Wednesday, and Friday and 2 P.M. to 4 P.M. on Sunday. The museum is closed Tuesday, Thursday, Saturday, and on major holidays. Admission is free. For information, call 205-845-5714.

To reach the Fort Payne Depot Museum from Interstate 59, take the Fort Payne exit (Exit 218) and follow Al. 35 to downtown Fort Payne. In Fort Payne, Al. 35 bears left onto Gault Avenue, which is also U.S. 11. For a few blocks, both Al. 35 and U.S. 11 follow Gault. At the intersection with Fifth Street, Al. 35 turns right while U.S. 11 continues straight on Gault. Make the right turn onto Fifth Street, following Al. 35. The museum will be on the left in one block. If coming from De Soto State Park, take County Road 89 to Al. 35 and turn right (west). Follow Al. 35 down the mountain. The museum will be on the right.

FORT PAYNE

Fort Payne

Fort Payne was named for its first commander, Captain John G. Payne. The tem-porary fort was built in early April 1838 to serve as a removal fort during the removal of the Cherokees in 1838. It was one of five removal forts in Alabama. There were thirteen removal forts in Georgia, eight in Tennessee, and five in North Carolina. Fort Payne was unique because it also served as an internment camp, the only one in Alabama. The other ten internment camps were located in Tennessee.

Surrounded by wooden stockades made of upright logs, both removal forts and in-

Fort Payne Depot Museum

ternment camps were used to hold the Cherokees during the removal process. Removal forts, also called removal stockades, were used to hold Cherokees temporarily during the first few weeks of the roundup in May and June. They were scattered throughout Cherokee country. From the removal forts, the Cherokees were then moved to internment camps to await emigration. The ten internment camps in Tennessee were located near the emigration departure points at Ross's Landing and the Cherokee Agency on the Hiwassee River. Most of the Cherokees outside of Alabama ended up spending the entire summer in these internment camps, experiencing horrible conditions. The Cherokees who were brought to Fort Payne during the initial stages were not taken to the Tennessee internment camps. They stayed at Fort Payne until it was time to leave for the West. Eventually, four detachments left Fort Payne under orders from General Winfield Scott.

For several years, a stone chimney located in a wooded lot in downtown Fort Payne was thought to be the chimney from the original stockade. However, according to DeKalb County Historian John Chambers, the chimney was constructed about 1909, and Fort Payne was actually located a few blocks away from the chimney site.

To reach the site of the temporary stockade which was called Fort Payne, take Exit 218 from Interstate 59. Then follow Al. 35 into town where it turns left (north) onto Gault Avenue. Continue on Al. 35 for another 0.6 mile before turning right (east) onto South Third Street. Drive down South Third Street and cross the railroad tracks. On the other side of the tracks, turn left onto Godfrey Avenue which parallels the east side of the tracks. Drive north about one block on Godfrey to 118 Godfrey Avenue South which will be on the right (east) side of the road. The stockade was located on property which is now occupied by the Fort Payne Improvement Authority's brick office building.

WILL'S TOWN MISSION

Fort Payne

The Will's Town Mission was established in 1823, by Reverend Ard Hoyt and Hoyt's daughter and son-in-law, William and Flora Hoyt Chamberlin—all of whom came from the Brainerd Mission. The ten-acre site was selected because it was on a main road and was close to the home of Major George Lowrey. Lowrey was a prominent Cherokee leader who was elected assistant principal chief in 1828. Ard Hoyt's son, Milo, married George Lowrey's daughter, Lydia. Sequoyah and David Brown, who assisted Sequoyah in translating the new testament into Cherokee, lived with George Lowrey while they worked on the translation.

The Mission complex was located in the 3700 block of Godfrey Avenue North. The cemetery and a smoke house from the original mission remain standing. From Interstate 59, take Exit 222 and follow U.S. 11 east for 1 mile to Fort Payne. Turn left on Gault Avenue and drive 1.3 miles to Thirty-Eighth Street. Turn right on Thirty Eighth Street and drive 0.5 mile to Godfrey Avenue.

BARRY SPRINGS

Broomtown

The abundance of water at Barry Springs is one reason the site was chosen for a removal fort. The large spring, named for settlers who arrived in 1838, feeds into nearby Mills Creek. The site was also chosen for a removal fort because it was located close to several Cherokee settlements, including Turkeytown, Wills Town, Broomtown, and Haweis Mission.

The hastily constructed stockade was a large circular structure built of chestnut logs. It was large enough to hold four hun-

Barry Springs

dred to five hundred families. Shade, water, and food were provided at the removal fort, but there were few other amenities. The Barry Springs stockade, like its counterparts in Georgia, North Carolina, and Tennessee, was used temporarily to hold Cherokees until they could be moved to larger internment camps located near the emigration departure points in Tennessee and Alabama.

To reach Barry Springs from Fort Payne, take Al. 35 south to Cherokee County Road 41 which is 4.8 miles north of Gaylesville. Turn east on County Road 41 toward Broomtown. In 4.8 miles, turn left (northeast) onto Cherokee County Road 99 and drive 4.4 miles to Barry Springs. Watch for a white metal sign for the Barry Springs site on the right. It will be on the side of the road in front of a field between the springs and Mills Creek. The springs are located to the right of the sign. They are on private property but are visible from the road.

FORT LOVELL

Weiss Lake

Fort Lovell was one of the stockades used during the round-up of the Cherokees in 1838. The site rests on Williamson Island in Weiss Lake, between Cedar Bluff and Centre, Alabama. The fort was originally called Fort Armstrong. It was built during the Creek War and located at the largest of all Cherokee settlements, Turkeytown. Turkeytown was known as Gun'-di'ga-duhun'yi, Cherokee for "turkey settlement." It was named for the original chief of the settlement, Turkey or Little Turkey.

During the Creek War, Pathkiller was chief of Turkeytown and principal chief of the Cherokee Nation. In October 1813, Turkeytown was in danger of being attacked by the Red Sticks, a hostile faction of the Creek Indians. Pathkiller sent runners to Andrew Jackson's army in the north with a plea for help. Jackson responded by ordering a detachment led by General James White, which included many Cherokee soldiers, to relieve the town.

By December 12 of that year, General John Cocke and the combined Cherokee and Tennessee forces had built Fort Armstrong on the Coosa River near the site of the Turkeytown settlement. At first, the fort was garrisoned by Cherokees, but the new commander, Colonel Gideon Morgan, had to decommission the Indians because their terms of service as Tennessee volunteers had expired.

To reach the general location of Fort

Lovell from Interstate 59, take the exit for Al. 68 and follow it to Centre. In Centre, Al. 68 turns north toward Cedar Bluff. As you approach Cedar Bluff, Weiss Lake will be on your right. Watch for a small pull-off used by fishermen on the right (east) side of the road, which provides a good view of Weiss Lake. This pull-off is 0.5 mile south of the junction of Al. 68 and Al. 9 on the south end of Cedar Bluff. Williamson Island will be southeast of the pull-off, near the north shore of the lake.

TURKEYTOWN CEREMONIAL GROUNDS AND PARK

Gadsden

The Turkeytown Ceremonial Grounds are located north of Gadsden, at the site of the original Cherokee settlement of Turkeytown. Located at the site is a well dating from 1810 or 1811, when Turkeytown was the largest of all Cherokee settlements.

Site of Fort Lovell on Weiss Lake

At that time, the village stretched for twenty to thirty miles along both banks of the Coosa River.

Pathkiller was chief of Turkeytown and a principal chief of the Cherokee Nation. When Pathkiller died in 1827, John Ridge, son of Major Ridge, served as executor of Pathkiller's estate, which included a ferry on the Alabama Road at the Coosa River in Turkeytown. Ridge bought the ferry from the Pathkiller heirs, as well as property on either side of the river. The property included one hundred acres of cleared land, most of which was bottom land, a peach and apple orchard, a large house, and several outbuildings including slave quarters.

Much of Turkeytown and Pathkiller's estate are now underwater. Pathkiller's grave is reportedly located at the Garrett Cemetery on a high bluff overlooking the Coosa River. However, a headstone with Pathkiller's name on it has also been placed at the cemetery at New Echota, Georgia.

The Turkeytown Ceremonial Grounds opened August 1993. Future plans for the site include development of a living Indian village, museum, and council house. An annual powwow is held at the Turkeytown Ceremonial Grounds the third weekend in

Turkeytown Ceremonial Grounds and Park

August. For information, call 205-549-0351.

To reach the ceremonial grounds, take Exit 183 from Interstate 59 and follow U.S. 431 (Meighan Boulevard) 4.5 miles through downtown Gadsden to U.S. 411. Drive north on U.S. 411 for 5.5 miles toward Centre. The ceremonial grounds will be found on the left side of U.S. 411, adjacent to Gaston High School.

NOCCALULA FALLS PARK

Gadsden

According to the legend of Noccalula Falls, the beautiful Cherokee princess, Noccalula, jumped over the falls to her death because she did not want to marry the Creek chief her father had chosen for her. This beautiful waterfall, named for the tragic heroine, plunges into a rugged sandstone gorge near the end of Black Creek, Lookout Mountain's southernmost creek. Lookout Mountain was called Chatanuga Mountain by the Indians. Chatanuga has been interpreted to mean "rock coming to a point." Chatanuga Mountain was the home of Creek Indians long before the Cherokees moved into the area in the eighteenth and nineteenth centuries. In addition to the falls, the Noccalula Falls Park features botanical gardens, a pioneer village, shops, picnic facilities, and a campground.

The falls are open year-round, from dawn to dusk. Some attractions at the park require an admission charge. For information, call 205-549-4663 or 205-549-0351.

From Interstate 59, take Exit 188 for Gadsden. Follow U.S. 211 for 2.5 miles up Lookout Mountain to the park entrance on the right.

Noccalula Falls

GUNTER'S LANDING

Guntersville

About half a mile northwest of Gunter's Landing was the location of an early Indian village of the Mississippian period, believed to have been inhabited around 900 to 1200 A.D. The village was located on the flood plain of the Tennessee River where it was protected by the river on one side and by a swamp and stream on the other. The people of the village supplemented these natural defenses by constructing a log stockade which enclosed their village and mound. Excavations of the village were conducted under emergency circumstances, with less than five weeks allotted for the excavation before inundation by waters from the Guntersville Dam. The results of the excavations revealed that the mound was 180 feet by 230 feet at the base, and 13 feet high. The mound was built in a series of stages, each with a rectangular building on top.

Long after the ancient village disappeared, the Cherokees started to move into north Alabama in the late 1700s. About 1785, a Scotsman named John Gunter came to live among the Cherokees and took a Cherokee wife named Catherine. They built a trading post and established a ferry along an old trading path. A thriving settlement called Gunter's Landing soon developed.

Gunter's Landing continued to thrive throughout the steamboat era, which began in earnest about 1820. The popular way to travel up the Tennessee River was to take a steamboat to Tuscumbia, then catch a train around the Muscle Shoals to Decatur, and catch another steamboat to the Tennessee River Gorge. At the gorge, one had to disembark because of the treacherous waters and take a canoe or smaller boat to Ross's Landing. Gunter's Landing was an

Gunter's Landing

important steamboat stop on the river. It was also located on the road known as Jackson's Trail, used by Andrew Jackson on his way to the Creek War in 1813 and 1814.

During the Cherokee Removal of 1838, steamboats carrying Cherokees stopped at Gunter's Landing for fuel and supplies. When the Cherokees began their move westward, a detachment of 1,090 Cherokees who were led by Chief John Benge crossed here after departing from Fort Payne.

The town of Gunter's Landing was located on the site of present-day Guntersville. The original town stretched from the ferry on the Tennessee River inland to the present city. The ferry sight is now underwater but was located on the north end of town at the U.S. 431 bridge over Guntersville Lake. From Huntsville or Gadsden, take U.S. 431 to Guntersville. After crossing the Tennessee River on U.S. 431, watch for the Guntersville Chamber of Commerce and Welcome Center on the right. The small park across from the welcome center provides a good view of the lake and the area where Gunter's ferry and the Mississippian village were located. There is also a historical marker at the welcome center indicating that Gunter is buried nearby.

Site of Creek Path Mission

CREEK PATH MISSION

Guntersville

Another prominent settler in the area was John Brown. Brown, whose Indian name was Yahnugungyahski, meaning "drowned by a bear," was part Cherokee and had three wives. Brown had business interests in the Nickajack and Ross's Landing areas, as well as in Brown's Valley at Guntersville. Brown established a village, which was known as Creek Path, on Brown's Creek on the east side of present-day Guntersville.

In February 1820, John Brown sent a letter to the Brainerd Mission—where his daughter, Catherine, and son, David, were students—requesting that the Brainerd missionaries establish a school at Creek Path.

The request was on behalf of all the Cherokee headmen in the Creek Path area. In the letter, they stated they had seen the benefits of education. They promised to send twenty or twenty-five children to the school.

The Brainerd Mission responded by sending Reverend Daniel Butrick and a Cherokee student named John Arch, also called Atsi. The Creek Path Mission was quickly constructed with the help of Cherokee men and children. Within two days, services were being held in the new building, which had interior dimensions of seventeen feet by twenty-two feet. Sunday school was held for Cherokees, whites, and blacks—the classes for the fifteen black students were held separately from the other students. The number of students increased rapidly. Catherine Brown was soon asked to leave her studies at the Brainerd Mission and start classes for girls at Creek Path. Emphasis was placed on reading, writing, spelling, and the study of scriptures. A church building was built at Creek Path in the fall of 1820. The mission continued to grow until several of the Cherokee families in the area voluntarily moved west. Creek Path Mission was finally abandoned in 1837.

Mary Alves Higginbotham, who has researched the Creek Path Mission, wrote in an article for the *Journal of Cherokee Studies* that all that remains of the Creek Path Mission is a magnolia tree on an island in the Tennessee River. The mission cemetery was inundated by the waters of the Guntersville Basin. There is a small island with a magnolia tree near the banks of the Tennessee in the general vicinity of the mission. Although it may not be the island Ms. Higginbotham referred to in her article, it is visible from an overlook.

To reach the overlook from either Gadsden or Huntsville, take U.S. 431 to Guntersville. On the south end of town, take Al. 79 southeast to the Cherokee Elementary School in the Crossroads community. A historical marker for Creek Path Mission is in front of the school. It indicates that the grave of Catherine Brown is 0.5 mile west. At the school, take Cherokee Valley Road 0.3 mile to Lake Shore Road and turn left (west). Go to the end of the road to the boat-launch ramp. A small island with a magnolia tree can be seen directly in front of this boat ramp.

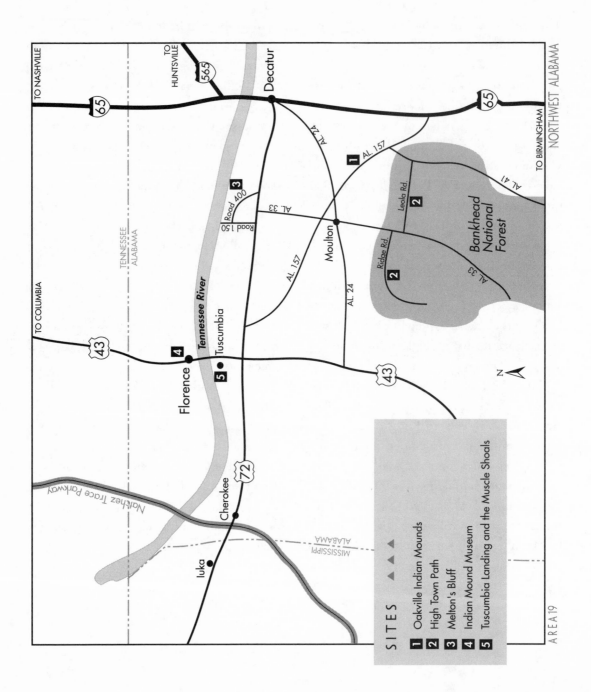

TO NASHVILLE

TO HUNTSVILLE

Decatur

565

65

65

TO BIRMINGHAM

AL. 24

AL. 157

1

Leola Rd.

2

AL. 41

Bankhead
National
Forest

Road 400

3

Road 150

AL. 33

Moulton

AL. 157

Ridge Rd.

2

AL. 33

AL. 24

TENNESSEE
ALABAMA

Tennessee River

Tuscumbia

TO COLUMBIA

43

Florence

4

5

43

72

Natchez Trace Parkway

Cherokee

MISSISSIPPI
ALABAMA

Iuka

N

SITES ▲ ▲ ▲
▲ ▲ ▲

1 Oakville Indian Mounds
2 High Town Path
3 Melton's Bluff
4 Indian Mound Museum
5 Tuscumbia Landing and the Muscle Shoals

Oakville Indian Mounds Park and Museum

NORTHWEST ALABAMA

▲ ▲ ▲

When the Cherokees were being pushed westward by Euro-American settlers during the late 1700s, several Cherokee towns were established along the Tennessee River in northern Alabama. Most of these towns were founded by Chickamaugans, followers of Dragging Canoe, who seceded from the Cherokee Nation in 1776. Dragging Canoe's people included refugees from burned-out

Cherokee villages in the Overhill, Middle, and Valley settlements in Tennessee and North Carolina. Many disenfranchised Creeks also became followers of Dragging Canoe. In eastern Alabama, Cherokee villages were founded at Crow Island (near present-day Stevenson), Long Island (near present-day Bridgeport), Gunter's Landing (near present-day Guntersville), and Brown's Valley (also near Guntersville). Further west, the Cherokees claimed the Chickasaw Old Fields at Ditto's Landing (near present-day Whitesburg, south of Huntsville) and established towns at Moneetown (on Fox Creek in Lawrence County), at Courtland, at Melton's Bluff, on Coldwater Creek (near present-day Tuscumbia), and on Town Creek (near Wheeler Dam).

Chief Doublehead, a Chickamaugan who became a successful businessman, established several different villages in northwest Alabama, including settlements at Bluewater Creek (near Wheeler Dam), on the south bank of Brown's Ferry (below Athens), in Limestone County (at the forks of Big Cypress and Little Cypress Creeks), and near Colbert's Ferry (on the Natchez Trace). Doublehead established a land agency called the Doublehead Company, which leased thousands of acres between the Elk River and Cypress Creek to more than fifty white settlers. The land Doublehead leased was in Cherokee territory, and as such, was not supposed to be available for this type of settlement. After Doublehead's death in the summer of 1807, the lease holders ran into legal problems which resulted in their eviction in 1811. Doublehead was also the father-in-law of the prominent Chickasaw chief, George Colbert, who operated the ferry on the Tennessee River at the Natchez Trace. Through land speculation and by controlling transportation routes, Doublehead and his followers controlled the Mussel Shoals (later changed to Muscle Shoals) area for many years. Doublehead's prosperous business interests made him an influential leader in northwest Alabama.

OAKVILLE INDIAN MOUNDS PARK AND MUSEUM

Moulton

The Oakville Indian Mounds Park and Museum are dedicated to several Native American cultures who lived in the Moulton area at various times—Indians from the Woodland and Mississippian periods, as well as the latter-day Cherokee,

Creek, and Chickasaw tribes. The mound at the site, which is about 20 feet high and 220 feet at the base, was a ceremonial and burial mound used during the Woodland and Mississippian periods. In later years, a cemetery for whites was established on top of the mound. It was located on the Black Warrior Town Trail which led from Melton's Bluff at the Elk River Shoals on the Tennessee River to the Creek Indian town of Black Warrior. The Creek town was destroyed during the Creek War in 1813.

A new museum, built in the shape of a council house, is located at the mound. At the time of this writing, the museum and mound, under the supervision of the Lawrence County Schools Indian Education Program, had not officially opened to the public. For information, call 205-905-2494.

From Decatur, take Al. 24, the Gordon Terry Parkway, toward Moulton, then turn left onto Al. 157. Follow Al. 157 south 5.8 miles to County Road 187 and turn left again. Drive through cotton fields on either side of County Road 187 for 1.1 miles to a sign on the left for the Oakville Indian Mound. If the gate is locked, you can still see the mound from the road, or park and walk back to the mound.

HIGH TOWN PATH

Bankhead National Forest

The ancient Indian trail known as the High Town Path ran from Charles Towne (Charleston, South Carolina) to the Chickasaw Bluffs (Memphis, Tennessee) on the Mississippi River. It generally followed ridges and watershed divides in order to avoid stream crossings and swamps. Another reason was because ridges were frequently used as boundaries between Native American tribes, whose villages were concentrated on rivers and streams. The trail was approximately one thousand miles in length, with the Indian village of High Town, near present-day Rome, Georgia, located halfway on the trail.

The High Town Path was a major trading path connecting villages in the East with those in the West. As white settlers moved into Alabama from Georgia and East Tennessee, they frequently used the High Town Path. Several important Cherokee villages were located on the High Town Path, including High Town, Turkeytown, and Brown's Village. Portions of the path appear on many old maps of the Southeast.

In Alabama, the High Town Path follows the Tennessee Divide— waters north of the

High Town Path

Tennessee Divide flow into the Tennessee River and eventually into the Mississippi, and waters to the south flow into Mobile Bay. The Tennessee Divide was a natural boundary used in several treaties. The ridge was used as the southeastern boundary of the Chickasaws in an 1816 treaty and in Chickasaw Land Claims in a treaty in 1786. The Tennessee Divide was also used as a northern boundary for Creek lands and as a southern boundary for Cherokee lands. In the Turkeytown Treaty of 1816, which ceded lands from both the Cherokee and Chickasaw territories to the federal government, the High Town Path was used as the southern boundary for the land cession.

In Lawrence County, Alabama, two forest service roads, the Leola and Ridge roads in the Bankhead National Forest and Black Warrior Wildlife Management Area, closely follow the old High Town Path. On the eastern side of the county, the path passes through the heavily logged wildlife management area, which includes a place called Indian Tomb Hollow. Indian Tomb Hollow was the location of a battle in the 1780s between Creeks and Chickasaws.

On the western end of the county, the road passes through the national forest where the scenic Kinlock Falls and Kinlock Rock Shelter are located. The Kinlock Rock Shelter is a prehistoric bluff shelter with petroglyphs carved into the stone. It is believed that the stone was used for ceremonial purposes.

To reach these portions of the High Town Path from Moulton, take Al. 157 southeast to Al. 36. Continue past this intersection on Al. 157 another 2.7 miles to Fulmer's Phillips 66 station. Turn right (west) on an unmarked paved road which is Lawrence County Road 200. Take County Road 200 for 2.5 miles to a dirt road which is County Road 198. Turn right and drive 2 miles to the forest service boundary. Here the signs change from county road signs to forest service signs and County Road 198 becomes Forest Road (F.R.) 272. From the forest service boundary take F.R. 272 west for 0.4 mile and turn right on F.R. 249. F.R. 249 is the beginning of Leola Road and the beginning of the High Town Path. From this point on, the roads will closely follow the old High Town Path.

Take F.R. 249 for 12.7 miles as it twists and turns through the country to Al. 33. There are two places where it may be difficult to follow F.R. 249. At 5.5 miles from the forest boundary, F.R. 249 turns left at a fork, and at 6.3 miles from the boundary the road turns right.

When you reach the intersection of

F.R. 249 and Al. 33, turn right onto Al. 33 and go north 1.5 miles, then turn left (west) at the brown national forest sign onto F.R. 213. This is the beginning of the Ridge Road. Follow F.R. 213 for 15.2 miles to F.R. 203. There are two points along F.R. 213 that may cause confusion. At the fork located 5.7 miles from Al. 33, go right. At 9.1 miles from Al. 33, there is a right (north) turn for F.R. 213. When you reach the junction of F.R. 213 and F.R. 203, turn left (south) onto F.R. 203 and drive 3.5 miles to F.R. 210. (There will be a sign for the Macedonia Church facing the opposite direction.) Turn left (southwest) onto F.R.

210 and drive 2.3 miles. On the right are signs stating "No Camping" and "No Alcohol." You can park here and walk back to old Kinlock Springs, or continue another 0.5 mile to the bridge at Kinlock Falls. Kinlock Falls is only a few hundred feet from the road but is best seen by taking a short path down to an overlook. From the falls, it is only 3.5 miles to where F.R. 210 runs into Al. 195. A right (west) turn on Al. 195 will take you out of the Bankhead National Forest to Haleyville. A left (east) turn will take you to Double Springs, where the Bankhead National Forest Service district ranger's office is located.

Kinlock Falls on the High Town Path

MELTON'S BLUFF

Courtland

Melton's Bluff is located at the Elk River Shoals on the eastern (upstream) end of the Muscle Shoals of the Tennessee River. Because of its strategic position at the head of the shoals, the Cherokees established a large village at Melton's Bluff. From this point, they could control river traffic. They even developed a reputation for river piracy.

Around 1780, John Melton, an Irishman who was married to a Cherokee woman, established a cotton plantation at Melton's Bluff that used black slave labor. In 1805, the Cherokees authorized the building of a road through Cherokee country which was called the Gaines Trace. It ran from the Tennessee River at Melton's Bluff to Mississippi. As a result of the Cotton Gin Treaty in 1806, the Cherokees at Melton's Bluff received one of the Mississippi Territory's first cotton gins and other concessions in return for ceding land north of the Tennessee River. To avoid persecution by fellow Cherokees for their involvement in the Cotton Gin Treaty, some of the Cherokees living at Melton's Bluff emigrated west in 1806.

As a result of the Turkeytown Treaty in 1816, many acres of Cherokee land south of the Tennessee River were ceded to the federal government, and many more Alabama Cherokees emigrated west. Melton's Bluff was the embarkation point for many of these emigrants. After the 1816 treaty, David Melton, John Melton's mixed-blood Cherokee son, sold Melton's Bluff Plantation and all the slaves to General Andrew Jackson. Melton's Bluff then became the seat of justice for Blount County in the Mississippi Territory.

During the 1830s, at least three groups of Cherokees passed by Melton's Bluff on flatboats as they emigrated west. After 1837, most of the Cherokees who emigrated west took a train around Melton's Bluff from Decatur to Tuscumbia.

To view Melton's Bluff, take U.S. 72/Al. 20 west from Decatur to C.R. (County Road) 400. Turn right (north), and take C.R. 400 to C.R. 418. Turn right (north) and go to the end of the road. There will be a Civil War monument, dedicated to General Joe Wheeler's cavalry river crossing, at the end of the road. This marks the western edge of Melton's Bluff Plantation. A portion of the Melton's Bluff Plantation property is partly owned by the Tennessee Valley Authority.

INDIAN MOUND MUSEUM

Florence

Before the Cherokees moved into the area in the late 1700s, the Florence and Mussel (Muscle) Shoals area had been home to many other Native Americans, including prehistoric cultures and the historic Chickasaws and Creeks. A thriving Mississippian culture, referred to as the Kogers Island People, built the Florence Mound on the Tennessee River sometime between 900 A.D. and 1200 A.D. Excavations revealed that "Wawmanona," as the Florence Mound is called, is a temple mound and not a burial mound. The large flat-top mound is 42 feet high, and the base is roughly 300 by 230 feet. These dimensions make it the largest mound on the Tennessee River.

In 1848, archaeologists E. G. Squier and E. H. Davis visited the Florence Mound and noted a semicircular earthwork, 270 feet from the base of the mound. The earthwork was 40 feet across at the top and 8 feet high. Squier and Davis suggested that it had originally been 12 to 15 feet high and had eroded to its lower height. Today, all traces of the earthwork have been destroyed by development in the area.

Although the mound was not built by Cherokees, a small museum located here

Indian Mound Museum

does display artifacts from several Native American cultures, including the Cherokees. Some of the tools and projectile points date back ten thousand years. The Indian Mound and Museum are open Tuesday through Saturday from 10 A.M. to 4 P.M. They are closed Christmas, New Year's Day, and Thanksgiving. When the museum is closed and the gates are locked, the mound can still be seen from the road. For information call, 205-760-6427.

The city-owned mound and museum are located in Florence, next to the bridge across the Tennessee River on U.S. 43 and U.S. 72.

TUSCUMBIA LANDING AND THE MUSCLE SHOALS

Sheffield

The area of the Tennessee River once known as Mussel Shoals extends from an area west of Decatur to Florence. The area was named for the freshwater mussels found in abundance along the river. This section of the river, which was later renamed Muscle Shoals, dropped 134 feet in 37 miles. The drop caused a series of rapids in the Tennessee River which made navigation very difficult. In the early 1830s, the Tuscumbia, Courtland, and Decatur Railroad Company built a railroad from Tuscumbia to Decatur as a bypass route around the shoals. People and goods traveling by water could be taken off the steamboats at one end of the shoals and transported via train to the other end.

During the Cherokee removal, several detachments of Cherokees were transported by steamboat or flatboat from Ross's Landing to Decatur, where they boarded trains for Tuscumbia. At Tuscumbia Landing, the terminus of the railroad, they re-boarded boats to continue their journey down the Tennessee River.

Tuscumbia Landing was located at present-day City Park West in Sheffield. The park is closed from December 1 to April 1.

From U.S. 43 in Sheffield, take Eleventh Avenue (the Jackson Highway) to Second Street and turn right. Go 2 blocks past Montgomery Street and turn left on Frankfort Street. Cross the railroad tracks and turn right on Georgia Avenue. Follow Georgia Avenue to Twentieth Street and turn left. Follow Twentieth Street around the Reynolds Aluminum property. Turn right onto Wilson Dam Avenue, then turn right on Blackwell Road at Jan's Store. The city park will be on the left in 0.1 mile.

BIBLIOGRAPHY

Alderman, Pat. *Nancy Ward: Cherokee Chieftainess & Dragging Canoe: Cherokee-Chickamauga War Chief.* 2d ed. Johnson City, Tenn.: The Overmountain Press, 1990.

Alexander, Lawrence, R. Bruce Council, and Nicholas Honerkamp. "An Archaeological Survey of the Proposed Outdoor Drama Amphitheater Site, Moccasin Bend, Chattanooga, Tennessee." The Jeffrey L. Brown Institute of Archaeology. The University of Tennessee at Chattanooga.

Allen, Penelope J. "History of the Cherokees." Unpublished manuscript available at the Chattanooga-Hamilton County Bicentennial Library.

———. *Leaves from the Family Tree.* Easley, S.C.: Southern Historical Press, 1982.

Anderson, William L., ed. *Cherokee Removal: Before and After.* Athens: The University of Georgia Press, 1991.

Armstrong, Zella. *The History of Hamilton County and Chattanooga Tennessee.* Vol. 1. Johnson City, Tenn.: The Overmountain Press, 1993.

At Home in the Smokies. Washington, D.C.: Division of Publications, National Park Service, 1984.

Banker, Luke H. "A History of Fort Southwest Point: 1792–1807." *The East Tennessee Historical Society's Publications* 46 (1974): 19–36.

Barclay, R.E. *Ducktown Back in Raht's Time.* New York: Van Rees Press, 1946. Reprint, Cleveland, Tenn.: White Wing Press, 1974.

Bass, Robert D. *Ninety Six: The Struggle for the South Carolina Back Country.* Lexington, S.C.: The Sandlapper Store, Inc., 1978.

Bogan, Arthur Eugene. *A Comparison of Late Prehistoric Dallas and Overhill Cherokee Subsistence Strategies in the Little Tennessee River Valley.* Ann Arbor, Mich.: University Microfilms International, 1985.

Boyd, Kenneth W. *The Historical Markers of North Georgia.* Atlanta, Ga.: Cherokee Publishing Company, 1993.

Brown, John P. *Old Frontiers: The Story of the Cherokee Indians from Earliest Times to the Date of Their Removal to the West, 1838.* Kingsport, Tenn.: Southern Publishers, 1938.

Brown, Joseph. "Captivity Narrative." *Journal of Cherokee Studies* 2 (Spring 1977): 208–18.

Brown, Richard Maxwell. *The South Carolina Regulators.* Cambridge, Mass:

Harvard University Press, Belknap Press, 1963.

Burns, Inez E. *History of Blount County, Tennessee: From War Trail to Landing Strip (1795–1955)*. N.p., 1957. Available through Mary Blount Chapter, Daughters of the American Revolution and the Tennessee Historical Commission.

Carberry, Michael. *Historic Sites of Blount, Cocke, Monroe, and Sevier Counties*. Knoxville, Tenn.: East Tennessee Development District, 1973.

Christian, George. "The Battle of Lookout Mountain: An Eyewitness Account." *Journal of Cherokee Studies* 3 (Winter 1978): 49–53.

Clark, Elmer T. *Methodism in Western North Carolina*. Western North Carolina Conference, The Methodist Church, 1966.

Clayton, Lawrence A., Vernon Knight, Jr., and Edward C. Moore, eds. *The De Soto Chronicles: The Expedition of Hernando De Soto to North America in 1539–1543*. 2 vols. Tuscaloosa: The University of Alabama Press, 1993.

"Comprehensive Management and Use Plan: Trail of Tears National Historic Trail." United States Department of the Interior, Denver, Colo., 1992.

Corkran, David H. *The Cherokee Frontier, Conflict and Survival*. Norman: The University of Oklahoma Press, 1962.

Corn, James F. "Conscience of Duty: General John E. Wool's Dilemma with Cherokee Removal." *Journal of Cherokee Studies* 3 (Winter 1978): 35–39.

———. "Sam Houston: The Raven." *Journal of Cherokee Studies* 4 (Spring 1981): 35–48.

———. *Red Clay and Rattlesnake Springs*. Cleveland, Tenn.: N.p., 1959.

Cornelison, John F., Jr., and Elizabeth Horvath. "A Report on the Phase I and Phase II Archaeological Testing of the U.S. Highway 58 Relocation Project at Cumberland Gap National Historic Park, Virginia." Southeast Archeological Center, National Park Service, Tallahassee, Fla., 1994.

Council, R. Bruce. "Ross's Landing at Chattanooga, A Cultural Resource History of the Chattanooga Waterfront." University of Tennessee at Chattanooga, 1989.

Creekmore, Betsey Beeler. *Knoxville*. Knoxville: The University of Tennessee Press, 1958.

Davis, Ren, and Helen Davis. *Atlanta's Urban Trails*. Vol. 2, *Country Trails*. Atlanta, Ga.: Susan Hunter Publishing, 1988.

De Bruhl, Marshall. *Sword of San Jacinto, A Life of Sam Houston*. New York: Random House, 1993.

Dickens, Roy S. *Cherokee Prehistory, The Pisgah Phase in the Appalachian Summit*

Region. Knoxville: The University of Tennessee Press, 1976.

———. "The Route of Rutherford's Expedition Against the North Carolina Cherokees." *Southern Indian Studies* 19 (October, 1967): 3–24.

Dickson, D. Bruce. "Archaeological Test Excavations at the Sam Houston Schoolhouse." *Tennessee Anthropologist* 2 (Spring 1977): 81–95.

Dixon, Max. *The Wautaugans.* Nashville, Tenn.: The Tennessee American Revolution Bicentennial Commission with the Appalachian Consortium, 1976.

Donnely, Polly W., ed. *James County: A Lost Colony of Tennessee.* Ooltewah, Tenn.: Old James County Chapter, East Tennessee Historical Society, 1983.

Dunn, Durwood. *Cades Cove: The Life and Death of A Southern Appalachian Community.* Knoxville: The University of Tennessee Press, 1988.

Eastern Band of the Cherokee Indians Planning Board. "Comprehensive Plan — Volume II, Environmental Reconnaissance Inventory." Eastern Band of the Cherokee Indians, 1974.

Ehle, John. *Trail of Tears: The Rise and Fall of the Cherokee Nation.* New York: Doubleday, 1988.

Evans, E. Raymond. "Fort Marr Blockhouse: The Last Evidence of America's First Concentration Camps." *Journal of Cherokee Studies* 2 (Spring 1977): 256–63.

———. "Highways to Progress: Nineteenth Century Roads in the Cherokee Nation." *Journal of Cherokee Studies* 2 (Fall 1977): 394–400.

———. "Notable Persons in Cherokee History: Ostenaco." *The Journal of Cherokee Studies* 1 (Summer 1976): 41–54.

———. "Notable Persons in Cherokee History: Stephen Foreman." *Journal of Cherokee Studies* 2 (Spring 1977): 230–39.

———. "Was the Last Battle of the American Revolution Fought on Lookout Mountain?" *Journal of Cherokee Studies* 4 (Spring 1980): 30–40.

Evans, E. Raymond, Victor P. Hood, and Loretta Lautzenheiser. "Preliminary Excavations of the Audubon Acres Site (U0HA84): Hamilton County, Tenn." Available through the Chattanooga–Hamilton County Bicentennial Library, Chattanooga, Tenn., 1981.

Evans, E. Raymond, and Vicky Karhu. "Williams Island: A Source of Significant Material in the Collections of the Museum of the Cherokee Indian." *Journal of Cherokee Studies* 9 (Spring, 1984): 10–34.

Faulkner, Charles H. *The Old Stone Fort: Exploring an Archaeological Mystery.* Knoxville:

The University of Tennessee Press, 1968.

Featherstonhaugh, George W. *A Canoe Voyage up the Minnay Sotor*. Vol. 2. Saint Paul, Minn.: Minnesota Historical Society, 1970.

Federal Writers' Project of the Works Project Administration. *North Carolina: A Guide to the Old North State*. Chapel Hill: The University of North Carolina Press, 1939.

Federal Writers' Project of the Works Project Administration for the State of Georgia. *Georgia: A Guide to Its Towns and Countryside*. Athens: The University of Georgia Press, 1940. Reprint, St. Clair Shores, Mich.: Scholarly Press, 1976.

Federal Writer's Project of the Works Project Administration for the State of Tennessee. *Tennessee: A Guide To the State*. New York: Viking, 1939.

Finger, John R. *The Eastern Band of the Cherokees: 1819–1900*. Knoxville: The University of Tennessee Press, 1984.

FitzSimons, Frank L. *From the Banks of the Oklawaha*. 2 vols. Hendersonville, N.C.: Golden Glow Publishing Company, 1976–79.

Folmsbee, Stanley J., Robert E. Corlew, and Enoch L. Mitchell. *Tennessee, A Short History*. Knoxville: The University of Tennessee Press, 1976.

Foreman, Grant. *Indian Removal: The Emigration of the Five Civilized Tribes of Indians*. Rev. ed. Norman: The University of Oklahoma Press, 1966.

———. *Sequoyah*. Norman: The University of Oklahoma Press, 1938.

French, Christopher. "Journal of an Expedition to South Carolina." *Journal of Cherokee Studies* 2 (Summer 1977): 275–301.

French, Laurence, and Jim Hornbuckle, eds. *The Cherokee Perspective: Written by Eastern Cherokees*. Boone, N.C.: Appalachian Consortium Press, 1981.

Frome, Michael. *Strangers in High Places, The Story of the Great Smoky Mountains*. Knoxville: The University of Tennessee Press, 1980.

George, David P. "96 Decoded." Booklet available at Ninety Six National Historic Park, Ninety Six, S.C., 1992.

Gleeson, Paul, ed. "Archaeological Investigations in the Tellico Reservoir, Interim Report." Report of Investigations No. 9, Department of Anthropology, The University of Tennessee, Knoxville, Tenn., 1971.

Godbold, E. Stanly, Jr., and Mattie U. Russell. *Confederate Colonel and Cherokee Chief: The Life of William Holland Thomas*. Knoxville: The University of Tennessee Press, 1990.

Govan, Gilbert E., and James W. Livingood. *The Chattanooga Country*

1540–1976: From Tomahawks to TVA. 3rd ed. Knoxville: The University of Tennessee Press, 1977.

Guthe, Alfred K., and E. Marian Bistline. "Excavations at the Tomotley Site: 1973–1974 & The Tuskegee Area: Two Reports." Tennessee Valley Authority, Knoxville, Tenn., 1978.

Hamel, Paul B., and Mary U. Chiltoskey. *Cherokee Plants and their Uses: A 400 Year History*. N.p., 1975.

Harris, W. Stuart. *Dead Towns of Alabama*. Tuscaloosa: The University of Alabama Press, 1977.

Hicks, Nannie Lee. *Historic Treasure Spots of Knox County, Tennessee*. N.p., 1964. Available through The Simon Harris Chapter, Daughters of the American Revolution, Knoxville, Tenn.

Higginbotham, Mary Alves. "Creek Path Mission." *Journal of Cherokee Studies* 1 (Fall 1976): 72–86.

Hodge, Cathy M. "The Revival of Roswell Mill." *North Georgia Journal* 11, no. 3 (Autumn 1994): 32–37.

Holmes, Tony. "Early Cherokee Ferry Crossings of the Eastern Tennessee River Basin." *The Journal of East Tennessee History* (1990): 54–79.

Hudson, Charles M. *The Southeastern Indians*. Knoxville: The University of Tennessee Press, 1984.

———. "A Spanish-Coosa Alliance in Sixteenth-Century North Georgia." *Georgia Historical Quarterly* 72 (Winter 1988): 599–626.

Hudson, Charles, and Carmen Chaves Tesser, eds. *The Forgotten Centuries: Indians and Europeans in the American South, 1521–1704*. Athens: The University of Georgia Press, 1994.

Hutchins, John. "The Trial of Samuel Austin Worcester." *Journal of Cherokee Studies* 2 (Fall 1977): 356–74.

Jackson, Olin. "Remnants of a Proud Past in North Fulton." *North Georgia Journal* 6 (Spring 1988): 18–22

———, ed. *A North Georgia Journal of History*. 2 vols. Alpharetta, Ga.: Legacy Communications, Inc., 1989.

Jefferson, Thomas. *Notes on the State of Virginia*. Trenton, N.J.: Wilson & Blackwell, 1803.

Jenkins, Gary C. "The Mining of Alum Cave", *The East Tennessee Historical Society's Publications*, no. 60 (1988): 78–87.

Keel, Bennie C. *Cherokee Archaeology, A Study of the Appalachian Summit*. Knoxville: The University of Tennessee Press, 1976.

Kelly, A. R., and Lewis H. Larson, Jr. "Explorations at Etowah, Georgia 1954–1956." Georgia Historical Commission, n.d.

Kelly, James C. "Fort Loudoun: British

Stronghold in the Tennessee Country." *East Tennessee Historical Society's Publications*, no. 50 (1978): 72–91.

Kelley, Paul. "Historic Fort Loudoun." Fort Loudoun Association, Vonore, Tenn., 1958.

King, Duane H. "Lessons in Cherokee Ethnology from the Captivity of Joseph Brown." *Journal of Cherokee Studies* 2, (Spring 1977): 219–29.

———. "A Powder Horn Commemorating the Grant Expedition Against the Cherokees." *Journal of Cherokee Studies* 1 (Summer 1976): 23–40.

———, compiler. *Cherokee Heritage: Official Guidebook to the Museum of the Cherokee Indian*. Cherokee, N.C.: Museum of Cherokee Indian, 1982.

———, ed. *The Cherokee Indian Nation: A Troubled History*. Knoxville: The University of Tennessee Press, 1979.

———, ed. "Primary Accounts of the Tsali Incident." *Journal of Cherokee Studies* 4 (Fall 1979): 213–33.

———, ed. "1835 Residences of Cherokees who Avoided Removal." *Journal of Cherokee Studies* 4 (Fall 1979): 240.

King, Duane H., and Jefferson Chapman. *Official Guidebook to the Sequoyah Birthplace Museum*. Vonore, Tenn.: Sequoyah Birthplace Museum, 1988. Reprint, 1993.

King, Duane H., and E. Raymond Evans. "The Death of John Walker, Jr.: Political Assassination or Personal Vengeance?" *Journal of Cherokee Studies* 1 (Summer 1976): 4–16.

King, Duane H., and E. Raymond Evans. "Tsali: The Man Behind the Legend." *Journal of Cherokee Studies* 4 (Fall 1979): 194–201.

King, P.C., Jr. *The Chattahoochee River*. Fort Gaines, Ga.: P.C. King, Jr., 1977.

Krakow, Kenneth. *Georgia Place-Names: Their History and Origins*. Macon, Ga.: Winship Press, 1994.

Lanman, Charles. *Letters from the Allegheny Mountains*. New York: George P. Putnam, 1849.

Lavendar, David. *De Soto, Coronado, Cabrillo: Explorers of the Northern Mystery*. Washington, D.C.: Division of Publications National Park Service, United States Department of the Interior, 1992.

Lewis, Thomas M. N., and Madeline Kneberg. *Hiwassee Island: An Archaeological Account of Four Tennessee Indian Tribes*. Knoxville: The University of Tennessee Press, 1946.

———. *Tribes That Slumber: Indians of the Tennessee Region*. Knoxville: The University of Tennessee Press, 1958. 9th printing, 1989.

Lillard, Roy G., ed. *The History of Bradley County*. N.p., 1976. Available through the East Tennessee Historical Society, Bradley County Chapter, Cleveland, Tenn.

Ling, E. Rodger. "Adventures on the Appalachian Trail in Georgia" *North Georgia Journal* 2 (Spring 1994): 8–13.

Livingood, James W. *Chattanooga: An Illustrated History*. Woodland Hills, Calif.: Windsor Publications, Inc., 1980.

————. *A History of Hamilton County Tennessee*. Memphis, Tenn.: Memphis State University Press, 1981.

Lowery, George. "Notable Persons in Cherokee History: Sequoyah or George Gist." Transcription by John Howard Payne. *Journal of Cherokee Studies* 2 (Fall 1977): 385–93.

Lumpkin, Wilson. *The Removal of the Cherokee Indians from Georgia*. New York: Augustus M. Kelley, 1971.

Marion, Francis. "Sowing Tares of Hate." *Journal of Cherokee Studies* 2 (Summer 1977): 333.

Martin, Isaac Patton. *Methodism in Holston*. Knoxville, Tenn.: Holston Conference of the Methodist Historical Society, 1945.

McDonald, Jerry N., and Susan L. Woodward. *Indian Mounds of the Atlantic Coast*. Newark, Ohio: The McDonald and Woodward Publishing Co., 1987.

McDonald, William Lindsey. *Lore of the River . . . The Shoals of Long Ago*. Florence, Ala.: Florence Historical Board, 1989.

McFerrin, John B. *History of Methodism in Tennessee*. Vol. 2, *1808–1818*. Nashville, Tenn.: Southern Methodist Publishing Co., 1871.

McKenney, Thomas L. *History of the Indian Tribes of North America with Biographical Sketches and Anecdotes of the Principal Chiefs*. Philadelphia, Pa.: D. Rice & Company, n.d.

Milling, Chapman J. *Red Carolineans*. Chapel Hill: The University of North Carolina Press, 1940.

Mooney, James. *Myths of the Cherokee and Sacred Formulas of the Cherokees*. Nashville, Tenn.: Charles Elder, 1972.

Moulton, Gary E. *John Ross: Cherokee Chief*. Athens: The University of Georgia Press, 1978.

Myers, William E. "Indian Trails of the Southeast." *Forty-second Annual Report of American Ethnology, 1924–25*. Government Printing Office, Washington, D.C.

Neely, Sharlotte. *Snowbird Cherokees: People of Persistence*. Athens: The University of Georgia Press, 1991.

North Carolina Atlas & Gazetter. Freeport, Maine: DeLorme Mapping, 1993.

Parish, Thurman. *The Old Home Place: Pio-*

neer *Mountain Life in Polk County, Tennessee*. Benton, Tenn.: Polk County Publishing, 1994.

Patton, Sadie Smathers. *Sketches of Polk County History*. N.p., 1950. Reprint, Spartanburg, S.C.: The Reprint Company, Publishers, 1976.

————. *The Story of Henderson County*. Asheville, N.C.: The Miller Printing Company.

Perdue, Theda. *The Cherokee*. New York: Chelsea House Publishers, 1989.

————. *Cherokee Editor: The Writings of Elias Boudinot*. Knoxville: The University of Tennessee Press, 1983.

————. *Native Carolinians: The Indians of North Carolina*. Raleigh: North Carolina Division of Archives and History, 1985.

Phillips, John Franklin. *The Indian Heritage of Americans*. Birmingham, Ala.: Birmingham Publishing Company, 1990.

————. *The American Indian in Alabama and the Southeast*. Nashville, Tenn.: Parthenon Press of the United Methodist Publishing House, 1986.

Pickett, Albert James. *History of Alabama and Incidentally of Georgia and Mississippi: From the Earliest Period*. N.p., 1900. Reprint, Spartanburg, S.C.: The Reprint Company, 1975.

Polhemus, Richard. "Archaeological Investigations of the Tellico Blockhouse Site: A Federal Military and Trade Complex." Report of Investigations No. 26, Department of Anthropology, University of Tennessee, Tennessee Valley Authority Publications in Anthropology No. 16. Published by the Tennessee Valley Authority, n.d.

Polk County Historical Association, Inc. *Polk County History*. Edited by D. William Bennett. Dallas, Tex.: Taylor Publishing Company, 1983.

"Position on Moccasin Bend." Chattanooga Intertribal Association, Chattanooga, Tenn., 1994.

Queener, V.M. "Gideon Blackburn." *East Tennessee Historical Society's Publication*, no. 6 (1934): 12–28.

Ramsey, James G. M. *The Annals of Tennessee to the End of the Eighteenth Century*. 1853. Reprinted, Kingsport, Tenn.: Kingsport Press, 1926. This book was reprinted for the Judge David Campbell Chapter, Daughters of the American Revolution.

Raulston, J. Leonard, and James W. Livingood. *Sequatchie: A Story of the Southern Cumberlands*. Knoxville: The University of Tennessee Press, 1974.

Remini, Robert V. *The Life of Andrew Jackson*. New York: Penguin Books, 1990.

Roberts, Bruce. *The Carolina Gold Rush*. Charlotte, N.C.: McNally and Loftin, Publishers, 1972.

Roberts, Ralph G. "Ancient Stone Fortifications at De Soto Falls, Little River, Alabama." *Tennessee Archaeologist* 5 (1949): 18–21.

Robertson, James. "Correspondence of General James Robertson."*American Historical Magazine* 5, no. 3 (Autumn 1994): 50–54.

Roper, Daniel M. "Does Anyone Know the Real Site of the Battle of Hightower Town?" *North Georgia Journal* 2, no. 3 (Autumn 1994): 50–54.

Rossman, Douglas A. *Where Legends Live: A Pictorial Guide to Cherokee Mythic Places*. Cherokee, N.C.: Cherokee Publications, 1988.

Royce, Charles C., *The Cherokee Nation of Indians*. Chicago, Ill.: Aldine Publishing Company, 1975.

Sakowski, Carolyn. *Touring the East Tennessee Backroads*. Winston-Salem, N.C.: John F. Blair, Publisher, 1993.

———. *Touring the Western North Carolina Backroads*. Winston-Salem, N.C.: John F. Blair, Publisher, 1990.

Saunders, William L., ed. *The Colonial Records of North Carolina, Vol. 10: 1775–1776*. Raleigh, N.C.: Trustees of the Public Libraries, by Order of the General Assembly, 1890.

Schroedl, Gerald F. "The Patrick Site (40MR40): Tellico Reservoir, Tennessee." Tennessee Valley Authority, 1978.

———. "Louis-Philippe's Journal and Archaeological Investigations at the Overhill Town of Toqua." *Journal of Cherokee Studies* 3 (Fall 1978): 206–20.

———, ed. "Overhill Cherokee Archaeology at Chota-Tanasee." Report of Investigations No. 38, Department of Anthropolgy, University of Tennesse, Tennessee Valley Authority Publications in Anthropology No. 42. Published by the Tennessee Valley Authority, 1986.

Shackford, James Atkins.*David Crockett: The Man and the Legend*. Edited by John B. Shackford. Chapel Hill: The University of North Carolina Press, 1986.

Shadburn, Don. L. "The John Rodgers Family." *North Georgia Journal* 5 (Spring 1988): 10–17.

Snell, William R. *The Councils at the Red Clay Council Ground*. Cleveland, Tenn.: Modern Way Printing Co., 1983.

———. "Candy's Creek Mission Station." *Journal of Cherokee Studies* 4 (Summer 1979): 136–84.

Spoden, Muriel C. *Kingsport Heritage: The Early Years, 1700 to 1900*. Johnson City, Tenn.: The Overmountain Press, 1991.

———. *The Long Island of the Holston: Sacred Island of the Cherokee Nation*. Nashville,

Tenn.: The Tennessee American Revolution Bicentennial Commission, 1977.

Stevens, William Bacon. *A History of Georgia: From its First Discovery by Europeans to the Adoption of the Present Constitution in MDCCXCVII*. Vol. 2. Philadelphia, Pa.: E.H. Butler & Co., 1859.

"Tellico Blockhouse: U.S. Garrisoned Fort, 1794–1807." Tennessee Valley Authority and Tennessee Department of Conservation, n.d.

Tennessee Atlas & Gazetter. Freeport, Maine: DeLorme Mapping, 1992.

Thomas, Prentice M., Jr., ed. "Archaeological Investigations at Fort Southwest Point (40RE11A), Kingston, Tennessee." Department of Anthropology, University of Tennessee, Knoxville, Tenn., 1977.

Tinney, Edward E. "History of Cumberland Gap National Historical Park." 1965.

Toops, Connie. *Great Smoky Mountains*. Stillwater, Minn.: Voyageur Press, Inc., 1992.

Walker, Charles O. *Cherokee Footprints*. Vol. 1. N.p., 1988.

Walker, Rickey Butch. *The High Town Path*. Moulton, Ala.: Lawrence County Schools Indian Education Program, 1992.

———. "Letter to the National Park Service, Branch of Long Distance Trails, on Melton's Bluff." 1991.

Walker, Robert Sparks. *As the Indians Left It*. Chattanooga, Tenn.: George C. Hudson & Co., 1955.

———. *Torchlights to the Cherokees: The Brainerd Mission*. New York: The MacMillan Company, 1931.

Walthall, John A. *Prehistoric Indians of the Southeast: Archaeology of Alabama and the Middle South*. Tuscaloosa: The University of Alabama Press, 1980.

Ward, George Gordon. *The Annals of Upper Georgia Centered in Gilmer County*. Nashville, Tenn.: The Parthenon Press, 1965.

Wheeler, William Bruce, and Michael J. McDonald. *TVA and the Tellico Dam, 1936–1979*. Knoxville: The University of Tennessee Press, 1986.

Wilburn, Hiram C. "Judaculla Place-names and the Judaculla Tales." *Southern Indian Studies* 4 (October 1952): 23–26.

———. "Judaculla Rock." *Southern Indian Studies* 4 (October 1952): 19–21.

———. "Nununyi, The Kituhwas, or Mountain Indians and the State of North Carolina." *Southern Indian Studies* 2 (April 1950): 54–64.

Wilkins, Thurman. *Cherokee Tragedy, The Story of the Ridge Family and the Decimation of a People*. New York: The MacMillan Co., 1970.

Williams, Max R., ed. *The History of Jackson*

County. Sylva, N.C.: The Jackson County Historical Association, 1987.

Williams, Samuel Cole. *Dawn of Tennessee Valley and Tennessee History.* Johnson City, Tenn.: The Watauga Press, 1937.

————. *Early Travels in the Tennessee Country, 1540–1800.* Johnson City, Tenn.: The Watauga Press, 1928.

————. *History of the Lost State of Franklin.* New York: The Press of the Pioneers, 1933.

————. *Tennessee During the Revolutionary War.* 2d ed. Knoxville: The University of Tennessee Press, 1974.

————, ed. *Lieutenant Henry Timberlake's Memoirs, 1756–1765.* Marietta, Ga.: Continental Book Company, 1948.

Williams, W. G. "Military Intelligence Report on N. C. Cherokees in 1838." *Journal of Cherokee Studies* 4 (Fall 1979): 202–12.

Wilson, John. *Lookout.* Chattanooga, Tenn.: Chattanooga News Free Press, 1977.

Woodward, Grace Steele. *The Cherokees.* Norman: University of Oklahoma Press, 1963. 10th printing, 1988.

INDEX